Connecting Leadership and Learning

Leading schools is becoming, almost daily, a more complex and demanding job. *Connecting Leadership and Learning* reassesses the purpose of schools, the nature of learning and the qualities of leadership that make schools authentic places of learning.

Starting with a review of what we can claim to know – and not know – about learning, leadership and their interrelationship, this book explores what it means to lead schools that place learning at the centre. Drawing on research from projects in seven different countries – including the United States, Australia and five European countries – the authors offer five key principles for practice:

- a focus of learning
- an environment for learning
- a learning dialogue
- shared leadership
- accountability – internal and external.

These key principles have been tested by teachers, senior leaders and school students and found to be applicable across cultural and linguistic boundaries. The challenges faced by in inner city schools, whether in London or New Jersey, prove a stern test for the five principles. Yet, as these schools testify, they bring a new sense of hope and conclude that learning is for everyone.

Based on rigorous research and thoroughly grounded in practice, this book aims to challenge the reader with big ideas about learning and leadership, and to break new ground in thinking about where leadership and learning meet so that practitioners can see how it works in school and classroom practice. It should be of interest to all school leaders and those aspiring to the role.

John MacBeath is Chair of Educational Leadership at University of Cambridge, UK.

Neil Dempster is Professor in Education and Professional Studies at Griffith University, Australia.

Connecting Leadership and Learning

Principles for Practice

Edited by John MacBeath
and Neil Dempster

Routledge
Taylor & Francis Group

LONDON AND NEW YORK

First published 2009
by Routledge
2 Park Square, Milton Park, Abingdon, Oxon, OX14 4RN

Simultaneously published in the USA and Canada
by Routledge
270 Madison Ave, New York NY 10016

Routledge is an imprint of the Taylor & Francis Group, an informa business

Transferred to Digital Printing 2010

Typeset in Garamond 3 by
Swales & Willis, Exeter, Devon

British Library Cataloguing in Publication Data
A catalogue record for this book is available from the British Library

Library of Congress Cataloging in Publication Data
    Connecting leadership and learning: principles for practice/
John MacBeath . . . [et al.].
        p. cm.
    1. Educational leadership. 2. Education–Aims and objectives. 3. School
improvement programs. I. MacBeath, John E. C.
    LB2831.6.C66 2008
    371.2–dc22   2007052723

ISBN10: 0–415–45292–9 (hbk)
ISBN10: 0–415–45295–3 (pbk)
ISBN10: 0–203–89464–2 (ebk)

ISBN13: 978–0–415–45292–2 (hbk)
ISBN13: 978–0–415–45295–3 (pbk)
ISBN13: 978–0–203–89464–4 (ebk)

Contents

Figures

Tables

Notes on contributors

John MacBeath OBE is Chair of Educational Leadership in the Faculty of Education at the University of Cambridge and Director of Leadership for Learning: The Cambridge Network. His research and consultancy brings together work with schools and with policy makers in Britain as well as internationally. He has worked in a consultancy capacity with the OECD, UNESCO and the European Commission and currently advises policy makers in Hong Kong on school self-evaluation and inspection. For a decade he has worked closely with the National Union of Teachers (NUT) and since 2002 has conducted four studies for the NUT with his Cambridge colleague Maurice Galton. He is currently President of the International Congress on School Effectiveness and Improvement.

Neil Dempster is Professor in Education at Griffith University and former Dean of its Faculty of Education. His research interests are in school governance and leadership, school improvement and the role that professional development plays in leadership, policy implementation, learning and organisational change. Neil is an Honorary Fellow of the Australian Council for Educational Leaders, a Fellow of the Australian College of Educators and its National President.

Sue Swaffield researches and teaches in the fields of educational leadership, school improvement and assessment. She has particular interests in leadership for learning, critical friendship and assessment for learning. Her work at the University of Cambridge Faculty of Education builds on her previous experience as a teacher and adviser.

Joanne Waterhouse has worked in Primary education for over twenty years and has worked as a headteacher and adviser. Her research and writing interests are distributed leadership, leadership for learning and the study of narrative for making meaning. Her work at the University of Cambridge Faculty of Education has involved participation in projects that have taken her overseas working with colleagues from various international settings.

George Bagakis is Associate Professor of Methodology and Programmes in Education at the University of Patras (Greece). He has worked on innovative projects for the Greek Ministry of Education as well as in international projects of educational leadership, school improvement and self-evaluation. He has also been a national representative in various international organisations (OECD, EU).

Jorunn Møller is Professor at the Department of Teacher Education and School Development, University of Oslo. She currently holds a position as Professor II at the University of Tromsø. Her professional interests are in the areas of educational administration and leadership, supervision, action research, and school evaluation. She is presently involved in research on educational leadership and policy change.

David Frost is a member of the Leading Learning for School Improvement team at the University of Cambridge Faculty of Education. He is the co-ordinator of the HertsCam Network and editor of the journal *Teacher Leadership*. His research and writing focuses on teacher leadership, organisational capacity and school improvement.

Acknowledgements

Our thanks to the 24 schools who accompanied us on the Leadership for Learning Odyssey and to the 22 schools who were still there at the end. We owe a debt of gratitude to the eight university teams who supported these schools for three and a half years and to those who organised the conferences in Copenhagen (Lejf Moos), Innsbruck (Michael Schratz) and Athens (George Bagakis). Thanks to David Perkins our critical friend for his gentle but incisive insights. None of this would have been possible, however, without the financial support and personal interest of Peder Wallenberg and the Carpe Vitam Board in Sweden.

Thanks also to Katie O'Donovan for organising the editorial team, and for proof reading the copy with good grace and good humour. And finally to Anna Clarkson of Routledge who commissioned the book and waited patently for it to be finally delivered.

The university teams

- Athens: George Bagakis
- Brisbane: Neil Dempster
- Cambridge: John MacBeath, David Frost, Sue Swaffield, Gregor Sutherland and Joanne Waterhouse
- Copenhagen: Lejf Moos
- Innsbruck: Michael Schratz
- Oslo: Jorunn Møller and Guri Skedsmo
- Seattle: Brad Portin

Introduction

Leadership and learning: making the connections

John MacBeath and Neil Dempster

Leaders lead and children learn, it's a simple as that. This recasting of a statement by a previous HMCI may be seen by some as self-evident and, for some, an accurate rendering of schools as we have known them. However, the times they are a-changing and the connections between leadership and learning are becoming increasingly difficult to capture in a simple aphorism. The richness and complexity of learning is matched by the multi-layered, often elusive quality of leadership, so that teasing out their interrelationship is not for the faint-of-heart. This book is about making the connections and about one particular endeavour: to define a relationship that would make sense to people in different parts of the world, in widely differing school cultures and in widely differing social contexts.

We start from the premise that context and culture matter and that school leadership is intrinsically bound in time and place. Yet in a globalised environment ideas travel fast and policies follow close behind. Perhaps, though, it is more accurate to say that policies tend to precede the thought, and that leadership is cast in a common mould and immediately recognisable wherever you are in the world. Much has been written about leadership – some of it in an international context – but there is very little which helps to make explicit what leadership for learning means and the differing forms it can take, both between and within countries. So, in our initial explorations of the connections, we started the journey aware of twin dangers: of paying too little attention to contextual and cultural conditions on the one hand and failing to perceive the common factors that travel well on the other.

As we came to research these issues further it was with a belief that wherever leadership is to be found in this globalised world it should not be simply a matter of status or position but a social and cultural process, embedded in its context. We conceived of it as a form of activity which we could study in its own ecological niche but, through a process of appreciative inquiry, hoping to identify those facets of leadership that transcend context and shine a new light on our own cultural practices. We shared a conviction: this is how change happens. In Chapter 3 we quote Czarniawska's notion of 'outsidedness', the process by which, as we come to understand others, we learn to know ourselves better as a consequence.

In every country to which our research has taken us, we find heads and principals experiencing the ambivalence of leadership: problems and opportunities, momentum and direction, frustration and fulfilment. All are touched by the managerialist and performativity agendas, struggling to put authentic learning first. So we start this book with three chapters that try to get to the bottom of the puzzle – how to make the connections real, meaningful and practical in the busy, intensified and complex life of schools and classrooms.

We start with learning. In Chapter 1 we try to answer the question 'What do we know about learning?' and consider why, after centuries of research the answer still remains so elusive. Perhaps it is because we continue to view it through the prism of school, institutional conventions serving to obscure the inherent impulse with which we are born and which continues, although often dulled and diminished, throughout out lifetime, yet very often not in school.

We may apply a similar analysis to leadership. The leadership impulse is equally in our genes but, like learning, may be inhibited by social and institutional conventions. It is naturally distributed through every population and in all of those populations there is a struggle for power and a desire to influence others. It expresses itself in friendship pairs and triads, in informal groups and gangs, in the home, in school, in sports, and competitive games. However, like learning, we sometimes find it hard to discern within institutions which by their vary nature create hierarchies, formalising leadership and followership, removing much of the fluidity and interchangeability that occurs spontaneously outside their rigid constitutions. The formalisation of leadership hierarchies also tends to individualise leadership inhibiting its potential for becoming a shared endeavour.

Our interest here, however, is with leadership in a school context and so in Chapter 2 Neil Dempster asks, and attempts to answer, the question 'What do we know about leadership? He questions the assumptions on which polices rest and explores the ambiguity and the essentially contested nature of what leadership 'is' and how it expresses itself in school settings. In so doing he affirms that in an educational context leadership always pursues a moral purpose. The most significant and enduring moral purpose of schooling is, as the 1996 Delors Report puts it – learning to live together, learning to know, learning to do and learning to be.

It is the human aspects of learning and leading that have defied researchers' attempts to demonstrate a causal link between what leaders do and what children learn, mediated by myriad influences within and outside schools. These tensions are explored in Chapter 3. Sue Swaffield describes leading and learning as natural bedfellows, conjoined by a sense of human agency, no longer seen as separate entities but as what human beings do in every social situation they encounter. Learning enhances leadership and leadership so infected cannot help but make learning its central preoccupying focus.

These first three chapters lay the groundwork for the Leadership for Learning Project, its sometime shorthand 'Carpe Vitam' descriptor, a reference to the name of its Swedish sponsoring body and exceptional leader Peder Wallenberg whose singular mission is to 'seize life' at every opportunity. The Leadership for Learning Project was in many ways an exceptional and ground breaking study. It involved 24 schools from eight cities coming together for the first time in Cambridge in 2002 and then in successive years in Innsbruck, Copenhagen and Athens. On each occasion, travelling deeper into a shared understanding of how leadership for learning plays out in classrooms, schools and networks.

Such was the diversity and individual character of schools as distinctive as Petropoulis in Athens or HBO in Copenhagen, we could have entitled the book '24 Schools'. In Chapter 4 we have tried to portray the cultural and political differences that are so crucial to our understanding of how leadership and learning interconnect, illustrating this through three short cases, in London, Brisbane and New Jersey. We hope these three short stories capture some of the vibrant nature of the communities in which these schools sit and the different kinds of challenges they face.

In Chapter 5 David Frost describes some of the challenges met in trying to establish a common language and a set of agreed conventions for researching schools in these very different settings, respecting the differing traditions that researchers from these eight countries' higher education sites brought to the process. As methodology could not be simply prescribed across national and cultural boundaries, we described it as 'emergent and eclectic'. For some, the project was a form of 'action research', for some it was 'co-inquiry' while others found 'action learning' a more palatable description. The common strand in all of these situations was school self-evaluation, a process of inquiry, not prescribed by government but arising from a need to reflect on and reframe current practice.

Chapters 6 to 10 set out the five principles that emerged from cross cultural discussions, school visits and exchanges across geographical, cultural and linguistic borders. In each case we attempt to illustrate ways in which these principles do not simply remain as lofty ideals or statements of intent but how they may be realised in practice. At the end of each chapter we raise questions for school staff, and students, to consider and discuss further. The living nature of those principles is taken further in Chapter 11 which describes how schools worked together to test and make sense of the principles in their own contexts. The first is a story of how a school in Whitby (England) and a school in Bakkaloka (Norway) found the common strands in their very different cultural settings. The second narrative centres on a group of schools in one Hertfordshire town embedding the principles in tools of inquiry and improvement planning.

We conclude in Chapter 12 with some defining features of leadership for learning and some of the messages that policy makers need to take on board if those connecting strands are to be put to the service of government's mission to 'raise standards', so that, hopefully, 'standards' will come to be seen in a much broader and richer sense.

Reference

Delors, J. (1996) *Learning: The Treasure Within*, Report to UNESCO of the International Commission on Education for the Twenty-First Century.

1 What do we know about learning?

John MacBeath

Schools are places for learning. Such a statement appears, on the face it, both trite and uncontentious. Yet beneath its surface appeal there are widely differing opinions as to its validity, plus a substantive body of research taking issue with the assumptions on which such a statement rests. The educational literature suggests seven differing kinds of challenge to the simplicity of the relationship between learning and schooling.

The first challenge comes from deschooolers and radical critics who contend that schooling is by nature anti-learning. Its very structures and conventions thwart learning, its institutional constraints limiting spontaneity and curiosity and what the father of the deschooling movement, Ivan Illich (1971), termed 'conviviality'. This view has a longer history going back to the idyll of the 'noble savage', epitomised by Rousseau who portrayed in the person of his character Émile, the unfettered learner following a path of his own inclination. In modern guise this view of institutions as oppressive and demotivating was particularly prevalent in the 1970s when numerous books and articles were published with titles such as Alan Graubard's *Free the Children (and Other Political Prisoners)*.

A second argument sees the deschooling movement as too overstated but concedes that the engagement with learning in school settings is highly variable. It points to a wide and substantive gap between those for whom school is a place for success and those for whom school represents a repetitive and demoralising experience of failure to learn. The arguments are developed in a stream of sociological studies which illuminated the interplay of class, race and gender in separating the winners and losers. Willis's seminal study in 1977, *Learning to Labour: How Working Class Kids Get Working Class Jobs*, depicted the role of class structures as disenfranchising a large minority, in which what was learned in school was, above all, one's place in society.

This leads in turn to a third body of critique, more overtly politicised in character and resting on assumptions as to the place of school in the political economy. The argument is rooted less at school level than at the level of the state which is depicted as legislating and authenticating certain kinds of learning as more or less valued currencies in terms of their economic return. To use government language, learning is 'delivered' through recognised agencies of the state, through an assessment and certification system which validates lower- and higher-order knowledge, primarily for its perceived instrumental value. Assessment thus becomes an instrument of government, driving the school's agenda, its priorities, its focus, its strategic direction, its accountability and the ways in which it represents to an external audience its quality and effectiveness. Schools, by this argument, find themselves caught between the twin agendas of high status 'academic' knowledge and low status vocational skills, having to exercise a delicate and problematic selection process. So learning itself is seen as having less and less intrinsic value but assumes greater proxy value, that is, as a form of benchmark for the efficiency of teachers, of school leaders and return on investment. In her book *Does Education Matter?* (2002), Alison Wolf explores the mythic relationship between school learning and the economy, arguing that the government's pursuit of the economic agenda has shrunk 'narrowly' and 'abysmally' the pursuit of learning.

A fourth and related critique locates the issues more centrally in the nature of curriculum. Patrick Lewis in his book *How We Think, But Not in School* (2007) describes the 'Hydra curriculum', as each head is lopped off another appears to take its place. Yet there is little wiggle room to accommodate new 'subjects' as the traditional core of the curriculum remains firmly in place. So, it is argued, teachers are pressed into covering content while what they are required to assess and account for less and less reflects what is important or relevant to the lives of children and young people growing up in the twenty-first century. Due to the nature of a standardised, sequential, age-related curriculum there is always a process of compromise between the learning needs and interests of the child and the demands of a bureaucratic system.

> Teachers may suggest a connection between learners' interests and experience and the school curriculum, but that is more of a ploy to motivate learners to absorb the meat and potatoes of the academic curriculum. Tests rarely ask for personal connections or commentaries; they want the curriculum rendered back in its pure academic form, untainted by personal associations.
>
> (Starrat, 1998: 5)

Reprising Herbert Spencer's tract 'What knowledge is of most worth', John White has edited a series of books inviting critics from a range of subject backgrounds to make an argument for or against the inclusion of their own pet subject in the compulsory curriculum. The publication of *Why Learn Maths?* in particular, provoked a heated response primarily because of the historic, hallowed and unchallenged status of mathematics at the core of the curriculum. We have become so inured to traditional canons of the academic curriculum, it is argued, that it is hard to see learning in any other way than through the lenses bequeathed to us by the medieval quadrivium and trivium.

As the nature and appropriateness of the curriculum comes under greater scrutiny it becomes increasingly difficult to know how to accommodate educational priorities which sit uneasily within a tightly timetabled collection of subjects. So emerging areas of concern such as environmental education, health education, personal and social education, education for citizenship and democracy all have to fight for curricular space. A fifth body of critique takes a more radical view of school purpose, seeing the core values of citizenship and democracy as ill served by an approach which simply adds more and more content to the curricular diet. Citizenship and democracy may be squeezed into the curriculum but the way in which these 'subjects' are taught is fundamentally in conflict with hierarchical structures, with authoritarian cultures and with selective mechanisms which exclude some children and which stream and set children into different social and ability groups. It is argued that learning which matters and is most powerful in shaping attitudes comes through the 'hidden curriculum', the implicit rather than the explicit messages that a school conveys to its students. Making learning explicit for, and through, democracy is the subject of Hartman Von Hentig's series of letters to a mythical nephew Tobias: in response to the question 'Why should I have to go to school?' in one letter he writes:

> In school you meet people different from yourself from different back-grounds, children you can observe, talk to, ask questions, for example someone from Turkey or Vietnam, a devout Catholic or an out and out atheist, boys and girls, a mathematical whiz kid, a child in a wheelchair . . . I believe wholeheartedly that the open school is there first and foremost to bring young people together and to help them to learn to live in a way that our political society so badly needs.
>
> (Von Hentig, 2001: 47)

A sixth perspective considers the wider purposes and contexts of learning, locating it less predominantly in classrooms, seeing it as crossing institutional boundaries. It charges schools with a failure to understand or build on the knowledge, skills and dispositions shaped by home, community, peer groups and agencies such as youth clubs and uniformed organisations. The nature of this complex weave is captured in Weiss and Fine's book *Construction Sites* (2000) which illustrates how learning is engaged and deepened through parental and family discourse in ways that cannot be addressed in the less intimate and less flexible classroom context. This conception of learning as 'constructed' in multiple different sites gave impetus to the full service school in the United States and extended schools in the UK, many local authorities re-inventing themselves as child and family services. In policy terms this is reprised in the five outcomes of the *Every Child Matters* agenda in England, which not only broadens thinking about outcomes but no longer casts schools as the sole arbiters of learning. However, the very nature of school to which we are 'locked in' militates against a more fluid open inclusive approach to meeting differing learning needs.

A seventh perspective comes at these issues through a different lens, starting not from the assumption that school learning is simply for children. Proceeding with the question 'Who is learning for?', it argues that to focus solely on the children's learning is to miss the point. Such a view, it is held, ignores the social interweave, not only of families, peer groups and communities but most pertinently the professionals who work and learn alongside their charges. Rather than as places for passing on knowledge to children, schools are portrayed as learning organisations, or learning communities – places in which pupil learning is inseparable from professional learning and the culture is one in which learning flows across boundaries of role and status. This seventh perspective owes much to corporate literature, for example Peter Senge, Chris Argyris and Donald Schon, their ideas transposed into a school context. The title of Senge's book, *Schools That Learn* (2000), shifts the focus of our attention from the pupil as learner to the school as learner. If schools do not or cannot learn then Illich and other critics may legitimately claim that schools are in an essential respect anti-educational.

Learning in the wild

When we view school-based learning through each of these lenses it raises a question of signal importance for leadership. What do we know about learning 'in captivity' and what do we know about learning 'in the wild'? The problem we confront is that we are never able to observe learning in a pure unadulterated form, as uncontaminated by the social structures we have created from cradle to grave. However, by studying learning as shaped and expressed in diverse contexts we find that we have still much to learn about learning and much to learn about how learning can be led, in and out of school.

Scientists eager to find the least socially constraining context for learning have celebrated the occasional discovery of wild children, often living with, or reared by animals. These are rare events but illustrate the importance of human socialisation and that uniquely human attribute, the power of language, which simply fails to develop without the simulation of human discourse. Without language these children have been deprived of the most essential of tools for giving shape to and extending experience, allowing thinking to abstract itself beyond the bounds of the present, and travel imaginatively among symbolic thoughtworlds.

Scientists have been afforded much wider scope for exploring asocial environments by studying what happens to children as yet unborn, the first nine months of their lives imprisoned in the viscous environment of the womb but with an awesome developmental task to perform. With sophisticated technology it has become possible to observe the beginning of learning close-up as the brain begins the intricate process of building highly sophisticated thinking and communication networks.

The growing child is not alone, however, connected to the social world through an umbilical tube, highly sensitive to environmental influences, nourished or deprived of opportunity not simply by the habits, behaviour and diet of the mother but by the environment she inhabits and the influence of those around her. One of the most dramatic effects of intellectual deprivation is Foetal Alcohol Syndrome (FSA) which impacts powerfully on capacity for learning and reveals itself in a generally unsuccessful childhood struggle to cope with the social, emotional and academic demands of the classroom. While the debate continues as to the nature and extent of genetic factors in ability and personality we do know that congenital (inter-uterine) effects combine in complex and powerful ways with genetic infrastructures to switch on and switch off gene activity, laying down some of the key parameters of human capacity.

Despite the heated and sometimes ideological debate about nature and nurture there is common agreement that these two complementary accidents of circumstance interact in and beyond the womb, and most significantly in the plasticity of the early years when children begin to discover themselves, start to reflect on who they are and begin the long journey of deciding who they want to be. So, child development studies furnish us with a source of valuable insights into the nature of learning. Many of the findings are surprising and counter-intuitive while some remain contested. In sum they tell us that small children are capable of much more than we have credited them with and are very often limited by the scope that their anxious parents, child minders and pre-school environments allow them.

Where the learning story begins

A large part of what we know about learning starts with the early years because this is one area in which there is complete consensus as to the vital influence of the formative period, up to and following conception. We arrive into the 'booming buzzing confusion' of the outside world, hard wired with a potential so vast that it makes a mockery of the school conceit of 'pupils developing their full potential'. In those critical formative years after birth the metaphoric description is of windows opening and closing as the extra-uterine environment nurtures or inhibits acquisition of skills and breeds, or inhibits, confidence in the world and those who inhabit it. Some children spend the early years in an environment shielded from the hazardous terrain beyond while others enjoy a wide latitude to experiment, to discover and to learn some hard lessons for themselves. Some infants form deep attachment to, and dependency on, their mothers while for others the mother may not be a central or permanent figure. What we know from 'stranger' laboratory studies is that from a very early age children respond quite differently to maternal separation and that attachment relationships vary widely between cultural contexts as well as within them. Lessons as to power, authority and trust are learned early and indelibly, often leaving a deep and permanent residue.

The emergence and stimulation of language plays a critical role in helping children to structure and add emotional colour to what they experience around them. From the booming buzzing confusion language singles out salient objects and concepts, and builds the tools through which children move from being acted on by their environment to acting on their environment. The child who reduces a newspaper to a hundred small pieces has effected a hugely satisfying expression of agency, although one which will become progressively set around with sanction and disapproval, particularly as emotive language labels become attached to certain forms of behaviour.

While language provides the most powerfully proactive of tools, its acquisition is a relatively slow process. We know less about the nature of learning in this pre-linguistic stage during which children make meaning from their experience, through imitation and trial and error exploration of their surroundings. But we do know that activity such as crawling is not only a swift form of locomotion but a powerful exploratory medium for forming and testing hypotheses about the world, relationships, cause and effect. It is one denied to some children because anxious, stressed or busy parents and carers confine babies to cots, playpens, baby bouncers or other corralled environments. The exploratory nature of trial and error in infancy is not, however, learning by the blind bumping up against things like the paramecium but a progressive cognitive structuring of the world, making the way for the conceptual added value of language and literacy. As Piaget showed, even before locomotion, children begin to work out causality relationships, pulling a carpet toward them to reach a target object, for example, then generalising this 'push–pull' schema to papers, sheets, tablecloths. With access to emergent language, children begin to attach labels to salient objects in the environment, progressively extending the world beyond the immediate horizons of the physical. The gulf between the richness and paucity of differing language environments has been shown to be huge and significant for later literacy acquisition.

For some literacy comes easily. For others the challenge of literacy is to learn to detach words from their affective relationship as words come to assume a more distanced and symbolic character. Words come to stand for things rather than being things and, if you have access to them, ideas are extended and exchanged through words, spoken and written. However, literacy comes as both a liberating and a constraining force. Patrick Lewis writes about schools 'drowning children in text' (2007: 46), missing opportunities to enrich and utilize oracy. He reminds us of Plato's warning that trust in written characters can silence the inner voice and undermine self-confidence and, more recently socio-cultural neuropsychologists who point to the essentially different mediating processes involved in the production of spoken and written text. Allowed to grow organically, and scaffolded by prescient parents and teachers, literacy adds to and enriches the repertoire or learning modalities. Constrained or force fed it may stunt and demotivate.

The boundaries of normality

Studies of child development whether in natural, laboratory or experimental settings have generated a plethora of theories as to what is 'normal' and 'abnormal', the latter a contentious label because the boundaries of 'normality' remain fuzzy and because the process of labelling itself creates a way of seeing, defining and creating intelligence. But the study of abnormality and extreme abnormality has also provided a rich field of scientific study, shedding light on the nature of learning difficulties while also opening our eyes to extraordinary intellectual powers of children with different kinds of 'special needs'. The thankfully disused term 'idiot savants' is a telling descriptor of the combination of 'subnormal' and genius intellect. There are accomplishments beyond the compass of our imagination such as Thomas Bethune, a blind retarded slave who at four years of age could play Mozart sonatas flawlessly, and whose repertoire as a teenager extended to over 5,000 classical arrangements having previously only heard them once. Or the American twins who could not add two and two but could instantly calculate the weekday of any date given to them back to the second century and beyond, in the process taking account of leap years.

In many special and mainstream classrooms there are children on the Asperger's spectrum whose obsessive motivation and attention to detail are a constant source of surprise to their parents and teachers. Their idiosyncratic behaviour is generally misunderstood and misinterpreted as many of the 'gifts' of autistic children continue to defy science. Brain imaging technologies have been able to shed some light on developmental processes which fail to install the mental filters protecting the average (one might say 'run-of-the-mill') human being from the barrage of information that allows synaesthetics to hear colours, feel numbers and see sounds while struggling to comprehend emotional expression. In his autobiography *Born on a Blue Day*, Daniel Tammet (2007) describes having to systematically learn the external indicators of emotion and how to read them in everyday social contexts.

Through investigation of conditions of aberrant brain behaviours neuro-science is helping to demolish some of the myths and folk wisdom, while adding substance to theories of learning. Technology which allows us to peer inside the brain is now able to identify patterns of cerebral activity and identify what it is that causes neurons to fire or misfire. The linking of thinking and feeling, motivation and demotivation can be observed at close quarters, revealing what makes the brain 'light up' within and between hemispheres and in the emotional centres of the amygdala and limbic system. As teachers and parents we know joy, hope and optimism when we see it but we are now gradually learning more about their physiological correlates and the electrochemical activity which accompanies challenge, engagement and euphoria. 'Hope fires a neuron in the brain', writes the physicist David Bohm (1983). Optimism and self-belief spark a bioelectrical network of activity which predisposes a learning, as opposed to a withdrawal, response.

From theory to practice

What we know about learning from various branches of social and medical science has taken us beyond the superstitions of bodily humours and studies of cranial indentations but nonetheless we are still in the realms of theory building, trying to match what we think we know to the situations in which children and young people find themselves. Learning theories have been highly influential in their impact on practice, embraced and then discarded as a new and better theory came along. Policy makers have laid the blame for school failure at the door of Piaget, Montessori, Dewey, and other heretics who, policy makers claimed, have misled generations of teachers and school leaders. Studies of infancy and childhood have, it is said, led to an embrace of ideas both doctrinaire and counter productive. Too simplistic an application of developmental theory construes children's progress through school as moving from the concrete to the abstract, from play to serious work, from childish theorising to adult fact.

The fallacy in stage theory, or its application, is that with developing intellectual and emotional maturity we do not put away childish things. Rather we have access to a wider range of modes of thought. An alternative theoretical stance, while accepting many of the valid insights from stage theories have problematised and reframed these, depicting them as modes of knowing which need to be applied more fluidly to children's progressive learning journey. For example, in his book the *Educated Mind*, Keiran Egan (1997) outlines a theory broadly developmental in nature but also recursive so that, he argues, whether as children or as adults, we constantly revisit ways of knowing, building not so much on what we know but how we know. As what we know becomes more deeply layered and more finely textured by the mental modes which we engage, we become more insightful and sophisticated in the way we apprehend and process knowledge – in other words we get better at learning how to learn.

Egan's five cognitive tools

Kieran Egan proposes five modes of understanding, cognitive tools which broadly follow a developmental sequence and although most characteristic of certain ages and stages are all facets of human attempts to comprehend the world.

Somatic understanding is in evolutionary and developmental terms the most primitive form of interpreting the world, yet essential to continuously feeling our way through life. It is memetic, a representational mode which does not rely on language but uses bodily sensation, rhythm and musicality to learn and communicate with others.

Mythic understanding is a fundamental mode of thought, most characteristic of early childhood in which the world is constructed of binary oppositions – good and evil, truth and lies, black and white. It is dominated by affective images rather than words, appealing to metaphor which graphically opens up new ways of apprehending causality and relationships.

Romantic understanding has its roots in the real world, made available by the tools of literacy and therefore offering a more distanced and complex version of events. The simplicity of binary oppositions is problematised and relationships are complexified. For young children it is 'the trek out of Eden to the adult's more prosaic world'. Yet it is a reality in which wonder, the exotic and the extreme exert a particular fascination.

Philosophic understanding is a product of a search for intelligible replicable truth that lies beneath the surface appearance of things. It is concerned with norms and the rules of argument, logic and evidence. It is systematic, abstract and dispassionate and moves beyond an interest in the particular to the general and generalisable.

Ironic understanding does not settle for the explanations of logic and science. It is reflexive and quizzical. It seeks to question not just what we know but how we know it. It recognises the tension that exists between an inherent sceptical approach to knowing and the need for a general knowledge schema within which it has to makes sense out of non-sense. Irony without philosophic capacity, however, is impotent.

Understanding in any one of these modes, argues Egan, does not fade away to be replaced by the next, but rather each properly coalesces in a significant degree with its predecessor. So as adults we have access to all modes, including somatic understanding which, although to the fore in infancy, continues to be deployed in adulthood. We accrue a wider repertoire of ways of understanding and a more highly developed social sensitivity as to when the somatic, mythic, romantic, philosophical or ironic mode is most appropriate. This ability to move around among modes of thinking is what systems theorists refer to as the principle of requisite variety. It describes the intellectual tool called into use so as to conform with the complexity of what it represents. In complex problem solving whether by scientists, philosophers, inventors or business executives at the cutting edge, learning is very often playful, romantic as well as philosophic and ironic, as much given to wrong answers as to right ones.

As adults we may find ourselves socially embarrassed when caught out in childish modes of behaviour, indulging the child in the adult, yet no matter how grown up we are we invent alternative magical worlds, fantasise and dream, enjoy adult fairy stories, science fiction and horror films and go to fancy dress parties. And even as philosophic and ironic adults, argues Egan (1997: 162), very often 'magic will trump science'. An alien paying a visit to a large news-agent might construct a theory of what preoccupies earthlings by scanning the 101 covers of adult magazines.

As adults we also create challenges for ourselves, in leisure, sport, the arts and music which we pursue with obsessive dedication, much of it competitive against others, much of it competitive against our own previous best. We pursue what Csikszentmihalyi (1990) terms 'flow' experiences, the psychological high we get from the meeting point of challenge and skill. We seek out cognitive challenges, through Sudoku, crosswords, jigsaw puzzles, chess and bridge problems, pub quizzes and video games because the progress from cognitive dissonance to cognitive resolution is intrinsically rewarding. Often persisting into adulthood are the collections we started as children – stamps, coins, comics and magazines, dolls, Dinky toys and train sets, military artefacts and other memorabilia to which we form a deep emotional attachment. The desire, or need, to collect, to compete the set, reach the next level is a powerful emotional driver.

It seems that human beings are never truly satisfied with the status quo and pursue higher levels of attainment and intelligence through the range of tools they have at their disposal. When we have access to what Vygotsky (1962, 1978) termed mediating intellectual tools, it opens up new ideas and alternative ways of understanding the world. Our restless inquiry prompts us not to settle for immediate reality, or the too easily known. The drive for novelty is always in tension, however, with the comfort of the familiar. As Mark Twain put it 'what gets us in trouble is what we think we know but it just ain't so'. Vygotsky described what he termed a 'zone of proximal development' (ZPD) to represent the sphere of knowing beyond our current understanding. The stimulus to move beyond what we currently know, or think we know, may come from the scaffolding of teachers but also from peers, parents or from our own psychological need to achieve, to know more, to do it better. In formal settings and conventional curricula the ZPD is often interpreted as the next linear step represented by pre-determined targets, rather than, as Vygotsky intended, a horizon of possibilities which may take us in new and uncharted directions.

Simply put, learning is its own reward and it is only as we institutionalise and ration learning that it requires extrinsic incentives and compensations such as gold stars and marks out of ten. The spontaneous multi-faceted learning that occurs in informal contexts contrasts with so much of what takes place in classrooms – sequential, cerebral, pre-determined. Objectives on the board at the beginning of the lesson tell us that the teacher is unlikely to be surprised into deviation or ambushed by children's spontaneous 'off-task' insights.

Dinosaurs and castles
In this English primary school teachers were nostalgic about no longer teaching topics that fascinated children but were no longer in the curriculum they felt obliged to teach. With the coming of a new head they were persuaded that it was better to start with what excited and fired children's imaginations, working back to, rather than from, curricular objectives. While teachers of 20 years' standing had, a decade ago, worked in this way the Primary Strategies, literacy/numeracy hours and key stage testing had blunted teachers' enthusiasm and confidence in their own professional judgement. A student on placement in the school given a box of dinosaurs didn't know what to do with them, having been trained to deliver curricular packages designed by someone else.

Assessment is geared to what we have been taught not what we have been enthralled by or learned about our learning. Learning is hard work, the term 'work' itself betraying its opposition with play. Yet, as adults, when we look back on school it is the peak moments of enjoyment and discovery that we recall. The memorable events are experienced anew with the emotional texture that gave rise to them. We recall teachers who weaved magic or made us laugh. Humour and laughter not only contribute to making learning fun but as Californian researchers Berk and Tan discovered, laughter makes us less susceptible to stress and disease. It lowers blood pressure, boosting immune function by raising levels of infection-fighting T-cells, releasing of endorphins and producing a general sense of well-being conducive to engagement with learning.

'Minds without emotion are not really minds at all. They are souls on ice', writes Le Doux (1998). He refers to cognitive science in the past as having limited itself as a study of only part of the mind, knowledge of the 'emotional brain' remaining shrouded in mystery and conjecture. Yet, as we now know, the relationship between depression, fearfulness, dependency and helplessness flows in two directions. A sense of empowerment and self-esteem stimulates learning while a positive learning experience in turn reduces dependency and depression. This is a virtuous circle with far reaching impact if sustained over a longer period. People who have had positive educational experiences tend to have a wider repertoire of interests and sources of fulfilment. They live longer and suffer less chronic illness. While this is not a simple correlation and one mediated by socio-economic factors, it is essentially about the ability to make informed choices, to believe that you are in control rather than being controlled by others. Following Hebb's famous dictum that that 'neurons that fire together wire together', not only do ideas build chains of association but they also become invested with emotional texture so that maths isn't maths but something to be dreaded, excited by or forever associated with a particular teacher of a particular place. How much of this we carry into adult life is graphically illustrated by Sarah Lawrence Lightfoot in her descriptions of parent–teacher meetings, conducted in classrooms 'saturated with immaturity'. Our memories of how, where and with whom we learned can take us back or they can take us forward.

Growing up absurd

A number of years ago Paul Goodman wrote a book entitled *Growing up Absurd*. It was about a world unfit for children. That assertion may be more powerfully endorsed in the third millennium. It is, in many respects, a more hostile place than it was when Goodman wrote four decades ago. The narrative of learning for young people today is how to survive and navigate a hazardous social terrain of inducement and threat. It might be argued that without the benefits of data, communication networks and the discoveries of neuroscience we were blissfully ignorant as to adolescent susceptibility to anxiety, depression, impulsiveness, aggression and self-harm. Or, is the explanation for the restless dissatisfaction of adolescence an artefact of contemporary society, which has created a whole new raft of afflictions unknown to previous generations? While there is now believed to be a genetic predisposition to aggression and depression (in Freudian terminology anger turned outward in aggression and anger turned inwards in depression), it is much more likely to be given expression in households, communities and peer relationships which are violent, chaotic and stressful. It is now widely accepted that abuse, poverty, neglect and sensory deprivation reset the brain's chemistry, a delicate balance highly susceptible to stress, lack of sleep, bad diet, chemicals, alcohol and drugs. This deadly cocktail has a far-reaching impact on learning behaviour in and out of school. The perennial challenge is to grasp what it means to grow up in differing social contexts and how to help young people bridge the move between these construction sites.

The more we venture into this tangled territory the more complex and contested becomes our knowledge of human learning and the greater our understanding of its social and emotional character. We develop a new appreciation of the precarious path that young people have to tread in order to attain a level of physical and mental health which enables them to engage with what schools offer them and begin to fulfil some, at least, of their uncharted potential.

What lies behind the façade that thirty or so young people present to their teachers within the classroom? What autobiographies connect the teacher to the individual lives lived out, or temporarily suspended, within the classroom? It is no longer possible to entertain the transmission or knowledge acquisition model, if we ever did believe that 'it is possible to achieve one to one correspondence between what is in the teacher's head and what the pupil learns'. And, adds Mary James (2008: 22), 'remembering things is fundamental. What is much more questionable is that pupils should, or can, remember things in exactly the same way as they are remembered by their teachers.'

Sticky knowledge

While teachers may use the terminology of getting knowledge to 'stick', we do know that knowledge is indeed 'sticky' but in a quite different sense of that term. The transmission of information between a teacher and student gets stuck in many places en route. It gets stuck in misconception because there is no prior knowledge on which to build. It remains faithful to old mental models because there is resistance to new or disturbing ideas. It fails to adhere because there is no emotional glue to hold it fast. It sticks because there is no disposition or apparent need to commit to the learning moment. It sticks because young people are deeply affected by the attitudes of their peers and wish to remain detached and 'cool'. As Maurice Galton found, 'If they volunteered too many acceptable answers too quickly, they could earn the reputation of being a 'buff'. If they offered too few answers they might be regarded as 'thick'. It was much safer, therefore, to get teachers to answer their own questions' (Galton, 2007: 62).

Perhaps above all, though, knowledge sticks fast because it is located deeply and singularly in the context of the classroom. 'Knowledge to go', as David Perkins puts it, is deeply problematic. Put simply, children can be taught with a high degree of reliability to solve problems when those problems are structured appropriately by the teacher and presented to students in the classroom context. Indeed it may be possible to achieve 100 per cent success with well-designed problem-solving tasks in the classroom. However, in an unstructured open field outside school the success rate may fall to as low as 5 per cent, says David Perkins (2006). This is due to three key factors. One, students have to be able to spot the problem. Two, they need to be motivated to want to engage with the problem. Three, they then need to have the ability to select and use the most appropriate tools to solve the problem. This is why Perkins places so much emphasis on dispositions, because without a desire to engage, learning will always be at second hand with a pitiable half-life in memory.

Howard Gardner reports similar findings. Research with college students on physics courses found that they could not solve the most basic problems if posed in a context slightly dissimilar to the one they first encountered it in. Gardner found that even successful students responded to problems with the same confusions and misconceptions as young children, reverting to their own implicit theories formed in childhood. This is depressing news for teachers, trying vainly to deploy every device and strategy to entice children into learning. Are their efforts frustrated because the legacy of schooling is to limit classroom endeavour to just one of Howard Gardner's 'intelligences', or to Egan's philosophic mode? Is it because we reserve expression of the other intelligences to drama and the 'creative subjects', those at the periphery of the curriculum or relegated to the 'extra' curricular domain? Is it because we have somewhere along the way lost the magic in learning?

Magic in the classroom

When John was at school he would rush carelessly through his homework in order to study his magic books, spending hours at a time, reading avidly and practising the high level of discipline to perform more and more elaborate tricks. As a teacher of maths he found it hard to motivate children until he was encouraged by his father to use his magic tricks. Not only did this engage and fascinate his pupils but he began to find lots of ways of using magic tricks to explore number, probability and equations. Most gratifying was the change in relationships with a class with whom he enjoyed a new-found respect.

John's story tells us something about the magic of engagement with learning. Learning is of necessity mediated in some form but all forms of mediation involve constraint as well as empowerment. So in whatever ways teachers try to structure their intervention they need to be aware of the critical balance of these two counter-field forces. We have a variety of terms to describe the process by which teachers entice pupils into learning, the hook, the lever, the affective tug, that pulls children into an activity, perhaps despite themselves. In Scotland in the 1970s, before the Educational Dark Ages, many primary schools used an approach called Storyline. It was founded on the belief that all learning is a form of narrative quest for deeper meaning and that all, or the greater part of, learning could be construed as a type of story telling. It was a thematic approach which engaged children by making connections between the external knowledge world and the inner world of their creative imagination. The classroom, indeed the whole of a school, might become an Amazon rain forest, a Victorian village, an island community or an urban street, the sterility of barren walls and regimented desks transformed into inspirational places, social places in which learning takes on the character of a shared adventure. Classrooms become places of surprise, welcoming of the unexpected and the unplanned.

Without the story form, argues Patrick Lewis, 'humans would have endless unconnected, chaotic experiences' (2006: 1). Such a view receives confirmation from neuroscientists who describe the cortex's narrative drive, its intrinsic need to make sense of, and weave stories out of, our disparate experiences. In Jerome Bruner's words we have a 'readiness or predisposition to organize experience into a narrative form' (1990: 45). Unless teachers are able to effect this and schools are structured as storied worlds children's experience of learning is liable to remain unconnected and dislocated.

Storyline is not the panacea. It can't repair the ruins of a sterile or fractured childhood. Nor is it the only approach to making schools congenial and stimulating places of learning. But, what it testifies to is the creative intelligence of children when freed from the numbing repetitiveness of much classroom routine, always with one eye on the ubiquitous test. It is, as Lave and Wenger put it, about 'the whole person acting in the world'.

10 lessons learned

- We are hard-wired as sophisticated learning machines.
- Our potential at conception is beyond imagination or measurement.
- In the critical months before birth we build the architecture of our brains but with highly variable success.
- Following birth the social, emotional and intellectual environment channels our genetic and congenital predispositions in nurturing or inhibiting ways.
- The quality, range and sensitivity to language plays a critical differentiating role in and out of school.
- The differential nature of experience creates a gap between high and low achievers well before children start school.
- School experience may act to reinforce and even exacerbate the achievement and attitudinal gap by the structures, attitudes and expectations which it employs.
- Our innate disposition to making meaning through narrative places an onus on adults (in school and home) to help children and young people achieve coherence in their learning.
- As children progress they extend the repertoire of their modes of thinking but early modes ('somatic' and 'mythic' for example) are not left behind.
- As young people and adults the child in us lives on. Curricular development, teaching and assessment need to represent this multi-vocal character of experience.

Leading learning

As leaders we need to recall and reflect on our own learning journey, the path it took and the modes and mental models which we grew intellectually and emotionally, remaining alive to the fact that the children, young people and adults that we aspire to lead may travel very different paths. Leadership for learning is ever open to surprise, leading in order to learn, learning so as to lead more effectively.

References

Alexander, R. (2006) *Towards Dialogic Teaching: Rethinking Classroom Talk* (3rd edition), London: Dialogos.

Argyris, C. and Schön, D. (1978) *Organizational Learning: A Theory of Action Perspective*, Reading, MA: Addison Wesley.

Bohm, D. (1983) *Wholeness and the Implicate Order*, New York: Ark Paperbacks.

Bramall, S. and White, J. (2000) *Why Learn Maths?* London: Institute of Education Publications.

Bruner, J. (1990) *Acts of Meaning*, Cambridge, MA: Harvard University Press.

Csikszentmihalyi, M. (1990) *Flow: The Psychology of Optimal Experience*, New York: Harper and Row.

Egan, K. (1997) *The Educated Mind: How Cognitive Tools Shape Our Understanding*, Chicago, IL: University of Chicago Press.

Galton, M. (2007) *Learning and Teaching in the Primary Classroom*, London: Sage.

Gardner, H. (1993) *The Unschooled Mind: How Children Think and How Schools Should Teach*, London: Basic Books.

Goodman, P. (1960) *Growing Up Absurd*, New York: Random House.

Graubard, A. (1972) *Free the Children (and Other Political Prisoners)*, New York: Vintage.

Illich, I. (1971) *Deschooling Society*, Harmondsworth: Penguin.

James, M. (2008) 'Assessment on Learning', in S. Swaffield (ed.) *Unlocking Assessment*, Oxon: Routledge.

Lawrence Lightfoot, S. (2003) *The Essential Conversation*, New York: Random House.

Le Doux, J. (1998) *The Emotional Brain*, London: Weidenfeld and Nicolson.

Lewis, P.J. (2007) *How We Think, But Not in School*, Rotterdam/Taipei: Sense Publishers.

McLuhan, M. (1964) *Understanding Media: The Extensions of Man*, Maidenhead: McGraw-Hill.

Perkins, D. (2006) 'Beyond understanding', Paper delivered at the Threshold Concepts within the Disciplines Conference, University of Strathclyde, 30 August.

Reimer, E. (1973) *School is Dead: An Essay on Alternatives in Education*, Harmondsworth: Penguin.

Senge, P.M. (1990) *The Fifth Discipline: The Art and Practice of the Learning Organisation*, New York: Doubleday.

Senge, P.M., Cambron McCabe, N.H., Lucas, T., Kleiner, A., Dutton, J. and Smith, B. (2000) *Schools That Learn. A Fifth Discipline Fieldbook for Educators, Parents, and Everyone Who Cares About Education*, New York: Doubleday.

Spencer, H. (1859) 'What knowledge is of most worth?', *Westminister Review*, July.

Starratt, R.J. (2004) *Ethical Leadership*, San Francisco, CA: Jossey-Bass.

Tammet, D. (2007) *Born on a Blue Day*, London: Hodder.

von Hentig, H. (2001) *Warum muss ich zur Schule gehen?*, München: Carl Hanser Verlag.

Vygotsky, L. (1962) *Thought and Language*, Cambridge, MA: MIT.

Vygotsky, L.S. (1978) *Mind in Society: The Development of Higher Psychological Processes*, Cambridge, MA: Harvard University Press.

Weiss, M. and Fine, L. (2000) *Construction Sites: Excavating Race, Class and Gender among Urban Youth*, New York: Teachers College Press.

Willis, P. (1977) *Learning to Labour: How Working Class Kids Get Working Class Jobs*, Farnborough: Saxon House.

Wolf, A. (2002) *Does Education Matter?* Harmondsworth: Penguin.

2 What do we know about leadership?

Neil Dempster

Introduction

This chapter seeks answers to the question: 'What do we know about leadership?' Ministries or Departments of Education would say 'quite a lot'. A quick scan of their websites in countries such as the United Kingdom, the United States of America, Canada, New Zealand and Australia tells us that most have defined leadership through 'Standards or Capabilities Frameworks'. These frameworks describe in detail the kinds of skills, competencies or dispositions employers believe their school leaders should have. The frameworks are used for a variety of purposes: as recruitment and selection instruments, as self-reflective devices for those considering whether they should make a move towards leadership, as guides for professional learning programmes and as formal assessment tools for promotion purposes. Most of these frameworks carry explicit messages about the type of leaders that school systems want to appoint by laying out expectations about what is acceptable.

As might be expected, the standards framework approach to leadership has attracted criticism in recent research literature (Leithwood *et al.*, 2002; Gronn, 2003; and Gunter, 2001), not only because lists are subject to omissions but also because the use of standards has not yet been grounded in empirical evidence.

Do standards frameworks enlighten us about leadership or have we justification to be sceptical about them? It is certain that lists of standards are the antithesis of the narratives described in Chapter 1 as an essential part of the way human beings make sense out of 'disparate experiences'.

How clear are the assumptions about leadership on which standards frameworks are constructed? We suggest that they are unclear and yet we know that the starting point for all school leadership should be its moral purpose. If enhancing or improving people's lives is the source of, or fundamental motivation for action by teachers and school leaders, then learning is the vehicle through which that moral purpose is achieved. When behaviourist sets of standards dominate leadership thinking and action in school settings, the moral purpose of education may well retreat into the background. Critical to keeping moral purpose centre stage is an understanding of the primacy of the learning needs, interests, abilities and aspirations of children, young people or adult learners, in fact all who at one time or another work with teachers and those in leadership positions.

To illustrate this point of view, we offer a narrative, a story which carries a message about the moral purpose of leadership which no standards framework could possibly cover.

> The story is about a young woman who worked as a school cleaner at her children's local primary school. She had been forced to take up this occupation after removing herself and her children from an abusive relationship with the man she had married as a teenager of 18. By the age of 21 she had three children and she was experiencing increasing domestic violence.
>
> Having left home at age 15, this woman, the youngest of 12 children, began her working life as a seamstress in a clothing factory in an Australian east coast regional township. As her marriage moved inexorably to failure, she saw the need to gain some economic independence from her domineering and violent husband. Unable to get the kind of work that would allow her to be close to her children after the Family Court awarded her sole custody of them, she jumped at the chance to become a school cleaner. At least that way, coupled with some waitressing, she was able to be close to her children for whom she became protector, in the face of a vindictive father who failed to meet any of the obligations for family support demanded by the court.
>
> This young mum, now a woman of 28, soon became well known in the school, taking on other tasks with teachers and children, so much so that she was spoken of highly by staff members as a future teacher aide. The principal however, had a different view. She saw in this young woman, a keen intellect, an inexhaustible drive, a love of reading and of the arts, particularly music, and an ambition to do better for her children.
>
> In occasional meetings around the school grounds and in classrooms during the day when the young woman helped children with reading difficulties, the principal encouraged her to think about going to university to become a teacher. She saw in the young woman, not only the potential to be a first class teacher, but to be a leader of the future – and she told her so. The principal was convinced the young woman had great potential, as yet unrealised. Her encouragement found its mark and the young woman took to adult studies like a 'duck to water'. She completed her senior certificate, gained university entrance and took out an education degree with first class honours, all the time supporting her family by cleaning the school and waitressing. However, she never taught in a school setting. Her first job following graduation was as an Education Project Officer with one of the Australian Divisions of General Practice. There she applied her education skills to the professional learning of doctors engaged in primary health care. She went on to complete a doctorate and to become the Chief Executive Officer of the Mental Health Council of Australia.
>
> (Dempster, 2006)

The concern shown by the principal for a parent who was an employee in her school is something for which the young woman and her children would always be grateful. What enabled the principal to offer the advice she did, is a professional commitment to improving the lives of people through education – in this case a person *most* would not expect principals' work to embrace. The story highlights the first of three leadership fundamentals which this and the following chapter discuss – *purpose, agency* and *context*. Leaders must be sure about and dedicated to the 'life-changing' bigger purpose of what they do. And there should be no doubt that all of their energies need to be directed to learning as the means through which individuals can change their lives.

The emphasis in our story on the moral purpose of education and therefore of educational leadership will come as no surprise to those who study leaders. Indeed, 'moral purpose' has appeared in the scholarly literature of the last two decades repeatedly (Sergiovanni, 1992; Fullan, 2003; Begley and Johansson, 2003). What is needed now is research knowledge which helps us understand what leaders in schools can do to maintain their focus on learning, not just for their students, but their teachers, parents and themselves. This brings us to the question to which the discussion in the bulk of the chapter is directed: 'What are the concepts and practices fundamental to an understanding of leadership?'

There is a simple answer to this question. Leadership is not a phenomenon that has any real meaning until it is attached to a particular context, and until it is directed to a particular purpose with particular people. These three central foci of leadership (context, human agency and purpose), however, belie the complexity every leader faces in creating the conditions in which people in known circumstances become agents working towards desired ends.

With its plot involving two key individuals, a principal and a parent, the story we told above is silent on a second message which is becoming much more prominent as a result of recent research. That work shows that there has been a change over an extended period of time from a concentration on leadership as individual action to leadership as collective activity. We believe that this change in thinking is in the right direction.

Two of the key concepts of leadership (*agency* and *purpose*) are included in the view of leadership put forward by Leithwood and Riehl (2003: 7) when they write: 'leaders mobilise and work with others to articulate and achieve shared intentions.' However, in the light of the third key concept, *context*, the definition should be amended for schools as follows:

> School leaders, understanding and accommodating the contexts in which they operate, mobilise and work with others to articulate and achieve shared intentions to enhance learning and the lives of learners.

In order to make sense of the view that leadership ties *context, human agency* and *purpose* together inextricably, we review recent, relevant literature to show where there is agreement and where thinking and action in education settings ought now to be focused. To do this, the focus on learning from Chapter 1 is taken as our point of departure. After all, the message from our story shows that in schools, the purpose of leadership should not be in dispute. It should be to enhance the opportunities for all to learn to the best of their talents and capacities. In short, leadership is for learning first and foremost as the definition above attests. How the context and the people in the school community are coupled to help achieve that purpose, are matters intrinsic to improving our understanding of school leadership and therefore these two concepts provide the focus for this chapter. We leave a discussion of leaders and their need for deep knowledge of learning and leadership and how to apply that knowledge for later discussion in Chapter 3.

The school context and leadership

There is a growing literature on the need for school leaders to understand the macro- contexts in which they work. Without that understanding, the research suggests, their capacity to balance various internal and external pressures on student learning is limited and learning and teaching are likely to suffer. In the section which follows, the context surrounding schooling (the macro-context) and local school contexts (the micro-context) are discussed in turn.

Understanding and accommodating the macro-context of schooling

Probably the most difficult thing for leaders to do is to reconcile teachers and local communities to the fact that the school is 'not an island' but part of a 'global village'. There are wider worlds in which schools work. We say 'wider worlds' because there are undoubted global influences on what school leaders do in their schools, as well as national legislative, policy and regulatory requirements. These are often construed as added interventions, some of which are not seen to be in the interests of student learning in the social and cultural settings in which they are located. The tensions created between meeting the needs of students and their families in the 'local' here and now, as opposed to serving the interests of distant governments concerned with comparative standards of performance (and an electoral future) have been well documented (Earley *et al.*, 2002; Groundwater-Smith and Sachs, 2002; Leithwood, 2005). In addition, there are never-ending reports exhorting governments to take on initiatives which are designed to address perceived shortfalls in education systems. The OECD Report of 2001 for example, emphasised the need for new responses to a changing social context which is characterised by the rise of the knowledge economy, growth in inequality and exclusion, and changing family and community life. It argued that questions such as the following needed urgent attention by education systems and ultimately by schools:

- Given the exploding trade in knowledge, is there a greater need for education based around personal development and citizenship than cognitive knowledge?
- Is the knowledge economy worsening social inequality, and if so, what are the implications for the role of the school?
- What are the implications of increasingly fragmented families and communities for schools? (OECD, 2001)

Questions such as these provoke bureaucratic activity, often resulting in initiatives to which funding is tied, or new legislation and regulations which mandate responses from schools. There is no doubt that the legislation affecting education in all western democracies has increased over recent years, most often with risk aversion in mind (examples include Every Child Matters, UK; No Child Left Behind, USA; The Children and Young People Act in Queensland, Australia, for example). School leaders must manage the implementation of any new requirements as well as the consequences of them in their school communities.

Moreover, there are a range of concerns or problems globally, which place pressure on school leaders because each problem embraced by government seems to carry an assumption that school systems, at best, will do something to educate the young about them, or at worst, will be prepared to respond in ways which combat the effects of some of the more pernicious problems abroad in society. Examples of global concerns or problems include: global warming, population increase, environmental protection and conservation, energy consumption, terrorism, global security, the inequitable spread of information and communication technologies, the transmission of infectious diseases, increasing substance abuse, 'new' or non-traditional family formations, family breakdown, poverty, child abuse, sexual harassment, and unemployment.

These problems are augmented for school leaders by a large number of global educational realities defined in the legislative and policy frameworks mandating what schools do around the world. These include government control of curriculum, national testing and assessment practices, school self-management, school accountability procedures, teacher education standards and accreditation, school governance structures, student behaviour codes, 'tightening' public funding and so on. Governments also require schools to gather and report on a range of matters related to the realities above, including student and staff attendance and absence, student, staff and parents' opinions of their schools, student performance on standardised tests against national and like school averages, financial management – and the list goes on (Groundwater-Smith and Sachs, 2002; Leithwood, 2005).

That global educational concerns are shaping daily school practices is neither surprising nor unwarranted. What follows logically, is that school leaders have to address both the matters their system 'masters' require and those to which they feel their student charges should be exposed. As can be seen from the lists above, there is a litany of problems and realities tied up in the macro-contextual influences on schooling. School leaders, irrespective of their countries of origin or their cultural settings, must be keen 'readers' of broad social, economic and cultural trends in order to enable them to interpret where and how the school's energies should be employed in the interests of keeping learning centre stage. Parents will always have the specific interests of their children at heart (rather than national or global interests) and so school leaders need to be armed with lucid explanations as to why they are required to implement some of the things governments demand of schooling or why a school places a particular emphasis on a specific global concern. Comprehensive knowledge of the influences on schools in modern society has been shown to be an asset to school leaders when leading change locally (Blackmore, 2004; Day *et al.*, 2001; Lingard *et al.*, 2002).

While over recent years we have seen that the context of schooling in many different countries is heavily influenced by global issues such as those above (MacBeath, 1998; Hargreaves, 2000; Leithwood and Riehl, 2003; Blackmore, 2004), there is a growing body of research concentrating on the ability of school leaders to be able to work well with others in the micro-context, to establish the conditions in which creative and effective student learning can take place. The research suggests that without supportive local conditions, the prime purpose of school leadership, namely, maximising student learning, is unlikely to be realised. In the following section we discuss some of the relevant research findings.

Understanding and accommodating the micro-context of schools

Understanding the micro-context of schools requires knowledge about the school as an organisation and the nature, aspirations and influence of the students' parents and the school's immediate community. Being a leader, therefore, necessitates different 'readings' in different contexts. Indeed Beccalli's (2004) work shows that most successful leaders have learned to behave differently in different places at different times. This finding is supported by the work of the National College for School Leadership (NCL) in one of *Seven Strong Claims about School Leadership*. Based on research findings that leadership involves the application of four common practices, the college argues that it is how those practices are employed to take account of different situations in different places which marks out the effective from the ineffective leader. The practices being referred to are 'building a vision and setting directions', 'understanding and developing people', 'redesigning the organisation' and 'managing the teaching and learning programme'. More is said about these practices later in the chapter.

The important point to be made is that when good leaders apply these practices in their school communities, they do so responsively rather than submissively. That is to say, leading effectively does not ask a leader to subjugate his or her aspirations for a school to the parochial interests of particular groups, whether inside or outside the school. 'Rocking the boat', the research suggests, is an important leadership skill able to be applied only when the capacity of the school community to 'come on board' has been calculated and enlisted. Failure to 'read' the context has been known to encourage the crew to 'scuttle the ship' or the community to 'mutiny', leaving the leader to 'walk the plank'.

Context-sensitivity, being able to 'read' organisational and community circumstances, relies on a number of personal attributes, not the least of which are the ability to be approachable, open-minded and flexible. Goffee and Jones (2003) show that the best leaders learn to use their most effective attributes through experience and that they are comfortable in interacting with a wide range of people in as many circumstances as possible.

To push home the point that understanding the micro-context of the school involves a type of 'lay sociological inquiry', we refer to the Price-waterhouseCoopers (PWC) *Independent Study into School Leadership*. That work adds the need for 'a certain amount of freedom' for the leader in a new environment to the need for the attributes of flexibility and open-mindedness.

Having spent some time describing the need for context-sensitivity by school leaders, we turn to some of the proximal school issues which are integral to informed school leadership. Inquisitive principals know this terrain well. They study local demography, local politics and economic trends. They seek out information on the composition of the parent body, their socio-economic, cultural and language backgrounds. They uncover action precedents to get a 'feel' for the nature of the parent community. Is it conservative in its outlook, is it experimentally inclined, is it aggressively supportive of innovation or apathetically disposed towards the school? Is aspiration muted or vocal? Answers to these questions form a backdrop for an analysis of the in-school context which involves the leader in gaining an understanding of:

- the composition of the student body;
- the attitude and experience of staff;
- the nature and scope of its curriculum;
- teaching and assessment behaviours;
- student behaviour and demeanour;
- learning experiences and opportunities;
- the quality of the school's buildings, surroundings and equipment;
- the extent of its discretionary funding;
- past levels of achievement by the students;
- data on the esteem in which the school is held by its teachers and students;
- the professional learning commitment of the staff;
- the present vision of the school and its priorities;
- its organisational structures and leadership; and
- the school's governance processes.

The list of factors influencing an understanding of any school's context is long. We make it part of the subject of Chapter 7 where we outline strategies and practices leaders use to address such factors in different cultural settings. Taken together, these factors illustrate how complex it is to understand any school context. Should a leader have thoughts of a 'quick fix' or of sweeping change, those thoughts should be put 'on hold' until comprehensive knowledge leads to understanding the capabilities of all concerned: students, teachers and parents. Doing things differently then requires strategies which match school community capability with vision and priorities (but as we said earlier, more on this later).

Of all of the factors involved in gaining an understanding of the school's immediate context, the most influential is the nature of the student body and its impact on what children and young people achieve (Mulford and Silins, 2003). In days gone by, as John MacBeath has pointed out in Chapter 1, the quality and characteristics of the student cohort were sometimes used as an excuse for lowering expectations and for arguing that it was difficult for schools to make a difference in students' lives, particularly when their socio-economic and cultural backgrounds were viewed as problematic. That is no longer the case. Understanding and accommodating the school context is a prelude to doing things which make a difference to the lives and learning of those who come into the school grounds. But putting life changing strategies into place requires leaders who are able to share a vision, pursue agreed priorities and directions with others, including parents and community members.

Summary

Our discussion of the macro- and micro-contexts of schooling has reinforced the view that understanding and accommodating contexts is a leadership fundamental. We feel that the school leader who tries to ignore the issues of the wider world, who puts up barriers to change, is of little benefit over the longer term to the school's students or their parents. As we said at the outset, no school should be an island and therefore no school leader should adopt a completely defensive attitude to what is happening in the world outside the school gate. Achieving balance between meeting the local needs of children, young people and their parents while having them engage in developing understanding about more distant matters is a struggle; but it is one that adds to the central purpose of education. The trick for school leaders is to manage the impact of some of the intrusive educational realities which have more to do with risk management, compliance and accountability than individual learning.

Having devoted time to a leader's need to understand and accommodate the context of schools and schooling, it is to the second of our trilogy of leadership fundamentals – human agency – that our analysis now turns.

Human agency and leadership

We reiterate, human agency is also a leadership fundamental. If the primary purpose of schools is to be achieved, it is only possible with and through others. Frost (2006), in a discussion of human agency, has defined it in common sense terms as people making a difference. As we have emphasised in this chapter, in schools, making a difference should always be linked with an intention to enhance learning. Watkins says:

> The exercise of human agency is about intentional action, exercising choice, making a difference and monitoring effects.
>
> (Watkins, 2005: 47)

Watkins' view of human agency provides us with a link to the four leadership practices we said we would return to earlier. In shorthand terms we are referring to *building vision, developing people, organisational structuring* and *managing teaching and learning*. Whilst we have argued that implementing these practices is context sensitive, we believe that they cannot be activated without cooperative human agency. Indeed no school leader should ever try to carry out these practices unassisted. If it is becoming accepted in the business world, where the focus is on the financial bottom line, that 'the cult of the charismatic chief executive appears to be coming to an end' (PWC, 2007), then in schools, where the focus is on people, relying on leadership charisma should be anathema. It should be replaced by a concern to embrace human agency and we suggest that this can be done by seeing the four practices above as needing collective action.

Our call for collective human agency in schools is supported by emerging research evidence on the distribution of leadership opportunities. When distributive leadership prevails, other benefits occur for staff, students and parents. To substantiate this assertion, we first discuss distributive leadership and its effects, before returning to our view that the four leadership practices outlined above must become collective agential activities.

Distributive leadership

There are at least two related bodies of research evidence (National College of School Leadership, 2006) about the benefits of distributing school leadership amongst people throughout the school. The first shows the influence of a leader on three aspects of staff performance, namely *capacity, motivation and commitment* and *working conditions*. A school leader's influence on student achievement is often only possible through indirect means and these three have been identified as significant. The research results show that the influence of a leader is strong on *working conditions*, moderate with respect to staff *motivation and commitment* and weak in relation to staff *capacity*.

The second shows that when leadership is distributed widely across members of staff, students and parents, the influence of this collective leadership construction is up to three times higher than that reported for an individual leader (NCSL, 2006: 12). For us, it is interesting to note that while school leaders make 'quite modest direct contributions to staff *capacities*' (NCSL, 2006: 10), it is well known that staff *capacities* have a strong influence on altered classroom practices and ultimately on pupil learning achievement (p. 10). Therefore, it is helpful to find research suggesting the substantial effects of distributive leadership. In a nutshell, shared or distributed leadership influences teacher *capacity* and teachers' *working conditions* and these in turn, when coupled with *motivation and commitment*, enhance student learning and achievement (NCSL, 2006:12).

These are encouraging findings; but while researchers seek further sub-stantiation, the findings are acting as a spur to school leaders who need support for innovatory practices that share leadership widely. Our work on the Leadership for Learning Project (LfL), for example, has led to the enunciation of a principle on shared or distributive leadership about which more is said in Chapter 9.

We return now to the four practices common to leadership and underscore the need for collaborative human agency in implementing them in a given school context. To do so requires leaders with sufficient confidence to expose the school's directions, functions, structures and resources, staff, student and community capacity, and teaching and learning programmes to a much wider group of people than might have been the case when 'heroic' leadership was the order of the day. Getting others to take on leadership roles within the school requires distribution that is both broad and deep (PWC, 2007). The structures for leadership must be put under a microscope so that positional leadership is augmented by leadership opportunities which reach deep into the organisation to engage teacher leaders and student leaders. At the same time, leadership roles should stretch across key functions of the school and be extended into the parent body and the community. At the end of the day, there should be deliberately shared leadership of *vision building*, *people development*, *organisational structuring* and *teaching and learning management*. As the PricewaterhouseCoopers (2007) report says:

> all of this means that school leaders now have to be much more outward looking than they used to be.
>
> (PricewaterhouseCoopers, 2007: 6)

Consistent with this theme, Miller and Bentley (2002) talk about widely distributed collective leadership so that local decision-making is shared. They predict a time when schools will no longer be structured as tight hierarchies, rather that they will be team oriented and networked with expertise drawn from sources outside the school's usual group of contributors (Miller and Bentley, 2002).

Leithwood and Riehl (2003) also predict flatter, team based leadership structures attaching particular roles to important school functions, adding parents and students as active players in school leadership

To get to this point, however, will not necessarily be easy. Schools will need to experiment with processes which move them along the continuum from formally delegated leadership to 'spontaneous' and 'cultural' leadership (MacBeath *et al.*, 2004) in which status and hierarchy cease to be a reference point for decision-making and anyone in the school – custodian, teaching assistant, pupil or teacher feels able to take the initiative in leading change. This is what is implied by a commitment to human agency.

Conclusion

To bring this chapter to a conclusion, we return to the story of the young mother motivated by her school's principal to study at university. In that story, there are major messages about two of the three leadership fundamentals on which our discussion has concentrated. The story showed that learning in schools extends to all with whom schools and their leaders come into contact, even parents. Leadership for learning therefore is inclusive. It is clear also that our story brought into the foreground, the driving motivation for those who lead schools – the moral purpose of education with its focus on the life changing potential of learning. Our discussion of the context of schooling showed that while macro or 'bigger picture' pressures are influential in what leaders can do, and are supported to do locally, it is micro-contextual knowledge which enables them to attune their senses to the needs and talents of all under the school's umbrella. However, reading the context with sensitivity and then developing strategies aimed at enhancing learning for all requires collective human agency. The principal alone had no hope of helping the young mother in our story to achieve as she did. Indeed, we have shown that principals acting on their own have little hope of releasing the potential of all of the students in their schools. Others must be involved.

This chapter has explained at a general level how leadership and learning are linked through a knowledge of the school's context and the power of human agency. In doing so, we have pointed to the need for strategies which shift leadership responsibilities from individuals to collectives and tactics which help leaders become informed readers of their schools' macro- and micro-contexts. Connecting the two concepts of leadership and learning theoretically and practically is the task of Chapter 3.

References

Beccalli, N. (2004) *When Style Matters in Leadership*, European Business Forum Special Report, January 2004, London: European Business Forum.

Begley, P. and Johansson, O. (eds) (2003) *The Ethical Dimensions of School Leadership*, Dordrecht and Boston: Kluwer Academic Publishers.

Blackmore, J. (2004) 'Restructuring educational leadership in changing contexts: a local/global account of restructuring in Australia', *Journal of Educational Change*, 5: 267–88.

Day, C., Harris, A. and Hadfield, M. (2001) 'Challenging the orthodoxy of effective school leadership', *International Journal of Leadership in Education*, 4 (1): 39–56.

Dempster, N. (2006) 'Professional standards for school leaders: a counter to orthodoxy', *Ed Ventures*, Canberra: The Australian College of Educators.

Earley, P., Evans, J., Collarbone, P., Gold, A. and Halpin, D. (2002) *Establishing the Current State of School Leadership in England*, London: Department for Education and Skills.

Feiner, M. (2003) 'Laws of leadership' in *Mastering Leadership*, London: Financial Times, PricewaterhouseCoopers LLP.

Frost, D. (2006) 'The conept of "agency" in leadership for learning', *Leading and Managing*, 12 (2): 19–28.

Fullan, M. (2003) *The Moral Imperative of School Leadership*, Thousand Oaks, CA: Corwin Press.

Goffee, R. and Jones, G. (2003) *Mantle of Authority in Mastering Leadership*, London: Financial Times, PricewaterhouseCoopers.

Gronn, P. (2003) *The New Work of Educational Leaders: Changing Leadership Practices in an Era of School Reform*, London: Paul Chapman.

Groundwater-Smith, S. and Sachs, J. (2002) 'The activist professional and the reinstatement of trust', *Cambridge Journal of Education*, 32 (3): 341–58.

Gunter, H. (2001) *Leaders and Leadership in Education*, London: Paul Chapman.

Hargreaves, A. (2000) 'Four ages of professionalism and professional learning', *Teachers and Teaching: History and Practice*, 6 (2): 151–82.

Leithwood, K. (2005) 'Understanding successful school leadership: progress on a broken front', *Journal of Educational Administration*, 43 (6): 619–29.

Leithwood, K. and Riehl, C. (2003) *What Do We Already Know about Successful School Leadership?* Philadelphia: Temple University.

Leithwood, K., Jantzi, D. and Steinbach, R. (2002) 'Leadership practices for accountable schools', in K. Leithwood and P. Hallinger (eds) *Second International Handbook of Educational Leadership and Administration*, Dordrecht: Kluwer, pp. 849–79.

Leithwood. K., Day, C., Sammons, P., Harris, A. and Hopkins, D. (2006) *Seven Strong Claims about Successful School Leadership*, Nottingham: National College for School Leadership.

Lingard, B., Hayes, D. and Mills, M. (2002) 'Developments in school-based management: the specific case of Queensland, Australia', *Journal of Educational Administration*, 40 (1): 6–30.

MacBeath, J. (ed.) (1998) *Effective School Leadership: Responding to Change*, London: Paul Chapman.

MacBeath, J., Oduro, G. and Waterhouse, J. (2004) *Distributed Leadership*, Nottingham: National College for School Leadership.

Miller, R. and Bentley, T. (2002) *'Unique Creation' Possible Futures: Four Scenarios for 21st Century Schooling*, Nottingham: National College for School Leadership.

Mulford, B. and Silins, H. (2003) 'Leadership for organisation learning and improved student outcomes – what do we know?' *Cambridge Journal of Education*, 33 (2): 175–85.

Nicholson, N. (2003) 'To the manner born', in *Mastering Leadership*, London: Financial Times, PricewaterhouseCoopers.

OECD (2001) *What Schools for the Future?* Paris: OECD.

PricewaterhouseCoopers (2007) *Independent Study into School Leadership*, London: Department for Education and Skills.

Sergiovanni, T. (1992) *Moral Leadership: Getting to the Heart of School Improvement*, San Francisco, CA: Jossey-Bass.

Watkins, C. (2005) *Classrooms as Learning Communities*, London: RoutledgeFalmer.

3 Leadership for learning

Sue Swaffield and John MacBeath

'Leadership and learning are indispensable to each other'

'Leadership and learning are indispensable to each other.' So wrote John F. Kennedy in a speech to be delivered in Dallas on what turned out to be a fateful day in November 1963. But how are leadership and learning indispensable to each other? What is the nature of the relationship?

With a little thought, a number of 'common sense' connections between leadership and learning come to mind. Leaders need to learn and leaders learn as they lead. Leadership of others involves being first able to lead oneself, a crucial premise of self-directed learning. Leadership and learning also share common skills, such as problem solving, reflection, and acting on experience. In educational organisations such as schools, leadership is needed to promote learning. In schools, learning should be the prime concern of all those who exercise leadership, and learning should both set the agenda and be the agenda for leadership. Leadership and learning are mutually embedded, so that as we learn we become more confident in sharing with, and leading, others. And as we lead we continuously reflect on, and enhance, our learning. Guy Claxton has suggested the new 'four Rs' of learning: resilience, resourcefulness, reflectiveness and reciprocity (Claxton, 2002). These dispositions are all as relevant to leadership as they are to learning, both of which are as much a matter of character as of skill. In talking about learning Claxton says:

> Being able to stay calm, focused and engaged when you don't know what to do is not merely a matter of technical training . . . Of course learning capacity is partly a matter of skill. But we also need a richer vocabulary that includes words like attitudes, dispositions, qualities, values, emotional tolerances, habits of mind.
>
> (Claxton, 2006: 4)

The same may be said of leadership.

When thinking about the relationship between leadership and learning it is possible to start with either concept, and then work towards the other. For example, we may start with leadership, scrutinising leadership roles and activities for their learning content. Or we may start by focusing on learning, which raises questions about forms of activity and the creation and sharing of knowledge. In turn this raises questions as to responsibility, locus of initiative, and about individual and shared leadership.

Little words make a difference

In education we seem to have a penchant for joining two big words with a variety of little ones. So, for example, 'teaching and learning' is used to refer to planned activity in the classroom. 'Coaching and mentoring' are often presented as conjoined twins or even a single entity, perhaps indicating a lack of clarity about their differences. Assessment *of* learning, *for* learning and *as* learning are three importantly distinctive concepts, where the little conjunction renders different meanings (Harlen, 2006; Earl, 2003).

So too can leadership and learning be joined by a variety of linguistic connectives, for example leadership *and, of, as* learning, or leadership *by, with, from* learning. Each connecting word creates a different phrase, some of which may be familiar, while others may surprise us into new insights. The focus of this chapter, and indeed of the whole book, is leadership *for* learning.

Another ingredient in the rich leadership soup?

How we construe 'leadership for learning' depends on our beliefs and understandings about leadership and about learning. If our conception of leadership is one that resides in a leader (in a school context the headteacher or principal), and if we believe that knowledge is transmitted or delivered from teacher to pupil, then leadership for learning is about the headteacher ensuring that the pupil learns what the teacher teaches. This appears to be implicit in the American use of 'instructional leadership', a mindset that may encompass the view that valued learning is measured by testing pupils and assumed to be a telling indicator of teachers' effectiveness. Leaders may be encouraged to act on this information, perhaps by awarding incentives and rewards for what is deemed to be 'successful' teaching and learning and taking remedial action when required. Another interpretation casts leaders as experts in fostering learning, proud of their hands-on expertise and deep pedagogic understanding. Others again concentrate more on putting in place structures and support for colleagues so that heads of department and team leaders take the direct lead in teaching and learning, while the principals prioritise shielding teachers from distractions to their focus on pupils' learning.

Leadership for learning viewed in this way is another category in the typology or 'alphabet soup' of leadership (Leithwood *et al.*, 1999; MacBeath, 2003; MacBeath, 2004). It perhaps most closely resembles 'learning-centred leadership', resonates with 'principle-centred leadership' and 'moral leadership', and has similarities with 'instructional leadership' and 'transformational leadership'

(Knapp *et al.*, 2003; Covey, 1990; Sergiovanni, 1992; Southworth, 2002; Hallinger, 1992).

There are, of course, differences among these various forms of leadership (otherwise the diverse labels would not have been coined), but a number of common threads among them may be discerned. They are all concerned with learning, primarily of pupils, but also of teachers and other members of the community whose continuous learning is in the service of student learning. There is a focus on process as well as outcomes, and a commitment to practice that reflects values such as trust and respect. Commitment, obligations and duties arise from individuals' beliefs as well as from professional and community ideals. Building collaborative cultures and increasing capacity and capital also figure large.

Despite a wealth of literature and a proliferation of adjectival prefixes, we believed there was more to understand about the nature of the links between leadership and learning. We saw leadership for learning not as an additional model of leadership competing for attention with a plethora of alternatives but as qualitatively different from other models. We hope to demonstrate that in the rest of this chapter and book.

Making the connections: an unfinished business

While the connections between leadership and learning may seem a matter of simple common sense and are taken as a given by policy makers, researchers will remain dissatisfied until they are able to identify empirical validation of the inter-connections. The quest for solid empirical ground has generated a considerable body of studies and metastudies over the last decade (for example, Bell *et al.*, 2003; Witziers *et al.*, 2003; Leithwood *et al.*, 2004) yet without definitive conclusion, as is evident from the subtitle Witziers *et al.* give to their paper: 'the elusive search for an association'. On the basis of her own extensive review Levacic concludes:

> Given the vast literature on educational leadership and management and the presumption of policy-makers that the quality of educational leadership affects student outcomes, the actual evidence for a casual relationship is relatively sparse.
>
> (Levacic, 2005: 198)

The multiplicity of studies over the last decade, nonetheless, make widely differing claims as to the leadership 'effect'. One of the most recent is Vivienne Robinson's 2007 metastudy which identified 26 pieces of research as meeting the empirical criteria for inclusion. She identified 'effect sizes' in the 0.3 to 0.4 range, which she describes as 'moderately educationally significant' (Robinson, 2007: 9). She concludes, however:

> . . . these connections need to be substantially strengthened if leadership literature is to deliver more reliable and more useful insights into the

particular leadership practices that create the conditions that enable teachers to make a bigger difference to their students.

(Robinson, 2007: 22)

The Australian literature is rich with studies. Reviewing these in 2008, Bill Mulford finds a fairly strong body of consensus among them, confirming the indirect relationship of leadership to outcomes, identifying the mediating factors as organisational learning, professional development, and a trusting, collaborative and risk-taking climate. This resonates with many other studies yet still leaves a number of questions unanswered, in particular the interplay of these within widely different cultural and political contexts. Mulford concludes:

> The context for leadership and school reform must be taken more into account with variables such as Education Department policies and practices, school location, school size, and home educational environment having been shown to have a clear interactive effect on leadership, the school and student outcomes.
>
> A key overall priority is broadening what counts as good schooling. Students' achievement in a knowledge society is increasingly being seen as wider than the cognitive/academic and involving both quality and equity. Not to measure the broader outcomes of schooling underestimates the net contribution that schools make to individual well-being and the wider society.
>
> Finally, the research and knowledge base on how school leadership interacts with a wide range of other factors to enhance student learning needs to be strengthened.
>
> (Mulford, 2008: 148)

Short of robust empirical data, what researchers can offer are 'strong claims'. In a metastudy for the National College of School Leadership Leithwood and colleagues (2006) offered seven such claims.

- Claim 1: School leadership is second only to classroom teaching as an influence on pupil learning.
- Claim 2: Almost all successful (school) leaders draw on the same repertoire of basic leadership practices.
- Claim 3: It is the enactment of the same basic leadership practices – not the practices themselves – that is responsive to the context.
- Claim 4: School leaders improve pupil learning indirectly through their influence on staff motivation and working conditions.
- Claim 5: School leadership has a greater effect on schools and pupils when it is widely distributed.
- Claim 6: Some patterns of distribution are more effective than others.
- Claim 7: A handful of personal 'traits' explain a high proportion of the variation in leader effectiveness.

These seven claims are, to a greater or lesser degree, problematic. For example, taken at face value and as a stand alone statement the first claim it is clearly untenable, as we know from four decades of school effectiveness research that the most powerful influences on learning are parents and peers, generally in combination with other factors which lie outside schools (Jencks *et al.*, 1972). While the school context is perhaps taken as implicit in Leithwood *et al.*'s first claim, nonetheless the 'compositional' or 'contextual' effect (what Thrupp, 1999, terms the 'social mix') has been repeatedly shown to be one of the most salient factors in pupil achievement and in attitudes to learning (Gray *et al.*, 1990; MacBeath and Mortimore, 2001).

While the first claim would find support in effectiveness studies which give primacy to the classroom and teacher effects (see Luyten, 2003 for an overview of the literature), distinguishing leadership and classroom teaching as two separate effect sizes carries more meaning as a statistical abstraction than it does in the somewhat messier milieu of schools and classrooms.

The second and third claims refer to effective headship practices as fairly consistent but in acknowledging their responsiveness to context it leaves open to question ways in which context may actually reconfigure and reshape what leaders do and the kind of leaders they become. The fourth claim, which reasserts a fairly consistent finding of leadership studies, also tends to suggest a unidirectional flow of influence. Further, are the fifth and sixth claims reconcilable with the seventh, which refers specifically to the 'traits' of the headteacher? While the ontological basis for 'trait' theories is dubious, we do know that attitudes, competences and effectiveness of headteachers do not remain stable from one context to another and that an effective head may not be equally successful in one school as in another. In schools with widely shared leadership a singular research focus on the individual may, in fact, divert attention from the internal dynamic and complexity of effects. As Levacic (2005) reminds us, most studies assume a one way relationship between leaders and learners whereas the effects are reciprocal. That is, leaders learn from students and from teachers, the subtleties of this process requiring fine grained qualitative study. Leithwood *et al.* (2008) acknowledge that we still have a lot to learn about the patterning of relationships which explain achievement.

While the evidence strengthens the case that some leadership distribution patterns are more helpful than others, it sheds little light on the range of patterns that actually exist in schools and, most importantly, the relative effects of these patterns on the quality of teaching, learning and pupil achievement (Leithwood *et al.*, 2008: 35).

It is the continuing pursuit of effect sizes that highlights one of the inherent problems with findings and claims derived from quantitative studies. This is because in order to measure 'effects' both leadership and learning have been subject to some form of quantification so that the qualities or competences of headteachers 'stand in' as proxies for leadership while student 'outcomes' are measured by tests and examinations. Thus, the best that can be offered is whether certain traits of headteachers can be tied in some way to student performance in examinations.

The equation is narrowed still further, however, by a general penchant for measuring curricular subjects that lend themselves most easily to quantification, hence mathematics becomes the most readily available proxy for learning, and is also preferred because it is less 'contaminated' by the home effect than other subjects. As music, art, drama, dance and other so-called 'creative' subjects prove too difficult to quantify they are, in general, simply ignored. Subjects that are most measurable are then adopted as indicators of school effectiveness and in the process assume high stakes status, so perverting the core purposes of the school and narrowing the curriculum, producing what O'Neill (2004) describes as 'perverse indicators'.

So it is argued (for example, Labaree, 1997; Lewis, 2007) that what tests purport to measure may in fact be anti-educational. They may be the products of tactical measures to push up a school's overall scores, often at the expense of those judged to be beyond redemption, while high stakes pressures can tempt teachers into cheating (Haney, 2000; Leavitt and Dubner, 2005; Nicholls and Berliner, 2005).

While attainment data are now generally complemented by attitudinal data through the use of student and teacher surveys, these are notoriously difficult to interpret without qualitative forms of follow up which explore the ambiguities in interpretations of language and the researcher's intent. Claims for connecting leadership and learning will derive their greatest value from studies which go beyond the quantitative and venture deeper into the hidden curriculum and the underlife of the school. Failure to take cognisance of the submerged body beneath the waterline risks sabotaging researchers' carefully planned direction of travel.

As schools respond to the rapidly changing social currents, the nature of both leadership and learning require radical rethinking. Both need to be understood as diffuse and distributed concepts. In England the trend towards extended and full service schools is breaking, or at least fracturing, the mould of the nine to four school. The remodelling of the workforce has led to a proliferation of leadership roles within the school and the community, extending leadership and the very nature of leadership into new arenas and new forms of activity. We have come to understand leadership as embedded in actions taken both individually and collectively within cultures that encourage and promote shared agency. Leadership activity may be actively promoted by the headteacher but may occur irrespective of the head by dint of a strong collegial culture and/or a core of committed change agents (MacBeath and Stoll, 2001). Connections need to be explained in qualitative terms, in what has been called 'thick description' (Geertz, 1973), a form of narrative which captures the texture of a school's activities, the dynamic of interpersonal relationships, the 'flow' of learning and the unpredictability of life in schools and classrooms. Liebermann and Friedrich (2008) consider the issue in these terms:

In many studies of leadership, one of the problems is that leadership is daily and takes place amongst a myriad of activities and actions that accrue over time. Typical data collection strategies – interviews, surveys, or even observations and focus groups – often fail to show the interconnections and variety of activities, strategies and tactics that people come to learn over time when they take on leadership responsibilities.

(Liebermann and Friedrich, 2008: 39)

Reframing and revisiting leadership and learning

As critiques of quantitative research reveal, both learning and leadership are contested and complex notions. Bringing them together entails more than an act of addition, or utilising one in the service of the other. However, before considering the connections let us first reframe and revisit the two key elements of leadership for learning. Lee Bolman and Terrence Deal (1991), the leading exponents of reframing, describe four frames, but here we confine ourselves to two which we call simply the 'old' and the 'new'. Taking leadership first, the 'old' frame is characterised by a charismatic individual in a high status position, directing many others. In the 'new' frame leadership is viewed as activity, both individual and shared, influencing and serving others, taking the initiative and making decisions for the greater good, whilst modelling learning and being sensitive to context (see Table 3.1).

In the new frame two fundamentals of leadership discussed in Chapter 2 – purpose and agency – are implicit, and are revisited later in this chapter. There is a third fundamental which became explicit and powerful within the Leadership for Learning Project which we discuss in the rest of this book, that is the significance of context. Both the micro-context of relationships, organisational structures and micropolitics, and the macro-context of government policy, priorities and resources exert powerful influences on behaviour and decisions.

Tom Sergiovanni (2001) argues that behaving rationally involves taking account of context, something to which leadership needs to be acutely sensitive.

Table 3.1 The old and new frames of leadership

Leadership – The old frame	Leadership – The new frame
Leadership as . . .	Leadership as activity . . .
The few leading the many	Influencing others
Larger than life individuals	Taking the initiative
High status	Offering a service
Appointed or elected roles	Taking decisions on behalf of others
Characterised by a set of special competencies	Modelling learning behaviour
Control	Making moral choices for the wider good
Control	Adapting to circumstance
A few 'best practice' model approaches, applicable to all situations	Sensitive to, and influencing, context

The same actions may have completely different effects in different contexts, depending on the people involved, their view of the world, previous experiences and current circumstances. According to Malcolm Gladwell, in his book *The Tipping Point*, 'the power of context says that what really matters is little things' (Gladwell, 2000: 150). He illustrates this with the observation that most people behave differently in a clean street than in one strewn with rubbish and daubed with graffiti. Michael Fullan provides an educational example, pointing out that generally we 'will pay attention to the plight of individual students if those around us are doing so' (Fullan, 2003: 2). However, we are not restricted to responding to context; we can also help shape it, especially at the micro-level of our immediate sphere of influence. The effect of context is what makes it such a strong contender for consideration by those exercising leadership – changing the situation can be both a stimulus and a support for altering behaviour.

Learning, like leadership, can be viewed through different frames (see Table 3.2). The old frame in its simplest form is represented by the naïve statement 'Teachers teach and pupils learn. It is as simple as that' (Woodhead, 2002: 15). By contrast, Elliot Eisner's first lesson in his 2000 paper 'Those who ignore the past . . .: 12 "easy" lessons for the next millennium' is that 'students learn both less and more than what they have been taught' (Eisner, 2000: 343) – a truism which resonates with teachers everywhere, all too aware that teaching does not always result in learning. We also know that the traditional or 'old frame' view of learning as being synonymous with schooling is flawed: in Chapter 1 we set out seven challenges to this assumption.

The old frame of learning has a tenacious hold on the public, policy makers, and some educators, perhaps worn down, blinded or inoculated against their experience and understanding by the dominant discourse. This is despite more enlightened views of learning than those represented by the 'old' frame having been promulgated from Socrates and Plato onwards. Every day we continue to learn more about learning, through technical advances such as neuro-imaging and through open-minded and thoughtful observation of young people in authentic situations (for example Carr, 2001; Drummond, 2003). Nevertheless we agree with David Perkins' contention that 'we are still in the foothills of our understanding of learning'.

Table 3.2 The old and new frames of learning

Leadership – The old frame	*Leadership – The new frame*
Learning as . . .	Learning as activity . . .
What happens in classrooms	Posing questions
Conducted by teachers	Analysing for understanding
Transfer of information from those who know to those who don't know	Testing ideas
	Portraying thought and feeling
Reproduced in tests and exams	Thinking about thinking
Compliance	Developing a learning identity
	Making moral decisions

Learning viewed through the new frame reflects much of this richer understanding, and recognises that learning, experience, emotions, identity, metacognition and decision-making are all inextricably linked.

As at the beginning of this chapter we noted the relationship between leadership and learning, so too we may note similarities between the new frames of leadership and learning, and perhaps between the learner and the led. Both have to be active in their roles and to exercise agency. Leaders often talk of 'empowering others' but in a statement that challenges much received wisdom George Binney and Colin Williams declare:

> You can disempower somebody but you cannot empower them. They will really begin to change, take initiatives, take risks, provide real feedback, learn from mistakes and accept responsibility for what they are doing when they feel sufficiently confident to do so and are provided with a clear framework.
>
> (Binney and Williams, 1997: 69)

Implicit in this statement is a sense of agency, a human drive that is released when the climate is such that leading and learning are natural bedfellows. Exploring the connections between leading and learning had already been chosen as the defining and organising concept for the work of our group at the University of Cambridge where we had established 'Leadership for Learning: The Cambridge network' in 2001 (www.educ.cam.ac.uk/lfl). Setting up a research project in order to giver greater purchase on these two big ideas was an obvious next step and in 2002 we secured funding from the Carpe Vitam Foundation in Sweden to undertake a three-year journey into this complex and fascinating territory.

The Leadership for Learning Project: a discursive process

In setting up the project our singular purpose was to identify in what ways leadership for learning is qualitatively different from other models. We wanted to both develop a more robust conceptual grasp of its meaning but also to test how it played out in practice and whether it was a tenable proposition in a range of different national contexts.

However much there was still to learn and find out about leadership, learning and their interrelationship, we were not starting from scratch. For the Leadership for Learning Project we drew on the experience of university and school partners with traditions of inquiring into and making sense of educational ideas. Literature and previous research informed the process, and academic experts in the field stimulated our discussions and thinking.

Our empirical exploration of leadership for learning was essentially a discursive process, grounded in values and moral purpose which nourished the discourse and helped to contextualise data and inform developing theory. Figure 3.1 is an attempt to illustrate how democratic values and moral purpose stimulate the discourse which is, on the one hand, fed by data, and on the other feeds into new theoretical constructions. These in turn provide the principles for practice. By framing each element in terms of activity – explicating, defining, stimulating, analysing, illustrating, shaping and transforming – we see these as iterations of the essential elements that unite both learning and leadership (MacBeath *et al.*, 2006).

The discursive process in which we engaged within the research team and with our school colleagues has parallels with Alfred North Whitehead's three stages of educational development and growth. In his essay *The Rhythm of Education*, Whitehead calls the first stage 'romance' – 'the setting in order of a ferment already stirring in the mind' (Whitehead, 1932: 29). We had some

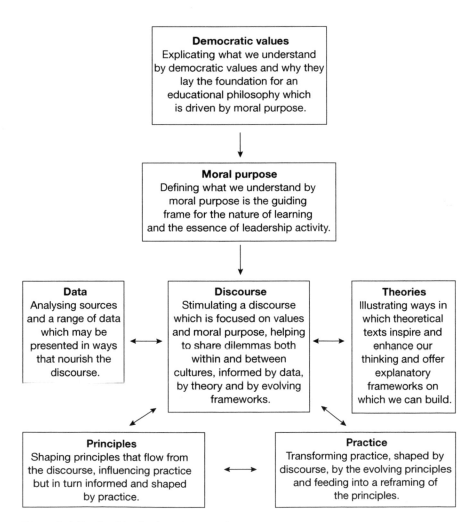

Figure 3.1 Leadership for learning – a discursive process

'stirrings in the mind' about leadership, learning and their interrelationship, and were aware of 'unexplored connexions with possibilities half-disclosed by glimpses and half-concealed by the wealth of material' (1932: 28). Whitehead's second stage is that of precision, and relates to the systematic analysis of data, integration with ideas, and detailed discussions that were the hallmark of much of the work carried out by the project's participants. His final stage is when the romance and precision come to fruition in terms of generalisation. For us generalisation took the form of principles. It is important to note that Whitehead referred to a cyclical process of continual repetition of the three stages, so that the principles lead into stages of further romance and precision, further 'stirrings in the mind' as they help us imagine and test new ideas and applications.

Our developing understanding of leadership for learning

Definition

Through the discursive process outlined above we developed our understanding of leadership for learning and have come to define it as follows:

> Leadership for learning is a distinct form of educational practice that involves an explicit dialogue, maintaining a focus on learning, attending to the conditions that favour learning, and leadership that is both shared and accountable. Learning and leadership are conceived of as 'activities' linked by the centrality of human agency within a framework of moral purpose.

We have sought to represent our developing understanding, ideas and applications in a number of ways, including various diagrams and models. All are somewhat unsatisfactory, to a certain extent due to the difficulty of representing in a static diagram what we conceive of as a dynamic process. This may be partly due to the limitations of a two-dimensional paper representation but owing more to the complexity of the interrelationships among key elements and to our continuing quest for deeper understanding. Nevertheless, these models both reflect and help shape thinking, and provide a route to connecting theory with practice.

Levels of learning and leadership

One model that we found helpful and has remained as leitmotif is the so-called 'wedding cake' model of Michael Knapp and colleagues (Knapp *et al.*, 2003).

Our adaptation, adding a fourth tier to the 'cake' (Figure 3.2) draws attention to the interrelated nature of learning, and the integral relationship between student and professional learning and the wider system in which they are located. Leadership is the connecting tissue which infuses learning at every level and makes the connections a practical reality.

The critical element in the four-tier model are the vertical connections which attempt to illustrate the flow of activities within and across the school in which learning is the central focus. Just as learning is the province not only of students but also of teachers, other professionals, schools and systems themselves, so too is leadership exercised in each sphere of activity. This is one important way in which leadership for learning is qualitatively different from other conceptions of leadership. It does not see leadership as synonymous with the individual at the apex of the school, whose influence extends 'down the hierarchy' from 'senior leadership teams' to 'middle leaders' and others with formal roles and responsibilities. 'Teacher leadership' (Frost and Harris, 2003; Lieberman and Miller, 2004) and 'student leadership' (MacBeath and Sugimine, 2003; Fielding and Bragg 2003; Rudduck and Flutter, 2003) have both come to prominence, acknowledging the contribution of these as playing a vital part in fostering learning and sharing leadership.

Distributed perspectives on leadership and learning

Sergiovanni (2001) writes about leadership 'density' as a measure of how far leadership extends within a school. Similarly, Coral Mitchell and Larry Sackney refer to a community of leaders and 'leader-rich' cultures (Mitchell and Sackney, 2000: 97). In the LfL Project these ideas prompted us to devise tools which would provide a measure of the extent to which different groups within the school community exercised leadership, and what it was that lent focus to their

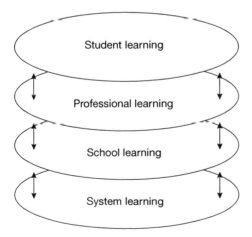

Figure 3.2 Interconnected levels of learning

leadership activity. While leadership as 'distributed' is often taken to mean that the headteacher or senior leaders 'hand out' or delegate certain roles and functions to others who carry out the work on his or her behalf, it is implicit in leadership for learning that people take on leadership as a right and responsibility rather than it being bestowed as a gift or burden.

This is what Jim Spillane proposes in his 'distributed perspective' on leadership – 'a framework for thinking about and analysing leadership' (Spillane, 2006: 10). For Spillane, leadership practice from a distributed perspective is 'a product of the joint interaction of school *leaders*, *followers*, and aspects of their *situation* such as tools and routines' (Spillane, 2006: 3) (italics in original). He puts the focus on practice, rather than leadership roles and functions or those responsible for them, and so supports the view of leadership as activity not a position. He stresses the importance of the interaction between leaders and followers, emphasising the role of followers in shaping leadership practice, and the way in which aspects of the situation contribute to defining the practice.

Spillane concentrates on two aspects of situation – tools and routines – although he acknowledges other aspects such as structures and culture. He defines tools as 'externalized representations of ideas that are used by people in their practice' (2006: 18) and gives examples of student assessment data, protocols for lesson observation, and lesson plans. Leadership routines are described as involving two or more people in repeated recognisable patterns of interdependent actions, for example student assessment regimes and professional development meetings, which constitute an integral part of school life. Spillane's point is that tools and routines are not just accessories of, or arenas for, leadership, but act to fundamentally shape leadership practice.

In his discussions of distributed leadership Spillane draws on activity theory (Engeström, 1999) while not specifically referring to it, while for Peter Gronn activity theory is explicitly referred to as a 'promising approach to the study of the work of leaders' (Gronn, 2000: 326). This promise is due to certain characteristics of activity theory, particularly that it takes a holistic perspective, has the division of labour as a central feature, and uses collectively performed activity as its unit of analysis. Adopting activity theory as his analytical framework, Gronn argues that 'leadership invariably takes a distributed form' (Gronn, 2000: 333). It is a form, he argues, whose time has come, and that will become more and more prevalent due to developments in technology that are increasingly facilitating collaborative work.

Activity theory is helpful in reframing our understanding of leadership as a distributed activity but is equally applicable to learning. There are important parallels and synergies to be found in research into distributed cognition and distributed intelligence (Pea, 1993; Cole and Engeström, 1993; Salomon and Perkins, 1998). David Perkins, for example, argues that 'human cognition at its richest almost always occurs in ways that are physically, socially and symbolically distributed' (Perkins, 1992: 133), and gives examples of each category including notes, portfolios and computers; learning in groups, pair problem solving and Socratic teaching; diagrams, concept maps and tables. In his book *King Arthur's Round Table*, Perkins relates the story of how the crew of the USS *Palau* used distributed cognition to bring the ship safely to anchor despite losing all power whilst in a busy narrow channel (Perkins, 2003). Disaster was averted by both parallel and coordinated thinking by many members of the crew. A highly structured command hierarchy dealt effectively with the emergency, not by one person making all the decisions, but by the captain ceding fine-grained control to others with the best requisite skills and in the key physical locations. As the drama unfolded, people who were in a position to see what was needed and to be able to do something took the initiative. Multiple solutions proceeded alongside each other providing back-up, and some more immediate responses being put into operation quickly while better procedures were prepared. The analysis of problems, devising of solutions and the accomplishment of action were carried out by people working in concert, using and building on ideas and information from others, giving and following directions, taking the initiative and trusting in others. Leadership, followership, learning and intelligence were all distributed.

Whilst rarely having to deal with an incident as dramatic as a ship underway with no form of steering, brakes or propulsion, it may also be a telling metaphor for schools adrift, having lost both the rudder of leadership and the compass of learning. Schools function best when all their members work together through a process of distributed cognition and distributed leadership. We are beginning to understand that the strength, resilience and capability of a school lie in its distributed intelligence, its shared leadership and its communal learning. This is what James Coleman (1988) described as 'social capital'.

Social capital

The concept of social capital adds richness to our developing understanding of leadership for learning in its emphasis on social networks and connections. It involves norms such as trust and collaboration, and varies in form depending on the frequency and quality of contact and the strength of bonding between people. Social capital theorists (for example Granovetter, 1973; Robert Putnam, 1999; and Simon Szreter, 2000) describe three forms of social capital – bonding, bridging and linking. Bonding social capital is characterised by relatively few, strong connections among people, creating strong groups but also leading to insularity. With bridging social capital the links are relatively weaker, but more numerous, having the advantage of being outward looking, connecting people with others beyond their immediate reference group, opening up new ways of seeing, relating and learning. Linking social capital is a form of bridging but instead of being collegial and 'horizontal' it is 'vertical', linking with others on different hierarchical planes, making connections between people with differing degrees of power and authority. It brings us back again to the 'wedding cake' model and the horizontal and vertical linking which are fostered by a quality of leadership in which the social capital is what is shared within communities of learners. Leadership for learning is concerned above all with keeping alive bridging social capital because it is the many and weak links that provide the scope and space for the exercise of agency in respect of both leadership and learning.

Agency

In further developing our understanding of leadership for learning we found the concept of agency helpful – in a sense the missing link between leadership as activity and learning as activity, leadership as dispersed and learning as distributed. Agency can be taken straightforwardly to mean 'the capacity to make a difference', but in his paper *The Concept of 'Agency' in Leadership for Learning* David Frost offers a fuller explanation.

> Being an agent or having agency involves having a sense of self encompassing particular values and a cultural identity, and being able to pursue self-determined purposes and goals through self-conscious strategic action.
>
> (Frost, 2006: 20)

He then goes on to discuss agency in relation to learning, free will, self-regulation, and self-belief, the essential characteristics that allow learning to occur and which characterise leadership. True learning, he argues, involves volition and purposefulness, and agency, whether exercised in learning or in leadership, involves moral choice as a corollary of free will. Anthony Giddens' theory of action posits a two-way relationship between individual agency and social structures and norms so that taking charge of one's own learning or influencing the learning of others is underpinned by a willingness to engage with the social or political structures which often serve to constrain and limit potential. The exercise of agency includes the monitoring, regulation and evaluation of how we learn and how we lead and the extent to which we push at the boundaries of conventional inhibitions.

When an individual or group grasp a sense of their own agency they may take the initiative to draw attention to something meaningful. They may spot the learning moment, helping others to see significance or new meaning in routine behaviour. They may discern leadership in the smallest classroom incident and celebrate it publicly. They may make learning or leadership visible to others. They may create a dialogue around those moments of insight or use them as something on which to plan and build alternative practices. Agency may take many forms with varied purpose. It may be exercised for good or for ill. As educators, however, we believe that as leadership and learning alike are infused with moral purpose, agency is the key ingredient that helps to share and shape that moral purpose.

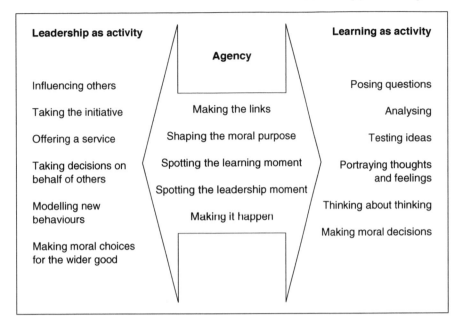

Figure 3.3 Agency linking leadership and learning

Moral purpose

Agency involves free choice, and as such is a moral issue. As Sergiovanni observes, 'Whenever there is an unequal distribution of power between two people, the relationship becomes a moral one' (Sergiovanni, 2001: 13). Not all leadership is 'good', nor is all learning. Neither is all leadership associated with valued learning. The actions of oppressive political leaders have caused suffering throughout the world, and young lives are blighted by gang leaders who exert strong influence on adolescent culture. Even leadership of a less obviously malevolent nature may be exercised in pursuit of undesirable ends, such as excessive consumerism or the cult of the celebrity. Much of what is learnt, formally and informally, detracts from rather than contributes to the individual and greater good.

The leadership and learning that we are interested in are not just neither malevolent nor neutral. They are positively benevolent. Leadership for learning is driven by moral purpose, based on values that underpin learning and infuse leadership. These are made apparent through behaviours and actions, and the conditions we create for students, teachers and parents.

Exploring *The Moral Imperative of School Leadership* Fullan states that:

> . . . the moral imperative of the principal involves leading deep cultural change that mobilizes the passion and commitment of teachers, parents

and others to improve the learning of all students, including closing the achievement gap.

(Fullan, 2003: 41)

He argues that the culture of schools and of the wider school system needs to become one in which sustainable, continuous improvement and reform are built in. This has resonances with John Dewey's view of learning as continual growth and the educative experience as one that promotes the possibility of having desirable future experiences (Dewey, 1938).

The learning that we value and promote is evidenced by the cultures we create. Fullan maintains that principals need to build new cultures based on trusting relationships, disciplined inquiry and action. He is careful to distinguish between a culture of discipline and disciplinarian leadership, and draws on Jim Collins' 2001 book *Good to Great* which identifies three aspects of a culture of discipline – disciplined people (which dispenses with the need for hierarchy), disciplined thought (which dispenses with the need for bureaucracy) and disciplined action (which dispenses with the need for excessive controls).

All three of Collins' disciplines infuse our actions and demeanour. We all make a difference to those around us, for good or ill, consciously or unconsciously, planned or by default. Our 'inner compass' (Covey, 1994) or sense of purpose can guide us if we continually ask ourselves the questions: Why did I become an educator in the first place? What do I stand for as a leader? What legacy do I want to leave? (Livsey and Palmer, 1999, cited in Fullan, 2003).

Distinctive features of leadership for learning

Grasping what leadership for learning means in theory and in practice has been, and will continue to be, a developing narrative. Concepts such as activity, agency and moral purpose each contributed something important to our understanding. We now see it as comprised of a number of distinguishing features (Figure 3.4).

As we continued to reflect, analyse data and engage in dialogue, we will further refine our ideas and understanding, as continuous inquiry and reframing are intrinsic to the very nature of leading and learning

Leadership for learning

'Leadership and learning are indispensable to each other.' *Leadership for learning* is an attempt to capture, define and illustrate this interdependency. This chapter has explored our current understanding of what we see as a dynamic concept centred around a particular form of educational practice. There is a lot to say and much still to learn about leadership for learning but in teasing our way through the five principles and prompts to action that follow in Chapters 6 to 10 we hope to shed some light on this complex and challenging concept.

1　There are explicit links between leadership and learning.
2　It is recognised that everyone has the potential for learning and for leadership.
3　Learning is at the centre of leadership activities.
4　The capacity for leadership arises out of powerful learning experiences.
5　Opportunities to exercise leadership enhance learning.

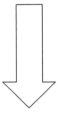

1　Leadership for learning is embedded in the culture.
2　Leadership for learning is value based and driven by moral purpose.
3　Evidence and contrasting perspectives are used to challenge leadership for learning practice.
4　There is a sensitivity to the differing contexts in which leadership and learning are.
5　Attention is given to the sustainability of leadership for learning.

Figure 3.4 Connecting leadership and learning

Leadership for learning:

Principled influential interactions arising from and resulting in valued learning.

References

Bell, L., Bolam, R., and Cubillo, L. (2003) *A Systematic Review of the Impact of School Headteachers and Principals on Student Outcomes*, London: University of London Institute of Education.

Binney, G. and Williams, C. (1997) *Leaning into the Future*, London: Nicolas Brealey.

Bolman, L. and Deal, T. (1991) *Reframing Organizations: Artistry, Choice and Leadership*, San Francisco, CA: Jossey-Bass.

Carr, M. (2001) *Assessment in Early Childhood Settings*, London: Paul Chapman Publishing.

Claxton, G. (2002) *Building Learning Power*, Bristol: TLO.

Claxton, G. (2006) 'Expanding the capacity to learn: a new end for education?' Keynote address British Educational Research Association, Warwick, 6 September.

Cole, M. and Engeström, Y. (1993) 'A cultural historical approach', in G. Salomon (ed.) *Distributed Cognitions*, Cambridge: Cambridge University Press, pp. 4–43.

Coleman, J. (1988) 'Social capital in the creation of human capital', *The American Journal of Sociology*, 94: S95–S120.

Collins, J. (2001) *Good to Great: Why Some Companies Make the Leap . . . and Others Don't*, London: Random House Business.

Covey, S. (1990) *Principle-Centred Leadership*, New York: Summit Books.

Covey, S. (1994) *First Things First*, London: Simon and Schuster.

Dewey, J. (1938) *Experience and Education*, New York: First Collier Books, 1963 edition.

Drummond, M.J. (2003) *Assessing Children's Learning*, second edition, London: David Fulton.

Earl, L. (2003) *Assessment as Learning: Using Classroom Assessment to Maximize Student Learning*, Thousand Oaks, CA: Corwin Press.

Eisner, E. (2000) 'Those who ignore the past . . .: 12 "easy" lessons for the next millennium', *Journal of Curriculum Studies*, 32 (2): 343–57.

Engeström, Y. (1999) 'Activity theory and individual and social transformation', in Y. Engeström, R. Miettinen and R.-L. Punamäki (eds) *Perspectives on Activity Theory*, Cambridge: Cambridge University Press.

Fielding, M. and Bragg, S. (2003) *Students as Researchers: Making a Difference*, Cambridge: Pearson Publishing.

Frost, D. (2006) 'The concept of "agency" in leadership for learning', *Leading and Managing*, 12 (2): 19–28.

Frost, D. and Harris, A. (2003) 'Teacher leadership: towards a research agenda', *Cambridge Journal of Education*, 33 (3): 479–98.

Fullan, M. (2003) *The Moral Imperative of School Leadership*, Thousand Oaks, CA: Corwin Press.

Geertz, V.C. (1973) *The Interpretation of Cultures*, New York: Basic Books.

Gladwell, M. (2000) *The Tipping Point: How Little Things Can Make a Big Difference*, New York: Little Brown.

Granovetter, M. (1973) 'The strength of weak ties', *The American Journal of Sociology*, 78 (6): 1360–80.

Gray, J., Jesson, D. and Sime, N. (1990) 'Estimating differences in the examination performances of secondary schools in six LEAs: a multi-level approach to school effectiveness, *Oxford Review of Education*, 16, (2): 137–58.

Gronn, P. (2000) 'Distributed properties: a new architecture for leadership', *Educational Management and Administration*, 28 (3): 317–38.

Hallinger, P. (1992) 'The evolving role of American principals: from managerial to instructional to transformational leaders', *Journal of Educational Administration*, 30 (3): 35–48.

Haney, W. (2000) 'The myth of the Texas miracle in education', *Education Policy Analysis Archives* 8 (41), http://epaa.asu.edu/epaa/v8n41/

Harlen, W. (2006) 'On the relationship between assessment for formative and summative purposes', in J. Gardner (ed.) *Assessment and Learning*, London: Sage.

Jencks, C.S., Smith, M., Ackland, H., Bane, M.J., Cohen, D., Gintis, H., Heyns, B. and Micholson, S. (1972) *Inequality: A Reassessment of the Effect of Family and Schooling in America*, New York: Basic Books.

Knapp, M., Copland, M. and Talbert, J. (2003) *Leading for Learning: Reflective Tools for School and District Leaders,* Washington: Center for the Study of Teaching and Policy, University of Washington (www.ctpweb.org).

Labaree, D. (1997) *How to Succeed in School Without Really Learning*, New Haven, CT: Yale University Press.

Leavitt, S.D. and Dubner, S.J. (2005) *Freakonomics*, London: Allen Lane.

Leithwood, K., Jantzi, D. and Steinbach, R. (1999) *Changing Leadership for Changing Times*, Buckingham: Open University Press.

Leithwood, K., Seashore Louis, K., Anderson, S. and Wahlstrom, K. (2004) *Review of Research: How Leadership Influences Student Learning*, New York: The Wallace Foundation.

Leithwood, K., Harris, A. and Hopkins, D. (2008) 'Seven strong claims about successful school leadership', *School Leadership and Management*, 28, (1): 27–42.

Leithwood, K., Day, C., Sammons, P., Harris, A. and Hopkins, D. (2006) *Seven Strong Claims about Successful School Leadership*, Nottingham: National College for School Leadership.

Levacic, R. (2005) 'Educational leadership as a causal factor: methodological issues in research on leadership "effects"', *Educational Management Administration and Leadership*, 33 (2): 197–210.

Lewis, P.J. (2007) *How We Think but not in School*, Rotterdam/Taipei: Sense Publishers.

Lieberman, A. and Friedrich, L. (2008) 'Changing teachers from within: teachers as leaders', in J. MacBeath and Y.C. Cheng (eds) *Leadership for Learning: International Perspectives*, Rotterdam: Sense Publishers.

Lieberman, A. and Miller, L. (2004) *Teacher Leadership*, San Francisco, CA: Jossey-Bass.

Luyten, H. (2003) 'The size of school effects compared to teacher effects: an overview of the research literature', *School Effectiveness and School Improvement*, 14 (1): 31–51.

MacBeath, J. (2003) 'The alphabet soup of leadership', *Inform No. 2*, Cambridge: University of Cambridge Faculty of Education.

MacBeath, J. (2004) *The Leadership File*, Glasgow: Learning Files Scotland.

MacBeath, J. and Mortimore, P. (eds) (2001) *Improving School Effectiveness*, Buckingham: Open University Press.

MacBeath, J. and Stoll, L. (2001) 'A profile of change', in J. MacBeath, and P. Mortimore (eds) *Improving School Effectiveness*, Buckingham: Open University Press.

MacBeath, J. and Sugimine, H. with G. Sutherland and M. Nishimura and students of the Learning School (2003) *Self-Evaluation in the Global Classroom*, London: Routledge.

MacBeath, J., Frost, D., Swaffield, S. and Waterhouse, J. (2006) *Leadership for Learning Carpe Vitam Making the Connections: The Story of a Seven Country Odyssey in Search of a Practical Theory*, Cambridge: University of Cambridge Faculty of Education.

Mitchell, C. and Sackney, L. (2000) *Profound Improvement: Building Capacity for a Learning Community*, Lisse: Swets and Zeitlinger.

Mulford, B. (2008) 'Learning about leadership in Australia', in J. MacBeath and Y.C. Cheng (eds) *Leadership for Learning: International Perspectives*, Rotterdam: Sense Publishers.

Nicholls, S.L and Berliner, D. (2005) *The Inevitable Corruption of Indicators and Educators through High Stakes Testing*, Education Policy Research Unit (EPSL-0503-101-EPRU), Tempe, AZ: Arizona State University.

O'Neill, O. (2004) *A Question of Trust*, Cambridge: Cambridge University Press.

Pea, R.D. (1993) 'Distributed intelligence and designs for education', in G. Salomon (ed.) *Distributed Cognitions*, Cambridge: Cambridge University Press, pp. 46–87.

Perkins, D. (1992) *Smart Schools: Better Thinking and Learning for Every Child*, New York: The Free Press.

Perkins, D. (2003) *King Arthur's Round Table: How Collaborative Conversations Create Smart Organizations*, Hoboken, NJ: John Wiley.

Putnam, R. (1999) *Bowling Alone: The Collapse and Revival of American Community*, New York: Touchstone.

Robinson, V.M.J. (2007) 'The impact of leadership on student outcomes: an analysis of the differential effects of leadership types', Paper delivered at the International Congress for School Effectiveness and Improvement, Auckland, New Zealand, 7 January.

Rudduck, J., and Flutter, J. (2003) *Consulting Pupils: What's in it for Schools?* London: RoutledgeFalmer.

Salomon, G. and Perkins, D. (1998) 'Individual and social aspects of learning', *Review of Research in Education*, 23: 1–24.

Sergiovanni, T. (1992) *Moral Leadership*, San Francisco, CA: Jossey-Bass.

Sergiovanni, T. (2001) *Leadership: What's in it for Schools?* London: RoutledgeFalmer.

Southworth, G. (2002) 'Instructional leadership in schools: reflections and empirical evidence' *School Leadership and Management*, 22 (1): 73–92.

Spillane, J. (2006) *Distributed Leadership*, San Francisco, CA: Jossey-Bass.

Szreter, S. (2000) 'Social capital, the economy and education in historical perspective', in S. Baron, J. Field and T. Schuller (eds) *Social Capital: Critical Perspectives*, Oxford: Oxford University Press.

Thrupp, M. (1999) *Schools Making a Difference: Let's Be Realistic*, Buckingham: Open University Press.

Whitehead, A.N. (1932) *The Aims of Education and Other Essays*, London: Williams and Norgate.

Witziers, B., Bosker, R.J. and Kruger M.L. (2003) 'Educational leadership and student achievement: the elusive search for an association, *Educational Administration Quarterly*, 39 (3): 398–425.

Woodhead, C. (2002) *Class Wars*, London: Little, Brown.

4 Seven countries, eight sites, 24 schools

Joanne Waterhouse and Neil Dempster

What we know about learning and about leadership grows almost by the day as new theories emerge, new texts expand the scholarly library, reframing and demythlogising, adding new terminology to an already bewildering repertoire. Yet the gap remains between what we claim to know and what we do on a day-to-day basis in schools and classrooms. We understand that children inhabit two different worlds – the world of school and the world of home and neighbourhood, the world of informal, spontaneous, social learning and the world of formal structured, sequenced and timetabled lessons. We referred in Chapter 1 to learning 'in the wild' and learning 'in captivity', a constant source of tension in the lives of children and their teachers. There are close parallels with leadership, expressed spontaneously by children and young people, often powerfully, in day-to-day transactions in the home, in neighbourhoods, peer groups, gangs, sports and games but petrified in school hierarchies, protocols and rules.

In Chapter 3 we briefly reviewed research studies which have tried to validate the connection between leadership and learning through quantitative methods, the desire for 'hard' evidence limiting their ability to provide deep insights into the contested nature and interplay of those two concepts. We described there how the Leadership for Learning Project grew out of a desire to make sense of these ideas and the dilemmas they pose in the real world of schools. Adopting the name 'Carpe Vitam' was a shorthand reference to the funding Swedish charity whose inspiration was the philanthropist and eternal optimist, Peder Wallenberg, who believed that 'seizing life' within the institutions of schooling could still be possible despite moribund institutional structures and political strictures which could often prove to be anti-life and anti-learning. He agreed to fund a three-year project in which learning, leadership and their interconnections would be put to the test.

We recognised that teasing out the connecting strands between learning and leadership in the 'real world' of schools and classrooms was a challenging proposition but multiplied tenfold in an international project which brought together schools, in a very literal sense, from across the world. Originally five countries agreed to take part, eventually becoming seven when Australia and Greece joined Austria, Denmark, England, and Norway and the two US states, New Jersey on the east coast and Washington on the west. In order to achieve some comparable baseline it was agreed to choose three schools in each of eight cities, all of which would have a cohort of 12 year olds. This gave us 24 schools to work with over the course of three years.

As Chapter 3 explains, we did not arrive with a blank slate but with ideas already formed, or half-formed, through Leadership for Learning: The Cambridge Network, and the accumulated wisdom of our partners in other countries. What remained to be tested, however, was how these ideas would play out in very different community contexts: in schools in different countries with different historical and cultural legacies; within quite different political administrations; and in cultures with differing linguistic registers which inevitably frame and constrain ways of understanding the world.

We could hardly have chosen a more culturally diverse set of cities and national cultures: from Athens, the site of the first modern Olympiad, to Newham in London, site of the 2012 Olympics; from Oslo and Innsbruck, both winter Olympic cities, to Brisbane in the balmy south, bordering the Gold and Surfer Paradise; from Copenhagen, cited as one of the 20 most liveable cities in the world, to an embattled inner city in New Jersey, cited as one of the most dangerous places in America.

In this chapter we try to capture the very different cultural settings of the project by examining what these schools might have held in common and in what ways they were could only be understood within their own historical legacies and cultural norms. To give more textured insights into the relationship between these schools and their communities we have painted three brief portraits of schools in Brisbane, Australia, New Jersey in the US, and in London, England. Having set the scene we then discuss some of the methodological challenges that this posed for eight research teams in their respective universities and research centres.

All of our 24 schools worked within their own policy context, each political administration exerting different kinds of pressures on these schools. During the course of the three and a half years of the project elections took place in all seven countries, in all cases observed with some anxiety by participants who feared a general and progressive trend to the political right.

Much of the anxiety centred on the autonomy of decision-making at classroom level and school level, seen to be subject to a continuing erosion. In Seattle and New Jersey the *No Child Left Behind* federal policy had introduced a form of policing of school standards, a source of external pressure not unfamiliar to staff in the London schools who, with their American counterparts, shared the politicisation of education as a legacy of the Thatcher/Reagan years. A key difference, however, is the devolution of power to individual school sites, a process which has progressed much further in England than in the US. For English observers the school district in New Jersey was redolent of a bygone age in which local authorities still exerted influence over staffing and student intake. In New Jersey the district superintendent moved staff around on the district chess board in an attempt to equalise opportunity and send the best leaders to the schools most in need.

While it might be said that England and the United States have learned to live with interventionist politics, the Nordic countries, Norway and Denmark, struggle to accommodate political directives within their long-standing democratic traditions, intolerant of hierarchy and new managerialism. These present a discomforting challenge to school cultures in which senior leaders and teachers have historically enjoyed a great deal of autonomy. Policy makers' enthusiasm for the 'Third Way' (Giddens, 1998), including among its advocates Tony Blair, has been less welcome in Nordic countries:

> This international trend that favours the reduction of the state and its public sector services presents a radical challenge to all Scandinavian countries that have been known for the value they place on equality. In educational policy discussions, schools are increasingly perceived as the unit of measurement, clearly implying new expectations of public reporting.
>
> (Møller, 2008: 215)

Autonomy within the classroom is also a strong feature of Greek schools, into which the long arm of government and the Third Way has still to penetrate. While Austrian schools have also been less constrained by political pressure, the election of a right wing government is slowly changing things and a programme for professional development of school principals is now a national strategy.

While Australian schools share many similar accountability demands to schools in England and the US in particular, the systemic provision and uptake of schooling is unlike any of the other nation states. In Australia, where private schools account for 40 per cent of all schools, there is a much more concerted attempt to address the balance than in other countries. Indeed in Norway, Denmark, Greece and Austria there would not be any thought about competing for students with the small number of private schools that exist in those countries. How schools attract students and the marketing they do with parents, while important in Australia, is not a matter on the agendas of countries where government schools are the dominant providers of education. In Norway, for example, 95 per cent of children attend public schools. However, the marketisation of education within the public sector has placed a higher premium on parental choice, its divisive effects felt most acutely in England.

The increase in consumer power which has been evident in global policy development in western economies has not bypassed schools. In education, governments see parents as the consumers, and schools as providers, selling their services and making transparent their achievements, benchmarked against national standards. This has been accompanied by efforts to bring parents more centrally into decision-making forums in schools. This thrust has not only proceeded at different rates in different countries but has assumed a quite different character in our LfL schools. In Austria there is a mandatory early warning system requiring parents to be notified when children are under-achieving, leading to a written agreements among parents, pupils and teachers with a view to putting supportive measures in place. The formal design is a matter for the individual teacher, but he/she is obliged to arrive at an agreement on the action to be taken. Parents receive a copy of the agreement.

Denmark and Norway have always seen parent participation as integral to a child's education and parents there are actively engaged with class teachers from the earliest years as a triadic class unit. This classroom level focus is accompanied by parental involvement in School and Community Councils which have a strong voice in what schools are mandated to do. In England, parent power is exercised through governing bodies which are the ultimate authority in schools and to whom headteachers are required to be accountable. There are parallels with School Boards in the United States but in that country the direct accountability to taxpayers has resulted in enforced changes to curriculum and reading materials, in some cases parents withholding taxes and so resulting in school closures. In Australia, some state jurisdictions have extended decision-making authority to school councils while others have moved towards structures which enable parents to provide direct advice on school matters. Parent power is a particularly important contextual influence when schools want to concentrate on learning and leadership because the key consumers in some cases have direct power over what might be done while in others their power is indirect.

Parental and family issues impact most powerfully on schools in what are now known as 'challenging circumstances'. Most, but not all, LfL schools faced a range of difficulties associated with low socio-economic status and welfare dependency, most acutely felt in schools in New Jersey and London. Many schools included children with second language learning needs and the cultural isolation that accompanies recent immigration, most markedly in Washington State, Australia and England. Still others had difficulty dealing with issues of leadership amongst teachers as a matter of cultural conditioning. In Greek schools teachers did not see themselves as having, or sharing, a leadership role, while in Denmark teachers flexed their leadership 'muscles' in response to policy directions they did not agree with.

While schools in each of the seven countries were subject to differing kinds of political pressures, some acute, some still to be fully felt, policy makers in all eight countries are highly sensitive to their nation's rankings within OECD reports and pressure on attainment targets is likely to increase rather than diminish. A commitment to leadership for learning as we pursued it within the project will continue to require a significant measure of courage and risk taking.

Three schools

A school in an inner city, USA

City High is an archetypical American high school. Its ancient brick building fronted by tall white colonial pillars consumes a large city block, a building large enough to house 4,000 of the city's youth who, out of school time, and often in-school time as well, take up their positions at every street corner. They may extend goodwill to those who pass by but to the wary pedestrian they are a threatening presence. It seems much safer to drive to the school than run this silently watchful gauntlet of young men.

The inner city is not a welcoming place. Year on year it wins an accolade as one of the most dangerous cities in the United States, most of the 30 or so annual homicides being gang related, a substantial number for a city of 84,000 people. Once described by James Madison as a 'dismembered torso bleeding into Philadelphia and New York', the city is easily accessible to these major centres by car or train and within easy travelling distance of the idyllic pastoral village of Princeton. The contrast with the inner city, sitting cheek by jowl with surrounding affluence, adds to the sense of embattlement. One local resident in less florid language than Madison's describes it as a 'socio-economically challenged' city in one the wealthiest counties in the state (Harvard Family Research, 2006).

The main campus of the High School occupies a symbolic space and the clock in the impressive white central tower marks the exact time. It was an expensive repair to restore the clock to its proper function after years of neglect but the incoming principal in 2000 saw it as a statement to the community that she and her staff meant business. A lower two storey red brick building in South Street is a second campus with its own principal.

In common with all inner-city schools, entrance is via a metal detector, the main target of which is knives and guns, a familiar armoury for young people for whom carrying arms is a necessary form of defence and a badge of membership. This is, of course, not true for all City High students, many of whom excel in one of the award, scholarship and honour programmes. Nonetheless, a serious minority are affiliated to one of the 50 or so gangs that inhabit the local community.

Despite the hallway guard, City High is a generally welcoming place. Efforts have been made to brighten the long traditional, otherwise bleak, tiled hallways that stretch into the middle distance and echo with the metallic banging of locker doors in between periods as students make the repetitive journey from one end of the building to the other. There is a vibrant atmosphere with students' work displayed in corridors together with posters bearing homilies and injunctions to strive and to excel. The school offers a breadth of opportunity through a spectrum of academic and vocational electives to complement the core requirements of language, math and science. There is a heavy emphasis on literacy and numeracy as students are, on average, well below state and national standards in the basic skills.

Teachers work hard to engage their students' interest in the face of an often uninspiring curricular diet within the core subjects and pressure to succeed within the draconian strictures of No Child Left Behind. In tenth grade they choose one of nine small learning communities which range from the Renaissance Academy to the Law and Justice Academy, all of these with a strong vocational bias. From a plethora of clubs students can choose hip hop, Bible club, basic Spanish dancing or a model UN club.

Sixty-seven per cent of students are African American and 27 per cent Latino. You are never far from reminders of race, racism and anti-racism. This is a predominantly African-American school and you better watch your language and your choice of iconography. On a conference day teachers pack the main hall and a visiting speaker makes the mistake of showing a video of an English school with all white children. He is kindly informed afterwards by three elderly female members of staff that this kind of fare does not go down well in City High.

The School District, 'committed to excellence and equity within an environment conducive to learning', enjoyed up until 2006 the superintendency of a visionary leader. An enlightened and unorthodox leader, he not only presided over a complex school district but invested a lot of time in educational matters. He wanted to keep abreast of thinking and encouraged his teaching force to read educational texts, convening regular 'book club' meetings to discuss a set reading. Unlike many of the schools in other countries, management is not devolved to school sites allowing staffing decisions to be made at district level. So, together with his team, he would pore over lists of school senior staff with his latest district intelligence to shuffle principals and vice-principals around to create the best blend of experience and opportunities for mentoring and professional development. It underlines some of the benefits of system leadership, which his counterparts in English local authorities no longer enjoy. The downside is felt at school level where staff express a desire for more local control over decision-making.

Three members of staff from City High participated in the LfL Project from its launch in Cambridge in 2002 up to its final conference in Athens in 2005. They were accompanied by two members of the School Board who were, in the latter days of the project, to hold the balance of power on the Board and influence key decisions. Through their influence and that of the Princeton-based research team, leadership for learning was adopted as district wide policy.

A school in Brisbane, Australia

Northside High which opened in 1970, is a government co-educational school situated on the North side of the river which splits the city of Brisbane on the sub-tropical east coast of Australia. The school grounds reflect the natural beauty of its environment, with landscaped gardens and seating areas to enhance the rich set of learning experiences offered to students. Buildings have been recently refurbished with new facilities and equipment added to enable specialist pursuits such as leadership, drama and music to be given high priority. Colloquially the school is said to be in a 'leafy suburb' and it is occasionally referred to as 'well heeled'. Both colloquial terms suggest a school at the higher end of the socio-economic spectrum. The current enrolment of approximately 730 students makes it a medium-sized Australian school. There are over 70 teachers working at the school, the great majority of whom have more than 10 years teaching experience.

The school is located in a well-established suburb where the community enjoys a strong sense of local identity. The suburb, developed in the main, during the 1960s and early 1970s, features well-kept brick homes all with their own free standing plots of land. Indeed, it could be said that Northside High stands in an area which typifies the idealised 'Great Australian Dream' – a home for every family, each with its own fenced garden, backyard swimming pool, veranda and barbecue area. Many children walk or ride a bicycle to school, though most take a bus or are 'dropped off' by parents travelling by car on their way to work. The school is a short distance from a small suburban shopping centre, so before and after school, clusters of students can be seen emerging from shops, standing chatting at the bus stop or just generally enjoyably 'hanging out'.

There have been some demographic changes within the area over recent years and these are stimulating some shifts in community views, particularly a growing avid interest in education, as younger families gradually replace an ageing population of original residents. The majority of residents in the area are professional people who belong to the middle and upper socio-economic range and many students have a family background where both parents work. Students tend to come from families 'where', as the teachers say, 'money doesn't seem to be an issue'. For the most part, the students have enjoyed a wide range of experiences in terms of travel and other outside school learning opportunities; thus the school community can be categorised as culturally rich. Such is the financial base within the community that many of those with a capacity to pay for education choose between Northside High and a number of local private schools. Competition for enrolment 'share' features frequently in conversations about the school's future. Indeed the school's performance is partly judged on its ability to attract 'a stronger enrolment share' than it had done during the 1990s when an increasing number of children 'drove past the school' on the way to a private education.

The school provides secondary education programmes from Year 8 to Year 12. While learning is portrayed by the principal and staff as the development of the whole person – the student's academic, social, personal, physical and emotional being – there is a special emphasis on leadership development for all students throughout the five years of secondary schooling. The focus is most visible in the school's leadership development centre. This is a purpose-built facility for the conduct of 'risk' and 'trust' based leadership training programmes. There, the students experience ropes courses, climbing walls, abseiling and general obstacle courses, always in teams and with varying or changing student leadership opportunities. These on-campus courses are supplemented by off-campus hikes, adventure style treks, excursions and camps under canvas.

In addition, and in direct competition with its private school rivals, a focus on academic excellence underpins the priorities of the school community. Over 70 per cent of students continue on to further education. Consequently, the school's main concerns about learning are related to promoting and encouraging students to be successful, first in the academic arena, and then in broader, or more general terms.

Since 2000, when the present principal was appointed, Northside High has enjoyed a high level of renewal and resurgence. Positive change has been achieved under his leadership with the support of a senior management team (a deputy principal and a number of heads of department) all of whom seem dedicated to fostering a process of continued improvement within the school. Whilst the principal provides strong 'top-down' leadership, school structures now encourage 'bottom-up' initiatives, with innovation and opportunities for democratic leadership at all levels of the school community, including students and parents. This was not the case at the outset of the LfL Project. Then the principal freely admitted his 'driving' style, a style which he has since modified to become more accommodating of leadership shared with others. At the outset, it was the principal who decided to take the school into the project, a decision for which he relied on a core of teachers, about a dozen in all, who were willing to be involved in exploring further the links between the school's professed interest in student leadership and its possible effects on learning. The commitment of these teachers, and the shared leadership which developed contributed to the project's impact on leadership in general classroom activities. The most tangible evidence that this approach produced benefits for students is seen in the school's receipt of a prestigious award for 'Excellence in the field of leadership' in the final year of the project.

A school in London, England

Hedgeworth Community School is a secondary school serving over 1,300 students situated in a London borough, one of the three ranked lowest on quality of life indicators. A recent television programme which named it as one of the worst places to live in Britain received an immediate response from young people and local residents, claiming that the programme had failed to perceive the warmth and hospitality of the local people.

The area is bordered by high-rise, council-owned accommodation, main urban thoroughfares and a railway line serving the capital. Some members of the local community work in the city nearby in well-paid jobs. Most are either unemployed or earning a low wage in shop and manual work. The high street is a long, never-ending cornucopia of small businesses serving the diverse community. There are market stalls near to the train station with costermongers working there perpetuating a family tradition that has existed for generations. Their customers today are largely Asian, from Pakistan and Bangladesh, although a range of languages and voices can be heard, including the familiar London cockney accent.

The school is located in a dense urban sprawl, approached through a series of narrow residential streets. There are rows of terraced homes and sections of brick, low-level flats. The sound of the high street fades and the atmosphere in the nearby streets becomes still and quiet. Some people walk the pavements, mothers pushing prams and elderly people making their way back from the shops. Mostly it is full of parked cars, mounting pavements, struggling for space and obscuring the view of the street.

There is no opportunity to get a long look at the school before you are upon it, turning another corner through the maze of pavement, patches of communal green and the walls of parked cars. The building is a rambling two storey concrete edifice lined with windows and edged with railings that seem unending. It has been extended in a series of phases since the 1940s. All is grey concrete and glass – windows too high to see either in or out. It is unclear where the entrance is until a walk around the railings reveals a bright, newly constructed reception area. This cheers the visitor, who is able to study the artwork of the students whilst listening to lively, busy chatter as the school day begins. There are several adults available to sort out the queries of a stream of elder siblings and parents, delivering late students, forgotten bags or explanations for recent absences. The community is cosmopolitan and multi-cultural and many parents speak languages other than English. The atmosphere in the reception area is welcoming and informal. There are several examples of creative strategies to understand the entreaties and needs of family members, including three-way conversations with youngsters translating for pairs of adults. Mostly there are smiles and assertions of understanding.

Between lessons, the students appear self-confident and move around the building in groups attending seriously to whispered conversations. There is a sense of marshalled energy. The students are constantly organised and monitored. Teachers are assertive and watchful. There seem to be layers of communication occurring simultaneously, between teacher and student, student-to-student, friend-to-friend, group-to-group. Occasionally there will be a flurry of activity and the suggestion of a scuffle. Almost wordlessly an adult attends to the group, a child is admonished and the group move on to their next class.

In lessons, the students can be hard working and keen to do well. The aspirations of many are to succeed in exams and be seen to do well by their peers, older siblings and parents. Their goals for success are typically short-term, to be achieved that week, or perhaps by the end of the year. The students demonstrate a confidence to talk to visitors and need little encouragement to express opinions. They are outwardly robust and self-assured. Their observations are sharp, astute and humorous.

The headteacher has been in post for seven years and expresses the sense that he is beginning to influence and fully shape developments. He has led an LfL agenda by promoting initiatives that create time for collaboration and supporting innovation. He is frustrated by a perceived timidity amongst some staff to see the big picture and insists that the entreaties from national government to be more creative and localised can be trusted. In the course of the coming year the school buildings will be demolished in stages to make way for a brand new edifice. In the view of the headteacher its grand design should be not so much a dictated architect's vision but built from the ground up to reflect the principles of leadership for learning.

Staff are concerned with the immediate needs of their students and the imperatives of exam success. They are proud of their departments and particular charges and demonstrate commitment to inclusive education. The curriculum is framed by national requirements and the teachers express frustration at the lack of time to develop work that could meet the needs of all students. Staff appear both enervated by the students and exhausted by competing agendas. There is a siege-like spirit, of success against the odds, of an indomitable commitment to the welfare of the children in defiance of unreasonable demands.

Learning is talked about at Hedgeworth Community School. Various members of staff and students talk readily and animatedly about the opportunities to have learning as a topic for discussion. Learning is increasingly promoted as the core business of the school and adults and students will discuss their learning. There are words for talking about learning. Staff meetings are scheduled for administration and for matters of learning. One teacher spoke about a recent series of meetings that had been focused on an initiative for curriculum development and that had pupil commentaries about their learning at the core.

Leadership, while a topic associated with formal positions of authority and tainted with rigid systems of accountability, is nonetheless dispersed as the school extends its compass within the community and has a plethora of new roles such as Assistant Head (Primary and Community Learning), Community Learning Manager, Student Support Centre Manager, Summer School Co-ordinator, Family Support Workers and Refugee Support Worker. Peer Mentoring and a Senior Students Scheme are aimed at increasing leadership opportunities for senior students who support younger students. Before selection they are given clear guidelines as to the skills and dispositions required and the tasks involved, including responsibilities at parents' evenings, assistance in setting up and running clubs, and managing podcasting and other forms of publicity about opportunities to learn in and out of school.

Leadership for learning is implicit, as the practice demonstrated by creative opportunities for new posts of responsibility and in the promotion of self-determination by students in lessons, is gaining momentum. Learning is at the centre of a strong discourse in the school, for students and adults. The conditions for learning are a matter for constant and continued reflection and debate. Sharing leadership is an espoused value for those in power and is matched by a range of change initiatives.

Conclusion

We chose three schools in order to convey something of the communities in which these schools were situated and the nature of the common and differing challenges they face. What brought them from these very diverse sites into the LfL Project was a shared desire to advance their understanding, to learn from schools in other contexts, other cultures, and ultimately to serve students and communities more effectively. As we enlisted schools on the understanding that they were able to subscribe to its underpinning values we started from a common base. All schools said they were able to endorse the centrality of learning, leadership and the links between them, the pursuit of learning and leadership as social rather than individual activities, and the distribution of leadership across all areas and levels within the school. However, once we were engaged in the project, we found that although there was commitment to participatory practices and shared leadership, time was needed to realise these within the day-to-day reality of school life and impatient policy pressures. Two examples from our accounts above illustrate this point. At Northside High, it took some time before the principal was able to let go of the reins, given that 'command and control' was his original default leadership position. In a London school, helping teachers move beyond the compliance mentality that accompanies the national curriculum and its assessment into a learning and leadership focused discourse required a leap of faith for many. Our observation of the project schools tells us that at the outset, many had an over-inflated view of their abilities to act out the values they said they espoused. Nevertheless, espoused theory became theory in action for most, as information about practice was discussed, decisions on development were made and leadership for learning principles were drafted.

When the take-up of global policy in each country, as we foreshadowed above, is added to local school contexts, it has shown that while there is some observable similarity in the way all schools deal with everyday problems, there are deep cultural differences which influence the approach taken to those problems and to newly emerging global issues. In addition, there are different responses expected by governments and the wider community to issues from that global policy environment.

Nevertheless, the differences amongst our project schools did not act as impediments to the development of shared principles for practice which explain connections between leadership and learning. In fact, we contend that the diverse school contexts from which the principles were derived give us a sense of confidence in their broader applicability. If linking leadership for learning was possible in 24 schools of such diversity, from differently endowed country contexts, then the principles for practice, we argue, are likely to have a robust generic quality. The process which generated the principles, and how we engaged with the 24 schools, is the subject of the following chapter.

References

Giddens, A. (1998) *The Third Way: The Renewal of Social Democracy*, Cambridge: Polity Press.

Harvard Family Research http://www.gse.harvard.edu/hfrp/, last accessed 29/1/08.

Møller, J. (2008) 'Living with accountability and mandated change: leadership for learning in a Norwegian context', in J. MacBeath and Y.C. Cheng, *Leadership for Learning: International Perspectives*, Rotterdam: Sense Publishers.

5 Researching the connections, developing a methodology

David Frost

Given the diversity and complexity of the cultural settings described in Chapter 4, we needed a way of working together that could cross national and cultural boundaries and respect the differing traditions and practices of our research collaborators and practitioners in the schools which we brought together for the first time in Cambridge in 2002. We needed a methodology which would have a number of key features not all of which were fully understood at the outset. We have described these as federalist, eclectic, emergent, practice-focused and educative.

A federalist approach

At the first meeting of the international research team we explored the variety of traditions and differences in the working practices represented around the table. We may have shared a set of values about leadership and learning but we didn't necessarily have a common language for inquiry. For some of us the Leadership for Learning Project was a form of 'action research' (Elliott, 1991). However, the word 'research', it was argued by some, was to be avoided because it might alienate practitioners; instead the term 'co-inquiry' (Palus and Horth, 2002) was suggested as more appropriate to the situation. For other members of the team, the term 'action learning' (Evans, 1982) was more palatable and more accurately described how practice in schools would develop. The language of 'school self-evaluation' was also at the forefront of some researchers' minds because of previous collaboration in American, Australian and European projects (MacBeath et al., 2000).

In order to accommodate these differences, we resolved that we would agree on a core programme of data gathering across the project as a whole but, beyond that, each national research team would pursue the aims of the project in their own way. At the heart of our thinking was the concept of subsidiarity, a term enjoying a wide currency in the European Union. This principle holds that it is desirable that decisions be taken at the most local level and only taken centrally where this is more effective. We therefore adopted an approach in which the eight research teams had their own methodology but shared particular strategies such as a large scale survey. While we recognised that this would throw up a number of challenges, for example with analysis, we put our faith in the possibility that everything could be resolved through reasoned discussion and negotiation.

An eclectic approach

Entering into a collaborative research project in which there are many voices reflecting a variety of beliefs and values about research may seem like a recipe for disaster but we preferred to see such diversity as a benefit. The particular interests of the experienced members of the research team not only brought a range of techniques and expertise to the table, but also provided the means to challenge our thinking and push us to articulate our taken-for-granted assumptions about professional practice.

An emergent approach

As a detailed, predetermined project design would have necessitated the imposition of a plan that may not have suited participating research teams, we chose instead to allow the design to emerge in response to the challenges that arose along the way. As the engagement with our collaborators in the schools grew, so fresh challenges emerged. For example, in the run-up to our second international conference, we were aware of a degree of reluctance on the part of some practitioners to learn from practice that was common in quite different kinds of schools in other countries. We therefore concentrated on the production of tools to support international exploration of practice. The idea of an emergent methodology has been rehearsed before and seen to be not only forgivable but to have clear advantages (Tom, 1996).

A practice-focused approach

In his extensive discussion of the nature of educational research, Martin Hammersley distinguished between 'scientific inquiry', which aims to contribute to what Carol Weiss called 'knowledge creep' (Weiss, 1997), and 'practical inquiry' which aims to produce practical knowledge recognised as such by practitioners and policy makers (Hammersley, 2001). In planning the project we were interested in the production of practical knowledge for two reasons. First, if practitioners were to expend time and energy on the project and to open up their practice to the scrutiny of others, they needed to derive direct and immediate benefit for their schools. Second, we wanted to be able to produce knowledge that could travel, that could be used by other practitioners in a wide range of countries and that could influence the thinking of policy makers in the global context. Our purpose was not to try to generalise about a wider population from a representative sample, but to initiate an experimental and discursive process; we therefore needed partner schools who shared our values and were open to challenging their practice.

An educative approach

Many years ago Lawrence Stenhouse posed the question: what is educational about educational research? In the paper cited above, Martin Hammersley makes the distinction between 'educative' research and 'informative' research, and questions whether projects designed to be both informative and educative may fail to do both effectively:

> educative action is aimed at changing people in some respect and is specifically designed to do this; informative action is aimed solely at providing people with information that is believed to be relevant to their concerns.
>
> (Hammersley, 2001)

We wanted the LfL Project primarily to be an educative process for all concerned and we also wanted to be able to say something with wider application. This, we recognised, would really be determined by the quality of the discourse that we created and would have to be subject to a process of collective interpretation in which pragmatic validity is paramount.

An action research perspective

The methodology of the project is closest to the concept of action research as described in Somekh's paper for the British Educational Research Association:

> . . . action research is grounded in the culture and values of the social group whose members are both participants in the research field and researchers. It may be instigated by an individual, but its momentum is towards collaboration, because the emphasis on social interactions and interpersonal relationships has the effect of drawing other participants into the research process.
>
> (Somekh, 1995: 342)

More fundamental, however, is the question of how the project would impact on practice. The essential defining characteristic of action research, according to one of its best known proponents, is as follows:

> The fundamental aim of action research is to improve practice rather than to produce knowledge. The production and utilisation of knowledge is subordinate to and conditioned by this fundamental aim.
>
> (Elliott, 1991: 49)

While our aims embraced the idea of improving practice in a direct and immediate sense, we also sought to build knowledge which could be abstracted in some way and brought into the public domain. We saw data as being used in two distinct but complementary ways: first to inform development work and second to feed the discourse. Informing the development work means using data for school self-evaluation and as a means to identify development priorities, using data as a stimulus to examine practice and discuss its value or effectiveness. This overlaps with the second purpose in that it feeds the discourse within the participating schools – something more than communication, conversation or debate – that social and linguistic space within which ideas and arguments flow. A discourse has some degree of coherence; embedded within it is a set of values and norms that can shape the thinking of those who inhabit that discourse. Our aim in the project was to disrupt established discourses of leadership and learning and to build a new one: a leadership for learning discourse.

Using data to feed the discourse refers to how we were able to present data at our international conferences so that practitioners and researchers could challenge their thinking, reflect on the issues and debate its significance in the light of their practical experience. In this way the data played a part in shaping the principles for practice that began to emerge as the project progressed. However, we did not begin the discursive process with data; we began by forming a social network.

Forming a social network

A dominant feature of the project was the structure of conferences that brought together the research teams, teachers, headteachers, principals and a few community stakeholders such as members of District Boards of Education in the US. We held four major international conferences during the life of the project, starting in Cambridge, then Innsbruck, Copenhagen and finally Athens. In between these three-day residential events there were regional gatherings, for example the Americans met in Seattle while the staff from the English and Greek schools met in Athens. The Australians, being in a region all on their own, participated in the between-conference meetings through the medium of telephone conferencing. Layered on this was a series of meetings of the research team through which the researchers fashioned themselves into the sort of learning community essential to an electric and emergent methodology. The community building aspects were vital; trust had to be built and we had to learn to communicate in a situation where we could not rely on the usual shorthand, the throw-away lines, familiar acronyms and local jargon. In an international grouping, we had to explain ourselves, demanding clarity and explicitness, in the process helping to clarify our own thinking.

Glimpses of practice

A natural starting point was to share portraits of the schools and of particular practices that reflected the LfL values. We asked practitioners to bring posters and other artefacts; images and symbols that represented what they valued in their schools and the challenges they faced. As we proceeded through the project, we refined the art of making practice visible to others. A key strategy was to invite practitioners to engage in portraiture which involves representation of an institution from various viewpoints drawing on a variety of types of evidence including documents, iconic material and physical or electronic artefacts (Lawrence-Lightfoot and Hoffmann Davis, 1997). These provided a basis for discussion across national, cultural and language barriers, posted on to the project website for the other schools in the project to view. They also had the potential to act as another vehicle for reflection as evidence was collected and selected within the school.

Making innovative practice visible was a continuing challenge throughout the project. At conferences we set aside space for displays and exhibits. We also began to produce vignettes of innovative practices, 400 words in length, compact but rich descriptions of practices which were then scrutinised in workshops in which the practitioners were cast as witnesses open to cross-examination rather than adopting the role of expert presenters. Vignettes were constructed to allow the reader to grasp the essential idea within a few minutes, identifying questions to interrogate it as relevant to their context.

At the final conference, practitioners came prepared to mount substantial exhibitions depicting connections between leadership derived from practices in their own schools. These impressive displays filled a small ballroom and became known as the Gallery Walk. David Perkins helped us get the most out of this by introducing one of his Visible Thinking routines (Perkins, 2003) which centres on the three key words – connect, extend, challenge – each of which constitutes a lens for viewing the materials exhibited. In other words, how does the practice represented connect with our own experience, how does it extend what we already know and how does it challenge our thinking? Participants were invited to write messages on Post-it labels to stick to the displays so that a dialogue could begin. In making practice visible in this way we were not expecting practitioners to mimic the innovative practices they had been exposed to in conference workshops or in visits to schools. As David Hargreaves underscored for us when he spoke to one of our regional conferences, professional knowledge cannot simply be transferred (Hargreaves, 2003), but innovation can travel when new practices are adapted for different contexts. Thus, making innovative practices visible both relied upon, and helped to build, a culture of development.

The development imperative

A key strategy to support development work was the allocation of critical friends, a concept with a good track record in school improvement and school self-evaluation (Swaffield, 2004) and one that featured in previous projects involving members of the Cambridge team (MacBeath and Mortimore, 2001; MacBeath *et al.*, 2000). Sue Swaffield sums up the defining characteristics of the role:

An essential distinctive element of critical friendship is a trusting relationship with a neutral outsider who brings an element of detachment and an alternative perspective. The critical friend operates predominantly through questioning as a catalyst for reflection and reappraisal on the part of the school colleague. Data and opinions may be offered for consideration, and while it is up to the school colleague how to respond to such input, the critical friend does not shy away from penetrating challenge if appropriate. The critical friend's prime and overriding accountability is to the school colleague and any others affected by the focus of the work.

(Swaffield, 2007: 11)

At our opening conference we outlined the concept and invited practitioners to discuss it and identify their own expectations for such a relationship, initiating a conversation that would help the schools to move forward with development work, informed by the research data gathered along the way. These conversations played an important part in the discourse that flowed through the project conferences and continued in networking among and within the participating schools.

Disrupting the discourse – injecting new ideas

A key strategy in our conferences was to invite speakers to challenge our thinking about leadership, learning and the link between the two. These contributions were designed to stimulate and provoke. For example, in Cambridge Judith Warren-Little from the University of California talked to us about the professional cultures that support leadership for learning and Lorna Earl from Canada, along with her co-author Louise Stoll, talked to us about the centrality of learning to school improvement; in Innsbruck, Mats Ekholm from Sweden gave us a characteristically Scandinavian perspective on the policy environment of leadership for learning; in Copenhagen Ciaran Sugrue from Ireland and Fibek Laursen from Denmark offered further perspectives on the nature of leadership; and in Athens, David Perkins from Harvard challenged us about our lack of attention to the role of the curriculum. It was essential that these theoretical perspectives were brought to the project from around the world and that they were processed through the multi-national debate within the conference workshops.

So far the impression may be that the Carpe Vitam project was largely a matter of practitioners coming together to discuss their practice with some stimulating theoretical inputs from visiting speakers. This is only half the picture. What is missing is the role of data in this discursive process.

The role of data

There was agreement that we would have a core programme of data gathering across all 24 schools in the project, establishing a 'baseline', a relatively objective and comparative analysis of capacity for developing a leadership for learning approach. This included the use of a questionnaire to school managers, teachers and students, interviews with headteachers/principals and teachers; shadowing of senior leaders and focus group meetings with parents. The primary function of these were as 'tin openers', a metaphor used to illustrate how data can be used as a basis for dialogue, a point of departure for further evaluation and research, and as a prelude to development.

The survey instrument was designed to gather data about respondents' perceptions of the importance of particular practices counterpoised with their perceptions of the extent to in which these occurred in actual practice. Identifying comparable populations of students and survey items was both challenging and a learning experience as we became more attuned to the nuances of language and the cultural meanings they conveyed. Leadership, learning and teaching do not translate simply from one language to others given that they are interpreted so differently in English. One obvious example is the German word for leader is 'Führer', a term so loaded with historical and political significance that it is not used as an equivalent to 'leader' in English. In the US, the term 'administrators' refers to managers while in Britain it refers to clerical and secretarial staff.

Quantitative data were fed back to the schools and discussed in meetings between key figures in schools and their critical friends, in some cases leading to new development priorities and in others informing ongoing development work. Alongside the survey each national research team agreed a programme of qualitative data gathering, difficult to standardise as each team had to negotiate its own relationship with their schools and devise their own programmes. Variation was inevitable but acceptable within our federalist approach.

Beyond the initial round of data gathering, schools were encouraged to update their school portraits and to invite researchers or critical friends to visit the school in order to help evaluate particular innovations. In the final year of the project a second survey and another round of interviews were carried out across the project as a whole. This provided an assessment of progress and left ·the schools with data that could be used to help identify next steps. As it became available, the data was fed into the discourse that ran as a continuous thread through the project. A key dimension was the use and continuing development of tools to give focus to our discursive activities, for example the workshop activity featuring a vignette of innovative practice, the project website on which participants shared accounts of practice, the 'learning wall' at conferences on which people posted challenging comments or the revolving PowerPoint display to which participants added slides during a three-day conference.

One of the most significant tools employed as an integral part of our international conferences was the structured school visit. Teams of project participants were invited to visit schools, provided with a framework with which to examine what they were seeing. As conceptions of leadership for learning took shape, the lens became sharper and fed into the drafting of a first of principles.

The emergence of principles for practice

While the research data we were gathering was of considerable practical use, it was not sufficiently reliable to support valid findings about the effectiveness of particular practices or the key issues for decision-making. Our solution was to draw on the idea of 'principles of procedure' (Peters, 1959, in Stenhouse, 1975) and adapt it to our purpose. Our principles for practice were derived in part from the range of theoretical perspectives introduced into the discourse by both research team members and visiting speakers, and in part from the early tranche of research data. We drew up the first draft of the principles midway through the project and used it as a framework for each of the activities during the third and fourth international conferences. Posters listing the draft principles were displayed in every room and in every workshop, as a frame for the discussion, to test, challenge and refine the draft principles. During this watershed conference, members of the research team observed the discussions and noted where the principles were upheld and where they were challenged. A year later at our final conference, the critique of the principles – now grouped into five umbrella principles – intensified and we emerged with a set of principles for practice that we could say defined our collective view of what leadership for learning could and should be.

Our five seminal principles represent our attempt to encapsulate what we have learned about leadership for learning that would be of practical use as well as theoretical interest. In offering the leadership for learning principles for practice to others we must be clear about their nature and purpose. They are first and foremost statements in which values are embedded. Second, they are an attempt to express in a sufficiently concrete way a vision of ideal practice which others can refine and develop. They are primarily an expression of pedagogical aims, a set of 'tin openers' and a tool for continuing discourse.

Despite the necessity of presenting the five principles separately in text, they are dynamically interrelated. *A focus on learning* and *shared leadership* are mediated by *conditions for learning*. *Dialogue* connects them, and all these four principles are framed by the fifth principle, *accountability* – to one another and to external groups and agencies that have invested faith and finance in our schools. *Moral*

---

1 Leadership for learning practice involves maintaining a focus on learning as an activity.
2 Leadership for learning practice involves creating conditions favourable to learning as an activity.
3 Leadership for learning practice involves creating a dialogue about LfL.
4 Leadership for learning practice involves the sharing of leadership.
5 Leadership for learning practice involves a shared sense of accountability.

Figure 5.1 Leadership for learning principles

Source: MacBeath *et al.*, 2006

purpose reflects the underpinning essential values, and the outer frame that brings all the elements into a coherent whole is *leadership for learning*.

Conclusion

The methodology of the Carpe Vitam project was only designed in part; it was also developed in action. It emerged. Our commitment to democratic values and to working in an international context led us down a path that was not as predictable as would be the case in a conventional research project. The central thread of the project was a discourse that gathered momentum, strength and focus during the three years between ICSEI (International Congress on School Effectiveness and Improvement) 2002 and ICSEI 2006. It is, of course, not concluded; it enabled us to offer a way of thinking about leadership for learning and a set of tools – including a statement of principles for practice – that can be used to take the conversation forward. As a response to global pressures that bear down on fundamental concepts such as leadership and learning, we need to continue to think creatively about ways in which researchers and practitioners can collaborate to create professional knowledge that has meaning internationally as well as in our own schools and classrooms.

References

Elliott, J. (1991) *Action Research for Educational Change*, Buckingham: Open University Press.

Evans, R.W. (1982) *The Origins and Growth of Action Learning*, London: Chartwell-Bratt.

Hammersley, M. (2001) 'Can and should educational research be educative?' Paper presented at the symposium on 'Do we Need a Science of Education?' at the Annual Conference of the British Educational Research Association, University of Leeds, England, September 13–15, 2001.

Hargreaves, D.H. (2003a) 'From improvement to transformation', Keynote lecture, International Congress for School Effectiveness and Improvement 'Schooling the Knowledge Society', Sydney, Australia.

Lawrence-Lightfoot, S. and Hoffman Davis, J. (1997) *The Art and Science of Portraiture*, San Francisco, CA: Jossey-Bass.

MacBeath, J. and Mortimore, P. (eds) (2001) *Improving School Effectiveness*, Buckingham: Open University Press.

MacBeath, J., Schratz, M., Meuret, D. and Jakobsen, L. (2000) *Self-Evaluation in European Schools: A Story of Change*, London: Routledge.

Palus, C.J. and Horth D.M. (2002) *The Leader's Edge: Six Creative Competencies for Navigating Complex Challenges*, San Francisco, CA: Jossey-Bass/Wiley.

Perkins, D.N. (2003) 'Making thinking visible', New Horizons for Learning. Online. Available HTTP: http://www.newhorizons.org/strategies/thinking/perkins.htm (accessed 13 November 2007).

Peters, R.S. (1959) *Authority, Responsibility and Education*, London: Allen and Unwin.

Somekh, B. (1995) 'The contribution of action research to development in social endeavours: a position paper on action research methodology', *British Educational Research Journal*, 21: 339–55.

Stenhouse, L. (1975) *An Introduction to Curriculum Research and Development*, London: Heinemann Educational Books.

Swaffield, S. (2004) 'Critical friends: supporting leadership, improving learning', *Improving Schools*, 7 (3): 267–78.

Swaffield, S. (2007) 'What is distinctive about critical friendship?', Paper delivered at the symposium Leadership for Learning: The Cambridge Network at ICSEI 2007, Twentieth International Congress for School Effectiveness and Improvement, Portoroz, Slovenia, 3–6 January 2007.

Tom, A. (1996) 'Building collaborative research: living the commitment to emergent', design, *Qualitative Studies in Education*, 9 (3): 347–59.

Weiss, C.H. (1997) *Evaluation: Methods for Studying Programs and Policies*, second edition, Englewood Cliffs, NJ: Prentice Hall.

6 A focus on learning (principle 1)

John MacBeath

Introduction

The first of our five Leadership for Learning principles we called 'a focus on learning'. It was a first principle not simply in a numerical sense but because everything else rests on this foundation. This principle, we might claim, was owed to an empirical grounding in work with schools, derived from our conversations with headteachers, teachers and school students in seven countries, but that would be a misleading gloss on what actually occurs in the interaction between research teams and schools. However grounded our theories, we always bring to them insights and theories, some well developed, some embryonic in character and what may be termed as propositional knowledge.

Our proposition, perhaps not yet well articulated at the outset of our collaborative inquiry with schools, was that leadership for learning must, by definition, frame leadership as learning-centred. Less clear, and still to be tested within and across diverse country contexts, is the question – what does this mean in the day-to-day practice of schools and classrooms?

What does it mean to focus on learning? As academics working in universities and within a world of constant theoretical debate we now bring our work with schools forward as a set of propositions about the nature of learning and what it might mean to focus on the nature and process of learning in the busy and conflicted environments of schools in widely differing contexts. This chapter explores the first of these.

Teaching with a focus on learning

We come to this task with a belief that teachers are not, or ought not to be, simply technicians, implementing or 'delivering' a curriculum. If they are truly to be seen as professionals their focus must be on learning, building their professional knowledge through observation, inquiry, discussion with colleagues, reading theoretical texts and keeping up to date with developments in the field – not just in their subject matter field but with an interest in the art and science of teaching. To effect this we also believe that leadership and critical friendship plays a key supportive and challenging role.

The most powerful tool available to classroom teachers is direct observation of pupils' learning. It is also by far the most sensitive and delicate of endeavours, requiring a high level of painstaking, and sometimes painful, insight. This is what Eliot Eisner (1991) has described as connoisseurship – the ability to perceive what is salient amid the complexity and simultaneity of classroom life. Some people, says Eisner, see everything and see nothing. The connoisseur has learned how to suspend preconception and judgement, to know what they see rather than seeing what they already know. Our sight is so suffused with the familiarity of classrooms, their conventions and daily rituals that to focus on learning seems not only unrealistic but gets in the way of the business, or the busyness, of teaching.

It may therefore be viewed as an indulgent luxury to take the time and make the effort to explore the learning of individual children. But when that opportunity presents itself, and when there is both will and skill to understand their thinking 'from the inside', it can be a shock to discover the dissonance between what we are trying to teach and the conceptions and misconceptions that are harboured in children's own inner space. Exploring children's misconceptions provides a fund of examples and anecdotes and every teacher can tell their own stories of how children get it wrong and then build subsequent knowledge on misconceived premises. However, there is a much more meagre fund of stories about teachers' misunderstandings and misconceptions. What is the teacher's response, asked Jerome Bruner (1987), to the pupil's calculation that two plus two equals five? It is, he suggests, the right answer but to a different question. In order to build on children's attempts to make meaning, therefore, the teacher needs to know what question the pupil is actually answering.

Exploring those mutual misconceptions can take pupils and teachers a long way in their learning journey and this lies at the very heart of good pedagogy. As pupils learn more about their own learning so teachers learn more about their own teaching and how to achieve a greater degree of consonance between what is taught and what is learned. The pressurised pace of classroom business and the overwhelming need to maintain control may, however, leave little time for such a learning discourse. In many circumstances there is not the order, the engagement or the linguistic resource to embark on such a mature dialogue. It is all very well, argues Maurice Galton (2007), to advocate wait time, or thinking time, but the novice teacher may well lose control if he does not follow the advice of his tutor or mentor to maintain the pace and stay firmly in control (Galton, 2007: 5).

Whether or not the teacher is able to sustain a focus on learning in the busy simultaneity of classroom life there are always opportunities in the tranquil spaces outside the classroom to study the products of pupils' learning. Their class work, homework or formal assessments may provide evidence to be reviewed not with a view to marking or grading but with a view to deepen understanding. In her book *Assessing Children's Learning*, Mary Jane Drummond (1993) cites a pupil conscientiously answering 36 questions on a test and getting a raw score of two correct. She writes:

We have little evidence from this test of his learning in the cognitive domain but we can see how much he has learned about the social conventions of school – how to keep his pencil sharp, how to stay in his seat, how to take a test, how to be a pupil. In the affective domain we can see Jason has learned not to express dissatisfaction or disquiet when meaningless demands are made on him. And yet we can also see signs – small but perhaps significant – that in limited ways left open to him, Jason is still struggling to make sense of what goes on around him in the puzzling world of school.

(Drummond, 1993: 9)

Studying the pupils' answers proves highly revealing as to some of the thought processes behind the wrong answers and his painstaking attempts to make sense of non-sense, and, 'the awful warning of what can happen to all children whose learning is not, for whatever reason, the prime concern and central focus of their teachers' attention' (Drummond, 1993: 9).

Making learning the prime concern and focus of the teaching task does, however, assume much, not only by way of time, energy and priority but also of expertise which might be deemed to lie more with educational psychologists than with subject specialists. Observation and interpretation of children's behaviour have proved challenging even for eminent researchers, so that most, if not all, teachers need the second or third eye, bringing colleagues and critical friends into the process of observation and reflection. Mutual observation of classroom life and shared discussion of pupils' work become a necessary professional adjunct to one's own individual interpretive efforts.

While such a collegial resource is not always to hand, what teachers can do is to mine the resource most immediately to hand, the pupils themselves. Soo Hoo (1993) writes, 'Somehow educators have forgotten the important connection between teachers and students. We listen to outside experts to inform' (Soo Hoo, 1993: 389). Teachers overlook their students for a number of reasons, but most significantly because without prior experience of consultation, children may be puzzled by the sudden interest shown in their views; they may lack the vocabulary or confidence with which to express their feelings, or they may find difficulty in adopting the stance needed to stand back from their experience in the form of critical inquiry.

A focus on teacher and pupil learning

Visiting a Cambridgeshire Year 5 classroom for a morning I was intrigued and hugely impressed by the mature quality of the conversation among young people and in dialogue with their teacher about their learning. These nine and ten year olds were reflective, analytic and challenging in their feedback to the teacher who herself modelled reflective behaviour, listening attentively to their comments, not reacting to the implicit criticism but, as was obvious from her body language and demeanour, genuinely interested in how they viewed the classroom and the relationships within it as a site for learning. It was in large part her own modelling of learning behaviour that created an ethos in which children were able to share their thinking in the way they did.

When I remarked at the end of the morning on the insights and maturity of these young people, the teacher responded – 'You don't think they *came* that way do you? This is the third year in which I have had these children and it has taken three years to get them to that level of confidence and access to a vocabulary through which to talk about their learning critically and constructively'.

In reviewing, documenting and recounting their classroom experiences, teachers use their own implicit theories of learning, but at the same time build on and modify their theories in light of those experiences. How teachers develop and test their theories of learning, suggests Maurice Galton (2007), is through a triangulation of craft knowledge, empirically observed practice and general principles. In the process, teachers come to recognise that general principles become refined, adapted and reframed in different contexts and with different learning purposes in mind.

No teacher could survive for long in a classroom without some implicit theory of how children learn, but it is only through making theory explicit that those assumptions can be tested, refined and developed. A pragmatic stance to theory would be to simply determine if it works or not but, as we have learned from teachers who focus on learning, the professional imperative requires a critical understanding of the validity and generalisability of theories and the value positions on which they rest. So, for example, behaviourist approaches certainly work within their own frames of reference. Children can be efficiently conditioned into desirable behaviour by appropriate forms of reward, and so behaviour can be shaped and moulded to the teacher's desired end. Similarly, deterring undesirable behaviour may be effected by graduated forms of punishment which also work in achieving a state of order and acquiescence so that children can be taught without disruption. However, a focus on learning, whether through direct observation, scrutiny of children's work, peer observation or collegial dialogue, brings us back to issues of values and a moral position, as Jerry Starrat (1998) has argued:

> The learning agenda of the school must connect to the central moral agenda of the learners during their thirteen or more years in school, namely the agenda of finding and choosing and fashioning themselves as individuals and as a human community. As human beings they are searching, and *must* search for the truth of who they are. Educators miss this connection because

they are accustomed to view the learning agenda of the school as an end in itself, rather than as a means for the moral and intellectual 'filling out' of learners as human beings. Schools assume that their learning agenda stands above and outside the personal and civic life of learners. By and large the message communicated to learners is: leave your personal and civic lives at the schoolhouse door – certainly at the classroom door.

(Starrat, 1998: 245)

We subscribe to the 41 articles of the UNICEF convention of Children's Rights, many of which rest on a moral base and, along with Csikzentmihalyi (1991) we believe that children are born with, and bring with them to school, a deep human drive to know, to explore their world, to become more skilled, more self-confident and to feel secure physically, mentally and socially. With a moral purpose in mind it is then incumbent on those who teach and those who lead to examine what may constrain and inhibit that innate learning drive and what may nurture and encourage it. This implies a sensitivity to structures, conventions, rules and norms which get in the way of creating a learning environment. It implies an alertness to the learning moment and how to capture and sustain it.

A focus on professional learning

As teachers pursue a focus on learning as applied to their pupils, it becomes clear that this principle applies as much to teachers as to those they teach. Indeed it may be argued that professional learning is an even higher priority than children's learning, as ignorance of how children learn and grow may be worse than no teaching at all. And, as we know all too well, bad teaching produces dysfunctional learners and justifies some of the criticisms of schooling discussed in Chapter 1. Teachers who can't or won't learn, or who do not acknowledge their role as learners when they are with their students, convey a powerful hidden, but easily decipherable, message. It is a message about the nature of authority – personal and institutional, and even more saliently, the authority of knowledge itself.

Lieberman and Friederich (2008) offers examples of how teachers learn from one another and how they learn to lead learning with and among their colleagues. In her vignette study, teachers took part in a summer writing project, writing about their own practice and their aspirations for their students' learning. As they did so they gained a new sense of their own authority and potential as agents of change and as leaders among their colleagues.

As we analyzed the vignettes and related data, we saw that these teachers adopted an *identity as a teacher leader* within their schools. This identity, shaped by their participation in the writing project, emphasizes doing what is best for students, taking responsibility for growing as a teacher and sharing practices with colleagues, and working in a collaborative manner.

(Lieberman and Friederich, 2008: 98)

A focus on learning ignites the will to lead because learning is restless and creatively dissatisfied and embraces change. Liebermann adds:

> As we analyzed the vignettes alongside the focus group interviews, we also began to understand the ways in which they *learned* a new set of skills and abilities that shaped their leadership and the roles they played as they carried out their work.
>
> (Liebermann and Friderich, 2008: 98)

A focus on organisational learning

Taking a focus on learning wider than pupils and teachers, our inquiry leads us to the nature of the organisation itself and how it manages and models learning. How an organisation learns may be a difficult concept to grasp as it has been argued (see Chapter 1) that organisations cannot learn, it is people who learn. Nonetheless, it is people who create structures; it is people who pass on ideas and leave legacies which become embedded in the cultural norms and day-to-day rituals of school or school life. So, the 'way we do things round here' is open to continuous and critical scrutiny. It is a process in which everyone has a voice and effective leadership has to be able to tune in to the changing acoustic of the school so that the very structures and modus operandi of the school itself are always open to learning.

A focus on organisational learning implies a deep capacity to respond to situations intelligently. It does, however, presuppose a reservoir of shared knowledge, a toolbox of strategies and techniques to apply flexibly and appropriately to the issues at hand. It requires an organisational memory and a distributed intelligence which feed back into structures and cultures which then assume a life of their own, independent of the individuals who inhabit them at any given time.

In this context Argyris and Schon (1978) make an important distinction between single and double loop learning. Single loop learning characterises much of the managerial and audit agenda, caught up in the self-perpetuating loop of targets, strategies, implementation and evaluation. This single loop may, however, lead to an unthinking and mechanistic place. As a school, reaching predetermined targets may provide a disinclination to learn, inhibited by what Cousins (1996) refers to as 'competency traps', that is, deeply embedded routines and ways of thinking which set up defences against thought and critique. 'Nothing fails like success', writes Senge (1990), implying that within a performativity agenda, success may prove to be the enemy of experimentation and risk taking.

A focus on learning implies risk, entering a double loop which is intolerant of routine and simplistic answers to complex issues. A focus on organisational learning addresses questions of values and purposes. It is concerned with the nature of evidence, truth and validity, subjectivity and objectivity, summative and formative assessment. Without access to more strategic ways of organising children's and adults' meta-learning much of the discourse remains at a reactive and intuitive level – dissipating energy rather than concentrating on what matters. To qualify as genuinely within the second loop, schools need to have the tools which enable them to reflect on their several and common experiences and to marshal these effectively.

> Clearly organisational learning can take place only through the actions and experiences of individuals. But what defines the organisation as unique is the way in which it is able to marshal the learning experiences of individuals, to draw effectively upon this collective body of knowledge and experience.
>
> (Tiler and Gibbons, 1991: 33)

Learning, as Cousins (1996) puts it, flows from 'organisational sensemaking'. It is a collective capacity, to learn about ourselves and to live with the inconsistencies, the contradictions, the cognitive dissonances that precede and characterise learning. 'The valuing of consistency leads to competency; the valuing of inconsistency leads to learning' (Argyris and Schon, 1978).

A focus on system learning

A fourth area of focus is system learning. This is a larger and broader concept than organisational learning because it reaches beyond the individual school and frames its interest in inter-school networks and agencies and the way in which information flows across the boundaries – not only school to school but also school to social, community and family services.

Of all four levels of challenge to understanding learning, it is the fourth of these that stretches the imagination and requires some radical rethinking and refocusing on what and who learning is for, where it best takes place and what we really mean by that much overused and misused term – outcomes.

When the government in England published its manifesto *Every Child Matters* and defined five outcomes (staying healthy, enjoying and achieving, keeping safe, contributing to the community, social and economic well-being) it struck a chord with many teachers for whom these had always been to the fore in their thinking and aspiration but who found it hard to conceive how they could take responsibility for children's safety or health and well-being when these lay largely outside the compass of the classroom and outside the school's purview. Nor could exhortations to work more effectively across institutional boundaries cut much ice when curriculum and testing were premised on maximal input of curricular content in minimal amounts of time bounded by one's own subject discipline and/or teaching objectives.

A focus on learning in an inter-agency context is one of the richest forms of discussion immediately available to teachers because it challenges inert ideas about learning and behaviour; it raises questions about the deeply institutionalised language we use, the language of assessment, teaching, outcomes, value-added, self-evaluation, culture, networking and the expanding lexicon of radical Conservatism and New Labour.

Working across agency boundaries teachers have learned from social workers that assessment may be seen not as what happens at the end of or in the middle of an intervention sequence but at the very beginning. While in the traditional mould teaching has started from where teachers are and what they want to teach, this is perplexing to social workers who pose the question 'How can we help you unless we assess where you are in your life and learning?' From community and youth workers teachers have learned about how successful achievers navigate their way through systems and that negotiation is ultimately more effective than command. Working with artists, musicians and craftspeople, teachers have learned about the buried creativity that is realised when children are coaxed into self-belief and offered alternative paths to learning.

A focus on learning: a matter of first principle

The Leadership for Learning Project provided a forum, or forums, in which to shape and test the first principle. A focus on learning was, on the surface, the easiest principle of the five principles to sign up to by participants in the project but it was also the most radical in its implications. All teachers could agree that learning is what schools are for and ultimately what school leadership has to be about, yet the vocabulary of learning, whether in English, German, Greek, Danish or Norwegian proved as often to inhibit thinking as to promote it. It has been rendered largely unproblematic, in part by its age old institutionalisation in schools, in part by its co-option by politicians and policy makers.

In all countries the everyday discourse within a school and its focus of concern is subject to policy pressures, to the demands of organisational convenience and by the competitive demands of curricular subjects. This makes it difficult for the prime consideration in the classroom to be on the nature and process of pupils' learning. Nor, in the busy and pressured lives of school leaders, can it easily be made the primary focus of leadership.

The fervour for immediate results

Senge's (1990) notion of organisational learning disabilities could be perceived to some extent in all participating schools at the outset of the project. In the early stages of the project the Greek research teams documented what they described as 'a fervour for immediate results', a comment which found a deep resonance in other participating countries. This was coupled, in the Greek context, with what was described as 'a widespread incomprehension of individual learning'. Despite goodwill and attention to pupils with learning difficulties, there was reluctance to risk departing from the set curriculum. The research team reported 'The overall impression is that the teacher is compelled to function according to the logic of the average student level and therefore adapts his/her teaching to the level of the class'. We suggest that this is highly likely to be the case for any school and any group of teachers actively addressing our first principle.

At the other end of Europe the Norwegian team were presenting a quite different kind of scenario but one also leading to a 'difficult conversation' with teaching staff. In these Nordic schools there was much less didactic teaching, rather classes replete with student activity, lively project work and engagement with information on the Internet. However, the research reported:

> By the end of the day we met with all the teachers participating in LfL and one from the leadership team. We discussed our observations, starting with the teachers' own views. They were quite satisfied because there was a lot of activity going on. The pupils seemed motivated. When we shared our observations with them and asked questions like: What kind of learning do you think was going on? What kind of results or end products do you have in mind in choosing project methods for this particular topic? What are the advantages and disadvantages of setting up groups of pupils at random? What are required by the teachers when pupils are working in projects? There were tendencies to apologies for not having enough time for planning, the school day was so busy, disciplining the pupils was sometimes difficult and so on. As such, this turned out to be a rather difficult conversation.

Schools in Innsbruck faced similar challenges. The Austrian team reported a slow and reluctant move 'from the traditional delivery by means of frontal teaching towards more open forms of learning ("*Offenes Lernen*")', but any change was dependent 'on personal initiatives of individual teachers or groups of teachers' and not something that could be easily mandated on a school-wide basis.

In a London school the senior staff spoke of their vision for a learning-centred school but one hampered by government prescription, ill-conceived inclusion policies and the slow nature of progress towards realisation of the vision.

> The nature of that vision and how it is shared and carried by others among the school staff is only available to us in glimpses but there is evidence of a more visionary embrace of learning as at the heart of the school's purpose. It is paradoxically both on the back of government policy and rhetoric well fuelled by teachers' ambitions that supersede what government appears to understand by learning-centred schools.

But, adds the headteacher, 'we've got a kind of vision of where we want to go. And I think we're always pushing that. Which is quite hard with all the stuff that goes on. But I think we're quite good at . . . Within that, of keeping focussed and keep pushing. And if we lose a few battles on the way, we're going to win the war . . .'

There are immediate parallels to be found with the vision in a Brisbane school. As a teacher described it in interview in 2003, midway through the project:

> Creating an intellectual climate that promoted learning demanded a new focus and direction for the school. The main thrust of that focus was risk-taking, that is the opportunity for staff and students to explore opportunities, take responsibility, set good examples and 'go out on a limb' . . . confident in what they are doing and helping others.

Meeting the challenge

It is only through the deepening of our understanding of where schools are that we can begin to tease out what we ourselves understand by a focus on learning and how it might begin to apply across the highly varied cultures and language contexts in which schools are working. From our cross-country research into principle number one, we have elaborated what we believe is implied by a focus on learning. Our five amplifications of the overarching principle are:

> Leadership for learning practice involves maintaining a focus on learning as an activity in which:
> * everyone (students, teachers, principals, schools, the system itself) is a learner;
> * learning relies on the effective interplay of social, emotional and cognitive processes;
> * the efficacy of learning is highly sensitive to context and to the differing ways in which people learn;
> * the capacity for leadership arises out of powerful learning experiences;
> * opportunities to exercise leadership enhance learning.

These five elaborations on the headline principle derive in part from the theoretical insights we brought to our work with schools but in equal measure from grounded evidence of how senior leaders and teachers make sense of a learning focus in their day-to-day practice. In many respects these five statements are already implicit in teachers' practice. Teachers understand that cognition is inseparable from the social and emotional context in which it takes place, however much the principle is observed in the breach. Teachers know that they are, and have to be, learners however difficult it may be to make that transparent to their students or colleagues. What may be less in teacher' consciousness is the way in which leadership takes its inspiration from learning or how leadership can ignite the spark of disciplined inquiry.

The evidence is strong, if uneven, that a commitment to focusing on learning grows in strength when it is made the school's primary focus. The evidence is also strong that teachers and school leaders know that it is always something to be worked at and worked for. It has to take account of the realpolitik of a performativity agenda, present in most of the education systems in the developed world, although with a quite different weight of impact. In a follow up questionnaire at the end of the Leadership for Learning Project we asked school staff to respond to an item: 'The nature and process of student learning is a focus for discussion among teaching staff', indicating whether they saw their schools as improving, declining or maintaining the status quo in relation to that statement. This item drew a generally positive response although there were differences between countries as well as within them. In one English school 78.2 per cent of staff attested to improvement in this respect while in two of the three Norwegian schools the figures were 65.2 and 61.1 per cent. Very similar figures came from an Australian school (64.3 per cent), a Greek school (66.7 per cent) and an Austrian school (63.2 per cent). In three other schools (Western USA, Australia and England) more than half the staff reported a positive trajectory on this item. In the US (New Jersey), the idea that there needs to be a focus on learning, while seen to be gaining ground amongst those actively engaged with the LfL enterprise, was yet to gain wide support. As the research team reported 'The evidence suggests that the mass of teachers are yet to be persuaded'.

The nature of the data relevant to these issues may be illustrated by staff responses in one London school (Table 6.1). While the pattern of responses is significantly more positive than negative on almost all items, it is the pattern of responses that speaks loudest. Although involvement in the project appears to have increased peer learning, risk is clearly seen as too risky not only for students but for teachers as well, perhaps related to item 19 – standing by your values in response to external pressures.

In all inter-school and inter-country comparisons the location, history and change trajectory of schools has to be taken into account and the nature of the struggle to maintain a focus on learning has to be weighed within the complexity of push and pull factors which drive schools forward and hold them back. We know and must take into account differences in school size, in structure, in family background, in socio-economic profile and ethnic mix, in teenage culture and media influence, and in political pressures on teachers' lives and work. As a report from the US (East) team in the LfL Project reveals, there is nonetheless a slow and uneven progress among the four schools.

> In response to the survey statement *Professional development in this school is primarily about learning*, over 30% of participants from 3 of the 4 schools believed that progress was being made toward this goal.

Yet in this school district attempts to address system learning are most apparent and most ambitious. Professional development focused on learning was made an explicit district-wide goal by the District Superintendent for whom this was a tangible demonstration of his belief that conversations about learning on the part of administrators and teachers are important planks of the transformation strategy. He continuously reiterated the principle of teachers being exemplary learners:

Table 6.1 Perceived direction of progress (n = numbers of staff)

		Direction of progress		
		↗	↔	↘
1	The nature and process of student learning is a focus for discussion among teaching staff.	23	32	4
3	Professional development in this school is primarily about learning.	22	25	12
4	The focus of leadership in our school is on student learning.	20	25	10
5	Teachers talk to one another about their own professional learning.	15	33	9
7	The culture of our school encourages everyone to be a learner.	22	34	3
8	Students are encouraged to learn in many places, not just in class.	20	27	9
9	Our students are encouraged to take risks in their learning.	9	37	12
10	Leadership encourages teachers to be adventurous and risk taking in teaching and learning.	9	37	12
13	Students collaborate with one another in their learning.	31	21	6
15	This school draws on the experience and expertise of students as a resource for learning.	16	34	8
19	In this school we stand by our values and principles in meeting external pressures.	15	32	11

> Unless you value adult learning . . . and demonstrate that, it's pretty hard to claim that you value child learning . . . unless we are all doing this together . . . Nothing keeps you closer to what it's like being a student than being a student yourself.

In accordance with this he negotiated contracts with teachers to increase opportunities built into the school day, for teachers to meet to facilitate the learning dialogue and planning and instituted regular reading and discussion groups among district staff.

To sum up, we argue that strategies designed to engage students, teachers, schools and the wider system in order to maintain a focus on learning do not happen by chance. Our experience tells us that they must be planned and deliberate, take account of the pressures and opportunities in local contexts and be continuous. We think it's a bit like preparing good meals. One superb dish for one dinner will not provide nourishment for all time. Constant attention to quality ingredients, careful preparation and variation according to individual needs and preferences are the hallmarks of healthy long term diets.

A diversity of strategies

All LfL schools in the seven countries and eight sites provide evidence as to a growing focus on new structures and built-in opportunities for staff to share ideas and practices through observation, systematic scrutiny of students' work, appointment of learning co-ordinators, creation of learning teams, learning exchanges with other schools or through feedback and challenge from project-based critical friends.

In Oslo, meeting the challenge of a focus on learning was attributed to the relationship established by critical friends. Their observation of classroom practice and questions raised about the nature of learning (cited above) had engendered a positive response from teachers and a reframing of their practice, as described by the critical friends themselves:

> When we visited the school three months later, a lot of things had happened. After they received the summary of our visit, the leadership team came together with the teachers involved in order to discuss our questions more in detail. They had decided to organize project work in a much more focused way. They had read and discussed an article we sent them after our visit in order to stimulate their thinking about leadership for learning. They had put up a plan for how they could monitor their work in a more systematic way and how they could share experiences. As a matter of fact, as critical friends we were quite impressed by the way they had taken on the critique in a positive way and used it as a basis for development . . . it seemed like we as critical friends managed to contribute, through our questions, to another way of framing the experiences.

A London school was able to use a grant from central government enabling the senior leadership team to appoint two experienced middle managers as 'learning coordinators'. They were given reduced timetables (50 per cent) and external training, and asked to focus solely on the development of learning. On the first day of term there was a short training session for staff on learning followed by the establishment of a working party (a third of the staff volunteered to be members), meeting monthly and launched with a weekend residential conference. Working party members then led a professional development day for all staff, with a focus on learning. Learning coordinators now plan with teachers, share lessons and keep parents informed of developments via the school's weekly newsletter.

The implementation of learning teams has been one of the most crucial aspects of the story of renewal in a Brisbane school. Discussion within the learning teams led to the restructuring of class groupings and staffing. With smaller classes and fewer teachers there were more opportunities to give a central place to a focus on learning.

> In their smaller groups, like they're in the same group from year 8 right through to grade 9 . . . they've got fewer teachers, who talk with one another about their student group and their learning and the relationships.

There's a lot less of the time spent now on kids playing off other teachers or knowing their way around the system because there really aren't the ways around the system, so we can focus more time on actually students' learning and the curriculum rather than a lot of other messy issues that swallow up time – that's probably had a big impact as well.

As the principal of this school has argued, 'The first thing you look at is what you want students to achieve and then you build your pedagogy and your teaching practice around that. With that in place, leadership and a leadership culture is created to support that focus on learning at the epicentre of the school's endeavour.' As it was said at a teachers' focus group in this Brisbane school:

> Through the journey, teachers have also become learners. At our learning team meetings there is always a consideration now of the learning that's actually happening and our teaching strategies to maximise student learning . . . we're actually talking about how kids are learning . . . we're actually probably talking about how we're learning in the classroom with the kids as well.

Something very similar took place in a Seattle school. Inspired by a visit to an LfL school in Copenhagen, senior leaders created a school within a school. The 'small school' as it became known was designed to focus on learning, bringing with it a changed relationship between teachers, students and learning. An interest meeting was publicised and held in June 2004 and more than enough teachers expressed a commitment to participate. A group of nine teachers was selected to serve as the team to teach in the small school. The small school was seen as a means to deepen the work of collaboration around student learning, and engage students more in their learning based on the ideas and principles that had emerged over the two years of working in the Leadership for Learning Project. Teachers began to interact in new ways with their students' learning, instituting regular conferencing at which teachers would meet with each student to reflect on their learning, establish or revisit goals and discuss their sense of belonging in the learning community.

In Athens, the strategy for a learning focus was to use the nucleus of teachers involved in the project as champions of change, through their focus on their own learning and that of their students, through the formal structures of weekly meetings, in the process promoting a cultural shift, a new discourse about learning and teaching and a broader distribution of leadership. The Greek research team wrote towards the end of the project:

> There are serious attempts for a broader distribution of leadership with the establishment of informal structures (weekly meetings of the project team after necessary re-arrangement of schedules), the exploitation of already existing extra-curricular activities for the development of project and innovative actions (theatrical workshop, environmental education, school newspaper, local history, museum education, etc.), the empowerment of

the Teacher and Parent Associations, the student councils (with joint activities, initiatives, participation of parents in celebrations, outings, educational visits).

And a final word from our teachers

At the end of the day it is through the testimony of teachers that we can see the extent to which a focus on learning touches hearts and minds. Many teachers commented that focusing on learning had changed both priorities and mindset. It had led them to ask different kinds of questions about their teaching and about the wider conduct of school life and leadership. As one school principal commented: 'Opportunities for learning enhance leadership and, setting in train a virtuous circle – opportunities for leadership enhance learning'.

A Norwegian teacher who had been part of the project from the start, wrote after the final conference in Athens:

> I have become more focused on learning in my own teaching, and I know that influences my work. I have also seen how important it is that we as teachers have time and space for discussing our teaching with colleagues, with a focus on learning.

A principal from the same country commented on how networking and support within a project such as this can 'speed up' a focus on learning:

> To be part of Leadership for Learning has 'speeded up' and provided a direction for focusing on learning in my daily practice. As a leader it has given me confidence in the importance of shared goals for school development.

This view is endorsed by an Australian principal who commented on the dangers of a focus on learning being seen as a luxury which can't be afforded when the focus is on the urgent:

> One of the things the project has done and what I hoped it would do was demand that we do reflection because I think a really important part of learning is taking the time to reflect . . . it's the thing that often we don't do in schools because it seems like a luxury, taking the time away from all those urgent things that are going on and do some of the important things.

The final word goes to a principal of a US East school, summing up his commitment to a continued focus on learning as lying at the very centre of leaders' concern:

> Leadership is concerned with student learning . . . everything we do should impact student learning and achievement. I've said it over and over again. No matter what we do, it's about developing better teaching and learning

Table 6.2 Questions for staff, school leaders and teachers

Principle No 1. Leadership for learning practice involves maintaining a focus on learning as an activity in which:	Question for staff and school leaders	Questions for students
1(a): everyone[1] is a learner	Is everyone in our school encouraged to be a learner? Do members of the senior leadership team see themselves as learners? Do teachers and teaching assistants see themselves as learners?	Is everyone in our school encouraged to be a learner? Do we see teachers and other staff in our school learning too?
1(b): learning relies on the effective interplay of social, emotional and cognitive processes	Does classroom practice in our school reflect a recognition that learning is an emotional and social process as well a cognitive one? Is it recognised in our school that our feelings and sense of well-being affect the way we are able to carry out our professional duties?	Do our teachers realise that how you feel about a learning activity makes a big difference to how well you learn? Do our teachers take into account our moods and our feelings? Do we have different kinds of groups and pair work activities in our lessons?
1(c): the efficacy of learning is highly sensitive to context and to the differing ways in which people learn	Do teachers consult students about how and where they prefer to learn? Do teachers adapt their teaching to take account of the different ways in which students prefer to learn?	Do teachers ask our opinions about how we prefer to learn? Do our teachers provide different kinds of learning activities to suit the different ways we prefer to learn?
1(d): the capacity for leadership arises out of powerful learning experiences	Does classroom learning help students develop the capacity to take responsibility and influence others?	Does what we do at school help us to take responsibility and influence other people?
1(e): opportunities to exercise leadership enhance learning	Do professional development experiences have a powerful effect on teachers' ability to exercise leadership? Do students have opportunities to express their views and influence the learning process? Do students have opportunities to take responsibility and to make choices in their learning?	Do we have opportunities to influence how we are taught and how we learn because our views are listened to and taken into account? Do our teachers give us opportunities to take responsibility and make choices in our learning?

1 'Everyone' includes students, teachers, teaching assistants, headteachers, the school as an organisation

strategies. This is our focus. I believe I try to model the importance of teaching and learning. This is my focus.

To assist others to make learning the central focus for everybody in schools, a series of questions linked to principle number 1 is included in the matrix (Table 6.2). They are aimed squarely at teachers, those in leadership roles and students. When these questions are seriously discussed they become prompts for the kind of action necessary to connect learning and leadership.

References

Argyris, C. and Schön, D.A. (1978) *Organizational Learning: A Theory of Action Perspective*, Reading, MA: Addison Wesley.

Bruner, J. (1987) *Making Sense: The Child's Construction of the World*, London: Methuen.

Cousins, B. (1996) 'Understanding organizational learning for leadership and school improvement', in K. Leithwood, J. Chapman, D. Corson, P. Hallinger and A. Hart, (eds) *International Handbook of Educational Leadership and Administration*, Dordrecht: Kluwer.

Csikszentmihalyi, M. (1990) *Flow: The Psychology of Optimal Experience*, New York: Harper Perennial.

Drummond, M-J. (1993) *Assessing Children's Learning*, London: David Fulton.

Eisner E. (1991) *The Enlightened Eye*, New York: Macmillan.

Galton, M. (2007) *Learning and Teaching in the Primary Classroom*, London: Sage.

Lieberman, A. and Friedrich, L. (2008) 'Changing teachers from within: teachers as leaders', in J. MacBeath and Y.C. Cheng (eds) *Leadership for Learning: International Perspectives*, Rotterdam: Sense Publishers.

Senge, P. (1990) *The Fifth Discipline: The Art and Practices of the Learning Organisation*, New York: Doubleday.

Soo Hoo, S. (1993) 'Students as partners in research and restructuring schools', *The Educational Forum*, 57: 386–92.

Starrat, R.J. (1998) 'Grounding moral educational leadership in the morality of teaching and learning', *Leading and Managing*, 4 (4): 243–55.

Tiler, C. and Gibbons, M. (1991) 'A case study of organizational learning: the UK teaching company scheme', in B.J. Cousin and L. Earle, *Participatory Evaluation in Education: Studies of Evaluation Use and Organizational Learning*, New York: The Falmer Press.

7   An environment for learning (principle 2)

Neil Dempster and George Bagakis

Introduction

This chapter addresses a number of the issues raised in Chapters 2 and 3 on how leadership and learning may be linked and how that knowledge may be translated into strategies and actions by school leaders so as to create and sustain a supportive environment for learning. We acknowledge that learning does not always have to be experienced as enjoyable or entertaining, although when this happens it is a source of added pleasure. Learning may sometimes be confusing, troubling, even painful and at times certainly not easy. However, when the pain or confusion 'barrier' is passed, learning is always accompanied by a sense of satisfaction. Getting to the satisfaction of achievement is in large part assisted by the quality of the environment in which learning takes place and part of that environment is created by the approach taken by teachers to learning.

To illustrate this claim we recount a story told by a colleague teaching physically disabled students in the Czechoslovakia of Iron Curtain days. She said that the most telling lesson about learning she gained from over thirty years with such children was the importance of *patience* in teaching and the significance of *small achievements* in the eyes of learners. She went on to say that watching skill acquisition for these children was hugely rewarding for herself and her teachers. It required a learning environment where patience had to accompany repeated attempts, repeated failure and repeated frustration; where support, encouragement and persistence had to be meted out with good humour; where laughter and frowns were the constant companions of struggling youngsters; and where no-one entertained any thoughts of giving up. The smallest of gains was great cause for celebration. For example, when trying to help severely physically disabled children to feed themselves, getting a hand even close to the object spoon was to be applauded; lifting it off the table unaided was a major achievement and getting it to the mouth, even empty, a gold medal result. We see quite starkly in this story two very important elements in the learning environment to which teachers and leaders needed undiluted commitment. Of course support and celebration would have had to be accompanied by other conditions for learning if the talents and capacities of children with disabilities were to be harnessed in learning for life.

Our discussion so far has hinted at what we mean by an environment for learning. We address this concept in the first part of the chapter, including a discussion of 'prompts' about how helpful conditions for learning are created, illustrating each with examples, ideas or vignettes taken from our experiences in the Leadership for Learning Project. In the second part of the chapter, we explain the role played by teachers, students, parents and school leaders in creating and sustaining these helpful conditions. We conclude the chapter by outlining a number of questions to provoke reflection on policy, practice and school evaluation.

An environment for learning

Our story above suggests that it is not the material spaces which constitute the environment for learning, nor the equipment or resources employed; it includes these, but it also embraces the knowledge, attitudes and skills of the staff and of the students, the teachers' feelings for their charges and the value the school places on learning. It includes the partnerships leaders, teachers, students and parents form with each other and the way in which teachers acquire, expand and use their professional knowledge. The environment for learning should be seen as a complex interplay of each of these components which, when taken together, create a culture, a technology and pedagogy for learning.

The second principle we developed to link leadership with learning during the project, and on which we now focus, sounds trite: 'Leadership for learning practice involves creating conditions favourable to learning'. The statement seems so obvious that it should almost be left unsaid. However, we follow it with five 'prompts' to action which grew out of discussions between teachers and researchers from the seven project countries. All would agree that the 'prompts' do not constitute a definitive list of 'helpful conditions' but equally, all would say that they provide a useful starting point, assisting schools to put in place supportive conditions for learning. We explain each of the 'prompts' below, referring to practical examples drawn from our experience during the project, principally from schools in Australia and Greece.

Prompt no. 1: school cultures should nurture the learning of everyone

In one of the Australian schools in the project there was clear evidence that attention was paid to creating and maintaining a school culture which valued learning, not only amongst the students, but also amongst the staff. At Southside High, the principal took great pains to explain the interconnections between teachers and administrative leaders in bringing the school's purpose, structure, function and culture into alignment. She explained these connections as a 'backward mapping' process, in this way:

> The model [backward mapping] says that the first thing you look at is what you want students to achieve; and then you build your pedagogy and your

teaching practices around that; and then you build your structures and your leadership and your culture in a way to support that; and that's the way I've tried to ensure that there is a link between what we do as leaders and what happens for kids in classrooms.

While a backward mapping approach might be easily employed when a school is settling on its intentions for students for the first time, when the school's organisational structures are already set however, it becomes a difficult task to deconstruct the school's existing purpose, function, structure and culture. Indeed, some schools have been travelling along in somnambulistic fashion for so long that their purpose is clouded, their functions not explicit, their structures historic and their culture is custodial. This was partly the case at Southside High, so to begin the backward mapping process required a school leader dedicated to ensuring that leading learning was the school's primary purpose and that aligning function, structure and culture with that purpose would need shared commitment and concerted action by teachers. The leader therefore had to initiate strategies which spread leadership for learning opportunities across the school. The principal did this by creating leadership teams, by focusing school discussions on evidence related to the conditions for learning experienced by students, and by expanding opportunities for teacher professional development, particularly professional development focused on pedagogy. These strategies together showed that the school was interested not only in the conditions for student learning but also the conditions for teachers' learning. Both are essential if our assertion that 'cultures should nurture the learning of everyone' is to stand scrutiny.

Three examples of how learning for everyone can be placed at the heart of a school's culture come from the Second Gymnasium School of Petroupolis. This is a public school in a middle income area of Athens. What is interesting about the school is that in the Greek system, which is heavily centralised, within-school monitoring processes generally are not substantial and pedagogical discourse is rather uncommon. The Second Gymnasium School, therefore, had to be a risk-taker to implement strategies focused on gathering information about learning.

First, the teachers did so by affording their students the right to make judgments about matters concerning their teaching. They did this through questionnaires devised by teachers, inviting students to comment on the quality of teaching. The questionnaires also provided students with the chance to gain an understanding of different aspects of the teaching–learning process because the data collected were analysed by teachers and students together in classroom discussions.

Second, the teachers agreed that to learn about their own teaching, a peer observation framework should be applied. Its basis was the assumption that improvement in learning is premised on improvement in teaching. Understanding difficulties and sharing good practice amongst colleagues was seen as an important means to achieve that improvement. However, the school needed to overcome practical difficulties such as finding the time for observation and collaboration, and the quite natural hesitation, inertia or resistance of some members of staff. To help in the process, a critical friend was engaged by the school to facilitate peer observation and to provide the necessary counselling and support to encourage participation.

Third, the staff of the Second Gymnasium School took a particularly bold step for Greek teachers. They opened up their classrooms to parents. They did so because they believed that the views of parents concerning teaching could be both challenging and stimulating for teachers while direct knowledge of classroom activity would enhance parents' understanding of their children's learning. We say more about this a little later.

As can be seen in the examples above, learning in a Leadership for Learning school should be for everyone: parents, teachers and students. Only when this happens, we argue, can a school claim that it has a learning culture – a fundamental precondition for creating conditions favourable to learning.

Prompt no. 2: everyone should have opportunities to reflect on the nature, skills and processes of learning

At Northside High School, we found that most students were keen to be involved in understanding their own learning. Indeed, in our survey of teachers and students we included a number of questionnaire items on the extent to which students were involved in determining the best way to learn for them, how frequently they received feedback on their learning, how they went about it, whether they felt their views on how to learn best were taken into account by teachers and whether they were able to be involved in the self-evaluation of their work. The comparison of responses to these issues provided us with a number of starting points for discussion. They opened up opportunities for staff and students to think about learning and to engage in genuine dialogue with one another. As those discussions proceeded, it became clear that the process of reflection by students was critical to effective learning, and a key lever in linking leadership with learning. During the project, Northside High's critical friend identified a number of learning skills that were common to leadership and learning. Three of these were selected as a focus – planning, problem solving and reflection. Since learning skills are known to be important academic enablers (Elliott, 2003), these three skills became the focus of the intervention pursued by school staff during the second and third years of the project. As reported elsewhere (Dempster, 2006), teachers from diverse disciplines such as mathematics, science, foreign languages, and the social sciences all incorporated the three leadership for learning skills in their classroom practice at appropriate times. We concentrate for the moment, however, on 'reflection'.

One example serves to illustrate the approach taken. Teachers across disciplines at Northside High played with a strategy to manage ideas, commonly called the 'Pyramid' strategy. It comprises three steps in which students work individually, then in small groups and then as a whole class. First, each student writes three responses to a 'starter' question on slips of paper (Post-it notes are good for this purpose because they can be attached to a chart later). Groups of five of six students are then formed. The teacher provides them with a chart on which a large pyramid is drawn. Taking turns, the students stick their responses at the base of the pyramid in clusters of similar ideas. As clusters are formed, a 'cover term' to identify each is agreed by the group. These cover terms are then written higher up on the pyramid for all to see. The third and final step involves the group in writing a one sentence answer to the question with which the activity started, using each of the 'cover terms'. This is written at the peak of the pyramid. Then as a whole class, the sentence produced by each group is read out. Questions for clarification are encouraged by the teacher and answered by the students. A second debriefing or reflective discussion follows stimulated by different types of questions such as:

- What have you learned about the formation of generalisations?
- To what extent was a group necessary in this activity?
- What do you think you have learned about leadership?

Using periodic reflective debriefings following classroom activities became commonplace at Northside High. These reflection sessions did not accompany every lesson but were undertaken frequently enough for the students to know that they were directly involved in developing understanding of the processes in which they were engaged. The connections between leadership and learning were thus brought quite explicitly into classroom discussions as were the nature, skills and processes of learning.

Experience in Greece at the Second Gymnasium School where 'teaching from the front' had been the predominant pattern, students and teachers began to grasp the possibilities provided by group work, engaging students in conversations about the processes of learning. Teachers commented on the greater ease with which dialogue about the nature of the learning process could be managed amongst students in groups of four or five. Moreover, they were able to probe more fully the limits of their teaching and students' learning, something not possible when teaching to the whole class. While this may not come as a revelation to teachers in some country contexts, it is noteworthy that a focus on reflection on the processes of learning can prompt action 'against the flow'.

A second illustration from Greece concerns the use of students as teachers in order to provide opportunities for them to understand better the difficulties of teaching and learning from the teacher's perspective. Students were invited to take the role of teachers by preparing lessons for the class. Students were encouraged in their lesson preparation to search for good strategies to help their classmates learn effectively. This required considerable thought and effort, concentrating on how their classmates might best be involved during the lesson. Added to this was the obligation of the 'student as teacher' to interact closely with all of his or her classmates and later, on reflection, being able to compare his or her lesson with the work of the teacher. Strategies such as this provide a real opportunity for students to reflect on the nature and processes of student learning in partnership with their teachers.

The opening up of classroom doors to parents, mentioned above was a third strategy aimed at increasing parents' understanding of the strategies and skills for learning and helping them to focus less on students' marks. Witnessing the struggles encountered in classroom activity as young people are introduced to new concepts and ideas threw new light on parents' perceptions of learning. When they participated in a class activity, they began to appreciate the demands on the teacher and the efforts made by teachers to help students achieve. In debriefing sessions with the teacher, parents were able to reflect on the targets that students were being asked to meet, the different nature of the challenges for different students, the individualised nature of learning, and the complexity of learning skills. In this way reflection helps teachers to enlist parents as allies in student learning.

Prompt no. 3: physical and social spaces should stimulate and celebrate learning

It has already been mentioned in Chapters 2 and 3 that the context for learning and leadership is a significant influence on what takes place in particular circumstances. Architects know that if clients have a chance to take part in planning forums about new buildings in which they will work, their ownership and acceptance of the spaces when constructed is heightened and improved effectiveness at work follows. When an environment is shabby and untidy, town planners know that it will attract graffiti and rubbish. When a public facility is dilapidated or derelict, police know that it will attract undesirable behaviour. These illustrations underscore the important influence of physical space on attitude and behaviour.

No less important is the influence of social space. By this we mean the nature of the social circumstances in which people interact in their daily lives. Nurses know that when they carry out their care of patients with a smile, a laugh or a concerned tone in their voices, that patients are more inclined to respond positively. Shop assistants know that businesslike service touched with interest in the customer is likely to enhance reputation and bring 'repeat trade'. Mothers know that being calm when children throw tantrums sends immediate messages about controlled reaction in the face of provocation. In short, the quality of social spaces is created through the way in which people conduct themselves in their institutional environments.

In the LfL Project, we sought students' views on the physical and social spaces in their schools through a series of school portraits and in responses to survey questions. In this way we wanted to bring to light the views of the users about important features of the learning environment. And we learnt much. For example, from the Northside High School Portrait, we learnt of the excitement young people feel for their first year of high school. We also learnt two years later that most still enjoyed their school, its surroundings and what it had to offer, contrary to the views of some hard bitten critics who generalise about adolescent alienation from school.

We also had reinforced for us the view that not only should physical and social spaces stimulate learning, but they should also be dedicated to its celebration. The presentation of a 'gold medal' for achievement to the youngster with special needs in our opening story is one way in which physical and social spaces for celebration are brought together. Ceremonies in school assemblies or informal gatherings where the real joy of achievement is shared add to the satisfaction of students, teachers and parents alike, while they reinforce this important aspect of a learning culture. In one of our Greek schools, informal celebration is seen, more often than not, through the presentation of student photographs, drawings and writing displayed on classroom or corridor walls. At school festivals, performances by students are always included and at national and international conferences, teachers' presentations of their school's activities are encouraged. There is nothing new in this as the impact of displays on human motivation and incentive are well known, provided that social space is made to accompany each display and they are used proactively rather than seen simply as wallpaper. In the film *Dead Poets Society*, the teacher (played by Robin Williams) takes his students down to the front hall of the school and asks them to look at the photographs that have always been there but students have never 'seen'. Time together to share student achievement with classmates, or opportunities for teachers to share their accomplishments with their colleagues is essential. In the busy lives of schools this can sometimes be overlooked.

Keeping the appeal and utility of physical space under review is something that should be a constant in schools. It is very easy to move into an uncritical routine about the physical circumstances in which students work every day. Decline in appeal is a slow process, moving imperceptibly along a continuum such as that from the 'fresh paint smell' of a new car to the eyesore of a 'rusty bomb'. Engaging with student critique of their school surroundings from time to time provides an opportunity for all to identify 'sore points' in the learning environment. Added to this should be an openness about students' views of the quality of the school's social space. School 'climate' and 'tone' are terms that have been used to focus attention on the kinds of attitudes, values and behaviours which characterise interactions of key players within schools and in relation to outsiders. Again, without periodically paying attention to the quality of the school's social space, it can deteriorate into a 'command and control' climate reinforced by an aggressive stance, often at cross purposes to the intentions of the school's leaders. Openness in communication, collaboration in decision-making and respect in interpersonal relationships deserve as much scrutiny as the physical environment of the school.

Prompt no. 4: safe and secure environments enable everyone to take risks, cope with failure and respond positively to challenges

There are both physical and social space imperatives tied up in the fourth 'prompt' which touches directly on the provision of a safe and secure environment for learning. Physical safety and security at school are matters that cannot be taken for granted. Indeed, over recent years much has been done to ensure students have a haven in their school, no matter their personal backgrounds or the social situations they experience outside the school grounds. It goes without saying that inside the school gates no one should feel that they will come to any harm. With this taken as given, we concentrate first on a different kind of 'safety and security' – namely the kind where students feel supported in taking risks in their learning, secure in the knowledge that they will not be emotionally 'harmed' through for example, ridicule, embarrassment or anxiety.

Physical and emotional 'safety' come together in the following example from Northside High School. There, prominence is given to leadership development and training for all students. Typical of much of this type of training is putting students into risk-taking situations. This is achieved in a purpose-built leadership centre in which students encounter climbing walls, ropes courses, obstacle courses and so on. It is well understood by the teachers that students will be unlikely to take the necessary risks to make best use of this facility if they do not feel safe. So, great attention to detail is given to safety management with all staff members and students playing important roles. It is also well understood that adolescents will be unlikely to take risks if they feel that their weaknesses, fears or failures will be subject to the taunts of their peers. So, close attention is given to the creation of a supportive emotional climate for boys and girls testing their 'wings' in new physical challenges. Celebration of success and effort are encouraged in equal measures. Persistence is rewarded with praise for achievement and failure is met with renewed determination to succeed.

The concept of a safe and secure environment should also be in evidence for members of a school's staff if learning for all is the goal. This means that a climate of trust must exist between those with power and authority and those without it – between the headteacher and the teachers, between teachers and teaching assistants. A climate without fear brings forth experimentation and innovation. In the Second Gymnasium School in Greece, the introduction of small group work amongst students, referred to earlier, was accompanied by times when class control became problematic, teachers experienced a failure to adhere to the timetable, and there was disappointment over lesson outcomes. Without a climate of trust, teachers would not have been able to work through these obstacles and further experimentation with group work would not have been feasible. As the teachers pointed out, if a condition of trust does not hold, then they would not dare to experiment or they would abandon experimentation with the first difficulties encountered.

Parents must also be able to interact with teachers, secure in the knowledge that they are partners with professional people working to a professional code of practice. Trust again figures prominently in this relationship. If parents are to learn about their children's progress or lack of it, then they should be certain that what they say to teachers is treated with respect and confidentiality. When teachers are implementing new ways of doing things, the views of parents need to be taken into account by the school. It is patronising to assume that innovations will be accepted without demur by parents no matter the quality of the parent/teacher relationship. Trust is maintained through the honest sharing of information and is at its best when failures are openly discussed.

Prompt no. 5: tools and strategies are used to enhance thinking about learning and the practice of teaching

Creating a flourishing school environment requires tools and strategies which facilitate thinking and discussion about learning and teaching. By strategies we mean the planned steps taken to ensure that learning and teaching are described, explained, evaluated and exposed to critique, to challenge and to constructive improvement. By tools we mean the mechanisms which form parts of different strategies to keep the learning environment under review. These mechanisms include data gathering instruments, sets of criteria, discussion processes, questioning techniques, photographic or video records, for example. We explain one of the tools and strategies employed during the LfL Project to illustrate the importance of views from students in creating optimal conditions for learning. Other examples of strategies and tools are discussed in Chapter 8 where their role in promoting dialogue is exemplified.

The strategy we feel has particular relevance to the creation of conditions favourable to learning is one dedicated to ascertaining student views of the physical and social spaces in their schools. Two strategies used were portraiture and photo evaluation. While all schools in the project used the former, photo evaluation was a feature in Austrian, Greek and American schools. Essentially students are given the task of presenting photographic evidence of what they believe are features in their schools that are helpful to learning or which create a stimulating environment. In other words, the strategy encourages students to look for and identify aspects of the physical and social environment which they find more or less conducive to their well-being. Problems or difficult situations which can be presented visually are also included in the photographic montage ultimately produced. Discussions amongst students followed by discussions with teachers unpack the strengths and weaknesses in the school's physical and social spaces and create a dialogue around reasons for singling out particular features in their snapshots. Using photo evaluation as a tool for school development is best achieved in a climate of trust and difficult to implement without it. This point was emphasised in one of our Greek schools where the teachers and students reported that the pictorial portfolio produced by students was 'magnificent' with very helpful 'unexpected' outcomes for school life derived from its use.

Having illustrated and discussed the five 'prompts' to action aimed at creating favourable conditions for learning, we turn to outline briefly the roles to be played in this set of processes by the members of the school community.

The role of teachers, children, leaders and parents in creating and sustaining an environment for learning

The importance of dialogue in creating and sustaining leadership for learning is examined in Chapter 8. There, its significance in defining qualitative differences between leadership for learning and other approaches to leadership are discussed with examples of how constructive dialogue is initiated, facilitated and managed. These examples carry messages about the roles of all involved in the school. Initiating and participating in conversations about the learning environment should be the ever present companions of discussions within and beyond the school. What role then should teachers play in these ongoing processes? How should students contribute to maintaining and enhancing their learning environment? What role should those in positions of leadership play in *creating conditions favourable for learning?* And what is the role of parents in supporting a quality learning environment?

This part of the chapter discusses the roles of the four key groups. First and foremost, however, we argue that all groups have an equal role in 'carrying a torch for learning'. By this we mean that all need to know and understand, as we have outlined in earlier chapters, that the primary purpose of the school is to foster learning, growth and change in everyone. Being able to articulate what the school is *for*, whether from a child's, a parent's, a teacher's or a leader's perspective is a capacity all should be encouraged to develop. It is a capacity which acts as a platform for conversations, debates, and decisions about the conditions for learning. Help with this comes from the role each group plays in a school dedicated to enriching its learning environment.

The role of teachers

Critical to the role of teachers in creating conditions favourable to learning is their willingness to open their practice to feedback from their students and other colleagues. Gathering evaluative data from students about classroom practice and student achievement and using these data to frame discussions with peers and with students is an important, but often anxiety provoking step to take. But our experience in the LfL Project tells us that it uncovers many pointers to practice which benefit student learning as well as the professional learning of teachers. Opening up classroom practice to peer review, feedback and ideas exchanges is likely to require a role shift for many teachers. That shift says that the effective professional is focused not only on teaching students and learning from them but also on teaching colleagues and learning from them. Sharing plans, aspirations and classroom realities about learning with parents is a final step to ensure that learning about learning from those with vested interests, is central to a teacher's pedagogy. While we acknowledge that this was not common to all schools in the Leadership for Learning Project, when it is embraced, it impacts on teachers in powerful ways.

The role of the teacher in contributing to the creation of favourable conditions for learning is therefore much more extensive when it is predicated on leadership for learning principle number 3 and the five prompts we have illustrated. Teachers need to be open to playing their part in nurturing the learning of everyone in an environment which is physically and emotionally safe and which stimulates and celebrates achievement. The five prompts can act as a useful set of stimuli for the necessary role reflection which is a concomitant of active professionalism and the continuous search for improved practice.

The role of students

What is the role of students in creating conditions favourable to learning? As we have already said, architects know that the users of spaces have a vested interest in the design, the planning and the implementation of ideas. 'User groups' are thus automatically composed and consulted when new buildings are being proposed. No less important is the role of students in contributing to their school environment than 'user groups' are to architects. So, students should be prepared and indeed encouraged to say what they think about the physical spaces in which they learn. More than this though, the concept of 'user groups' should be extended so that students see that they can play a vital role in the provision of feedback and in the generation of new ideas about the social spaces in which they interact. As we have already suggested, students learn from both their social and their physical surroundings. Teachers and school leaders play an instrumental role in establishing a climate in which the students' voice may be heard and in enabling the proactive student role to become a reality.

Second, students have a key role to play in ensuring that the conditions in which they learn at school are safe and secure. This dictum more often than not, is directed at student behavioural issues such as harassment and bullying and safety issues related to movement around the school and road safety outside the school gates. While the role students play in reinforcing safe and orderly conduct is important, it needs to be complemented by the role they play in understanding and accepting differences in learning capacity, supporting effort and repeated attempts in others seeking to break through a learning barrier and doing so with respect, tolerance and sincerity.

Prompts numbers 3 and 4 can be used in discussions amongst teachers and students when the student role in creating and sustaining good conditions for learning is the agenda. They can also be used by students themselves in 'user groups' like those foreshadowed above.

Finally, the student's role extends to cover prompts numbers 2 and 5   tools and strategies for reflection on the processes of learning. Becoming a reflective learner is essential if a student is to stimulate the conditions of his or her own learning as well as the learning conditions of others. In other words, understanding what learning *is*, becomes a prerequisite to adding helpful ideas to the conditions which facilitate it. Students need to know and be able to use the type of strategies and tools which aid the meta-cognitive analyses necessary in learning how to learn.

The role of parents

Teachers know that parents are the first educators of their children. However, by the time children have reached secondary school, parents also know that their role in learning is primarily one of support. While their modelling of behaviours, attitudes and values continues to act as the focus for one important dimension of their children's learning, the acquisition of subject knowledge and learning skills are matters which require professional experience and practice matched to students' developmental needs.

In a school where learning is the shared mission, parents can make their contribution to the conditions for learning by creating a home environment where learning is valued, whether through mistakes or successes, where failures are understood as pointers for improvement, where stretching self through challenging situations is encouraged and where achievement is celebrated. In other words, the role of parents in creating favourable conditions for learning mirrors that of the school in many ways. However, the parent's role is distinguished by acceptance of the responsibility to maintain a home environment which supports children's learning whether inside or outside the school. Each of the prompts to action can also be used by parents to reflect on the nature and extent of their role.

Finally, the role of parents should include a responsibility to participate in providing information about how the school's learning environment is perceived by them, and how it is reported by their children. For some it will also involve taking part in discussions about improvements to school conditions whether physical or social, sometimes leading to the implementation of initiatives to effect those improvements. No school concerned with enhancing its conditions for learning can do so without the direct and indirect input of its parents. Creating the conditions where this is known to be encouraged, supported and valued by the school helps pave the way to bring leadership and learning together in the role parents play.

The role of leaders

Chapter 3 has signalled the distinctive differences between leadership for learning and other forms of leadership. At the heart of this difference are the layers of leadership and the bridging social capital created when those with positional power and authority share leadership roles openly and freely with the less powerful. Nevertheless, the role of those in official leadership positions in creating and sustaining favourable conditions for learning is somewhat different from the roles played by students, teachers and parents. First and foremost, those in positions of leadership must genuinely wish to move beyond hierarchy and to place centre stage a school-wide commitment to shared leadership. In this sense, those in positional authority are no more nor less significant in implementing action on leadership for learning than teachers, students and parents. What is different is that positional leaders are responsible for school resources, such as time, space, equipment and funding and it is they who are able to facilitate bringing these to bear on improving the conditions for learning. To do so requires appropriate information, selective judgement and decisions based on the shared understanding of those whom the conditions affect.

In Chapter 2, attention was given to the need for those in leadership positions to pay critical attention to the micro context of the school. Such attention, it was argued, enables the school leader to understand where school resources should be directed if the learning environment is to be enhanced. Our experiences from the LfL Project show that the most important strategies school leaders can employ to develop an understanding of the conditions for learning cover the gathering of information, the evaluation of that information and the development of decisions from it; but *most* important of all, is that these three tasks are carried out *not* by those in positions of power but collectively, involving parents, teachers and students as appropriate. In addition, where a school may not have the necessary expertise to provide the kind of information which has an important bearing on the environment for learning, critical friends, university researchers or colleagues from neighbouring schools have been shown to be helpful in adding outside perspectives or 'benchmarking' information for local judgements and decisions. Together with the teaching staff, the school leader should employ school resources to ensure that there is reliable, accurate and comprehensive information about the conditions which contribute to learning so that informed decisions may be made about students, staff and the school as an organisation itself.

In some countries, systematic strategies to gather information on the school's performance such as cyclical reviews or annual audits are mandated. However, these are not the only ways of gathering information about a school's environment for learning. School leaders, teachers, students and parents need to employ a range of non-positivistic means to develop an understanding of the conditions for learning fostered in their schools. By keeping their 'daily antennae' directed to the receipt of opinions, ideas, criticisms or congratulations, cumulative qualitative data are 'tucked away' for future reference. As issues arise, school teams then have the ability to act as 'lay sociologists' – gathering informed input, before 'laying it out' in discussions, rather as connoisseurs do when talking about their particular specialities. Connoisseurship alone, however, is insufficient as is a systematic approach aimed at quantitative data gathered through more 'scientific' means. School-level judgements should be made on the information needed about particular situations known to have an impact on the conditions for learning.

Just as we began this brief discussion of the role of positional leaders, so we should conclude it. We do so by arguing that teachers, students and parents play a key role with their appointed school leaders in the provision of information about the conditions for learning and ultimately in its analysis and use. After all, in a leadership for learning school, their combined knowledge and experience enables them to make a shared contribution to understanding *better* how to maintain and enhance an environment favourable to learning.

Conclusion

The principle and the prompts we have discussed in this chapter are all considered instrumental in helping schools create the culture, technology and pedagogy that are intrinsic to a supportive learning environment.

First we say that a school must be devoted to creating a culture which is about learning, with all adopting a posture of inquiry into the knowledge, skills and attitudes needed to achieve at their best. This means that the school must have senior leaders, teachers, students and parents, all sharing a vested interest in making learning and the environment for it a key focus. For teachers, it is ongoing learning about their students and their pedagogy. For students, it is learning about their subject, about how they learn and how to develop effective learning strategies. For parents, it is willingness and opportunity to learn about how their children learn best.

Second, we say that a school must have access to technologies which are learner friendly in order to sustain the kinds of learning experiences, activities and environment considered vital to young people's development. Beyond a school's physical plant and equipment, strategies and tools which put leadership and learning under the microscope constitute an essential part of a school's technology.

Third, teachers' pedagogy must be shared, engaging, matched to need, interest and ability, and reflect students' feedback about how they learn best. It must draw on tried and trusted experience and quality research about learning. Finally, it must use sound evidence of student performance in diagnostic and formative ways to aid individual achievement.

To bring the chapter to a close, we offer a series of questions drawn from the 'prompts to action' described above. We list these questions in two columns, one for teachers, the other for students suggesting that they can be used in at least three ways: (i) to 'kick start' discussion about a school's environment for learning; (ii) to provide an ongoing set of questions helpful in self-evaluation of the conditions for leadership for learning practice; and (iii) to act as a springboard for questions to exercise the minds of parents about their role in creating conditions favourable to learning.

To judge whether these questions developed during the Leadership for Learning Project have wider application in different contexts, we turn back to the story with which we commenced this chapter. There, in a school for severely physically disabled children, could our questions for teachers be used to help focus attention on the environment for learning? We believe they can, every one of them; and with a little help from teachers and parents, the students' questions too can bring children into a leadership for learning partnership to enhance their learning environment and their sense of belonging to it.

Questions for teachers	Questions for students
1 Does the culture of our school nurture the learning of everyone?	1 Does the way that we do things in our school support the learning of everyone?
2 Do the learning tasks set for students provide the right level of challenge?	2 Do the learning tasks our teachers give us really make me think?
3 Does everyone have opportunities to reflect on the nature, skills and processes of learning?	3 Do we have opportunities to think and talk about how we learn?
4 Are students provided with feedback that helps them improve their work?	4 Do our teachers give us feedback that helps us to improve our work?
5 Do the physical and social spaces in our school stimulate and celebrate learning?	5 Does our school's design – the buildings, rooms and other spaces – help us to learn?
6 Do we actively try to create an environment in which it is safe for students to take risks, cope with failure and respond positively to challenges?	6 Do we know in our school that it is OK to make mistakes or not succeed at something because we can learn from this?
7 Do teachers in our school respond positively to challenges even where it means taking risks and dealing with failure?	7 Are our teachers able to try out new things and is it OK if they don't all work out?
8 Do we use tools and strategies in our school which enhance thinking about learning in classrooms?	8 Do the teachers in our school use a lot of different activities to help us think about the way we learn?
9 Do we use tools and strategies to support professional learning in our school?	

Figure 7.1 Questions for teachers and students

References

Dempster, N. (2006) 'Leadership for learning: possible links at the Gap State High School', *Leading and Managing*, 12 (2): Spring/Summer, 54–64.

Elliott, S.N. (2003) 'Academic enablers and the development of academically competent students', Paper presented at the 1st Annual International Conference on Cognition, Language and Special Education, Griffith University, Surfers Paradise, Australia (December, 2003).

8 A learning dialogue (principle 3)

Sue Swaffield and Neil Dempster

Introduction

This chapter discusses what we have learned about the importance of dialogue in leadership for learning and how to encourage and facilitate it. While language is fundamental in creating and sustaining culture, it is also a central feature in human agency. It provides the connection between people, enabling them to develop the shared meanings so critical to action on common purposes. In Chapter 2 the argument was made that if leaders are to mobilise people to work together to achieve a common purpose, then they have to create shared meaning, common vision, and helpful strategies that can be employed individually and collectively. When leadership and learning are intrinsic to the roles that *all* play within the school, we have found that none of these things can be achieved without dialogue. Since the purpose to which leaders in schools should be committed is 'learning for all' and since all, as leaders within the school, should embrace this purpose, conversations about how learning and leadership can be brought into a reciprocal relationship are essential.

In Chapter 3, we underscored the significance of dialogue in 'bridging and linking social capital' in schools. Ensuring that people engage with others beyond their immediate group, and that people with positional power and authority engage with those without it, is essential to the view that all are leaders of learning; and all learn as leaders in an LfL school. In other words, dialogue involving people from different sections and levels of the school helps to put the concepts of 'broadly' and 'deeply' distributed leadership into action. Dialogue relates to models of learning that emphasise constructivist and social approaches, and, according to Chris Watkins, defines the sort of talk that is most closely 'associated with rich learning, development of understanding and building of community knowledge' (Watkins, 2005: 120). Robin Alexander's extensive research in different countries and cultures leads him to characterise dialogic teaching as collective, reciprocal, supportive, cumulative and purposeful (Alexander, 2004) – five adjectives that describe the dialogue we sought to encourage and found to be productive in the Carpe Vitam Leadership for Learning Project.

Added to this depiction of dialogue and its relationship with social capital is the argument about human agency, as disciplined people engaged in disciplined thought and action. We say that while dialogue is the means through which leadership for learning is enacted, it is of a particular kind which may be thought of as 'disciplined dialogue'. By this we mean that discussions about leadership, learning and the relationship between them are not trivial, trite, piecemeal, or sporadic. They are not derogatory, censuring, destructive or coercive. They are positively focused on the moral purpose of schools and they are all-embracing. Conversations are not irrationally based on stereotype or hearsay, but on reason and values, stimulated by helpful qualitative and quantitative data. In this sense they are constructive conversations carried in 'disciplined dialogue'.

Reaching a point where 'disciplined dialogue' infuses professional conversations in schools is not necessarily easy, nor surprisingly is putting into practice the view that all in the school are leaders of learning. We illustrate this claim by recounting experiences from one of the Australian schools in the LfL Project where, at the outset, neither shared leadership nor shared dialogue were in evidence at all.

At Northside High, the principal seemed initially to be the only individual who had an interest in the Leadership for Learning Project. He reported that it was he who made the decision to become involved. It was not a staff decision. He wanted a vehicle through which his ideas might gain more influence in a school with a very stable staff, a great majority of whom had been there for many years before his appointment.

In preliminary discussions, we were able to establish that the principal held the view that if all students were afforded greater leadership opportunities during their five years of high school, their learning outcomes could be improved. He had no evidence that student leadership experiences enhanced learning, but he believed that there was an integral connection. While this view was not shared by all of the staff, it was shared by a number. It was these people the principal approached to form the core of the LfL Project team. He then had to step back, not by choice in the first instance, but because his workload did not allow him to take the kind of 'hands on' leadership role that he would have liked. In other words, he was usually reluctant to share control.

Because of the other demands on his time, quite early in the project, his 'driving' style to keep up the project's momentum changed to one of 'support where and when necessary' as the teachers began to shape the project and eventually to lead it themselves with their colleagues across the school. This 'taking up of the reins' by teachers did not occur quickly at Northside High. It slowly grew as teachers began to discuss students' views of the school, engaged in deeper conversations about learning and about what students found most helpful. This in turn stimulated discussions about what might be done differently if the school was to capitalise on its focus on student leadership. The principal's main contribution to these conversations was to provide the meeting space and time for his teachers and ensure access to helpful resources, such as a critical friend and research data. In this way the principal shifted his approach to leadership significantly over the three years of the project, but then so did the teachers and students. Throughout the project at Northside High, discussion about learning and leadership was stimulated by rich data about students, teachers and the school. While the teachers may not have used the term 'disciplined dialogue' to describe their project discussions, there is no doubt that extraneous or irrelevant matters were all but expunged from the agenda, leaving space and time for concrete conversations about matters germane to the school's moral purpose.

At the conclusion of the LfL Project at Northside High, the principal summed up his views about what had been achieved in a presentation to an audience assembled at an annual schools' Showcase Day. He reported that key questions about leadership, learning and how they might be linked now had a strong place in Northside High classrooms, while theory and practice were informing one another as a consequence. He admitted that it could not be assumed that leadership roles would be taken by all to whom they were extended. At his school, for many, time and space were required before ownership of ideas began to take hold. But it was a particular use of time and space which counted. Reflection through talk in teams, he argued, was essential and for this to occur, he as principal, needed to provide the necessary support (for example, timetable relief, funding when needed and follow-up documentation after meetings). He also spoke about his personal learning, acknowledging his initial 'driving' style, which, he said, had shifted to support for teacher leaders and teams. This emphasised for him the importance and power of staff relationships as well as relationships with students and others outside the school. He concluded by saying that he had himself become a learner, indeed a student of leadership, as a result of the project.

The principal's presentation contained a number of points which help us in seeking to understand how leadership and learning are connected. His reference to the place that key questions about learning and leadership hold in the school points to a determined focus on the school's moral purpose. His reference to the power of professional relationships reinforces the concept of bridging social capital and its capacity to help people transcend traditional positional authorities; while his identification of the need for time and space for reflection in teams of teachers underlines the 'merit' in not being told but in finding out together. We argue that none of these outcomes, nor those in which he identified the need for further research data and links between theory and practice, would have been possible without 'disciplined' dialogue.

Our experiences in this Australian school and in other LfL Project countries led us, through international dialogue (which we say more about later), to principle 3:

> Leadership for learning practice involves creating a dialogue about leadership for learning.

This principle, however, must be applied with a conviction about the enabling effects of bridging social capital. When this happens, teachers, positional leaders and students are afforded an equal opportunity to engage in 'disciplined dialogue' about the connections between leadership and learning. The creation of this kind of dialogue should be deliberate, planned, and central to professional conversations as our experience shows that it is not in any way possible through happenstance.

Scaffolding disciplined dialogue

In a multi-site collaborative venture involving many different groups of players (students, parents, teachers, school principals, board members, critical friends, academics, invited contributors) it is to be expected that communication would have a key role, but in the Leadership for Learning Project we explicitly fostered particular kinds of exchanges and discussions. As the project progressed and we became even more aware of the important role of disciplined dialogue than we were at the outset, so scaffolding techniques became even more focused and refined. 'Scaffolding' is important because we know that dialogue about learning and leadership does not necessarily occur without a conscious stimulus in the busy daily lives of teachers, students and parents. The process of 'scaffolding' is therefore very important. It is the means by which particular types of conversations are initiated, supported, 'fuelled' and sustained so that aspects of leadership and learning become the life-blood of focused conversations.

Dialogue, however well scaffolded, rests on certain foundations – understanding, trust and purpose. The first two are closely interrelated, and take time to develop. In a project where the participants speak at least five different national languages – seven if the differences among English, American and Australian 'English' are considered – a pre-requisite for dialogue is being able to understand what others say. Perhaps counter-intuitively, the multi-lingual aspect of the Leadership for Learning Project could in fact be seen as a benefit, not a hindrance, to communication, since it was obvious that we all had to work at understanding not just the words others used but also the meaning lying behind them. It was far more accepted than it seems to be in monolingual situations to express lack of understanding and to ask for clarification. Whatever the situation, however cross cultural or within a single school setting, speakers need to recognise the onus to express themselves in ways that make meaning transparent. Of course this will not always be achieved, but we have found that when the purpose of dialogue is agreed by all in the conversation, trust grows, misunderstanding is exposed easily and the search for meaning is pursued in very practical ways, as well as at more theoretical levels.

In addition to language, another imperative in effective communication is the understanding of context. Differences among classrooms in individual schools or amongst different school sites all have implications for the joint pursuit of leadership for learning. We suggest that dialogue concerned with awareness and understanding of difference can be scaffolded by creating opportunities and incentives for participants to share information about their own classrooms, and views of their school and the education system of which it

is part. We suggest that the aim is not that everyone should know and understand all aspects of each others' contexts, but rather to accept that there may be
deeply rooted differences that strongly influence surface features of practice and
perception. So attitudes of openness and the suspension of judgement are more
important and practical than encyclopaedic knowledge of other contexts when
disciplined dialogue is the norm.

Trust is closely related to understanding, and the voluntary nature of joining
the Leadership for Learning Project meant that there was an initial bank of
good will on which to build. This relates to O'Neill's (2002) category of trust
based on role, which may in time develop into trust in the individual, a form
of trust that Bottery (2003) refers to as 'identificatory trust'. Certainly we saw
many instances of deep trust and genuine friendship developing over the course
of the project. The residential nature of conferences, with their social elements
and periods of relaxation as well as formally structured activities, assisted the
building of relationships and the forging of trust between individuals. So to us,
there are social aspects which must accompany conversations if disciplined
dialogue is to flourish

Another condition for the development of dialogue is a purpose that matters,
and relevant subject matter. The central concepts of leadership and learning are
of course the raison d'être of schools and universities, and so it is not surprising
that participants in the Leadership for Learning Project were motivated to
contribute, at least in a broad sense. However, this interest and engagement had
to be won as school colleagues varied in their outlook, and in their willingness
to assist the collective longer term goal of understanding leadership for learning
while at the same time addressing their specific development agenda. It was not
unanticipated that we found some participants more narrowly focused on their
immediate concerns and displaying an instrumental orientation. We know that
this phenomenon is likely to emerge whenever conversations about persistent
problems or hoped for action take place. We also know that goodwill has a
'shelf-life', all the shorter if agreement on explaining why something is as it is
takes too long, or when taking necessary ameliorating steps results in rhetoric
rather than productive action.

Much dialogue during the LfL Project was scaffolded around the broad topic
of practice, which was examined and described in a variety of ways. Initially we
set up opportunities for school colleagues to present their own practices to
others, and in turn to learn about theirs. The questionnaire administered soon
after the beginning of the project yielded data that enabled each school to
discuss and learn about various perspectives on themselves (provided by
students, teachers and staff with differing responsibilities). This was extended
through comparison of each school's data with the aggregate of all the project
schools in their country, and in an even wider circle, with everyone in the
project. These comparisons enabled teachers to consider their own situation
within a broader context. Once the project was underway and understandings
and trust were developing, we set up structured activities at the international

conferences through which people could examine particular aspects of practice more closely, including very detailed consideration of an issue or dilemma.

School visits were an integral part of the conferences, enabling visitors to get a real feel for the country context, to see practice at first hand and to talk with, and listen to, students. In this way the visitors came to understand not only more about the practices themselves, but also the assumptions and values that underpinned them. They could see and hear about the factors that promoted and inhibited leadership and learning, and think about the transferability of practice. The hosts had a glimpse of the familiar through the eyes of the visitors, and got a sense of the way others saw them from the outside, rather than seeing the world only from their own viewpoint. Some colleagues found these visits so useful that they arranged additional visits to participants' schools beyond the conferences. In some instances these became reciprocal exchanges, incorporating a particular and agreed focus for inquiry. In a London school, for example, visits for teachers and students were arranged to New Jersey and to Oslo with influence on the design of a new school building to facilitate leadership for learning in mind.

Along with school visits, and conferences of all types (annual international, periodic regional and local, and a week-long virtual conference), in-school development was another crucially important setting for dialogue about leadership, learning and their interconnection. Critical friends and researchers supported each school in pursuing its own particular developmental agenda linked to leadership for learning. The external perspective of critical friends, and the feeding back of data from researchers, were very influential in shaping and progressing the work. Through its central features of questioning, reflecting back, and providing data and an alternative viewpoint (Swaffield, 2007), critical friendship both uses and generates dialogue, often resulting in reappraisal on the part of school colleagues. Dialogue at school level obviously took place in the first language, so issues could be examined in depth, nuances of meaning explored and complexities exposed.

In an Athens school the principal described how the individual voices that had existed in the school before the project 'came together' and staff began to have systematic discussions about school improvement with a focus on learning and leadership. While much of what was said was not new, dialogue brought latent ideas to the fore, considering them in new ways and applying them to classroom practice. Progress made was attributed in large part to the influence of the critical friend who acted as a catalyst for the school to discover, in the principal's words, 'the paradise that was actually around us'. Engagement in the dialogue was extended to parents through joint activities and structured occasions such as weekly discussions with teachers involved in the LfL Project.

There was an obvious developmental course in the dialogue around practice, summarised by Portin (2004) in three stages and by Swaffield (2006) in a nine-category typology. Comparison and contrast were powerful catalysts for dialogue, resonating with Czarniawska's notion of 'outsidedness' (Czarniawska,

1997), and Richards's process of separation, encounter, homecoming and dis-embedding (Richards, 1999).

As the project moved into its later stages and the five principles for practice became widely known and discussed, they provided another way of looking at practice. In short, the principles were used as a lens. They gave us a language that enabled the dialogue to move beyond exchanges of practice. The school visits also became more structured as time went on, with specific prompts based on the principles shaping the visit and scaffolding the subsequent dialogue.

Having spoken in general about scaffolding as the means of initiating, supporting, 'fuelling' and sustaining disciplined dialogue we now discuss some of the ways in which this was effected in more detail, underscoring the importance of techniques or tools which aid a better understand of how leadership and learning may be connected.

Tools for disciplined dialogue

Throughout the LfL Project we used a range of tools to support dialogue. Many we had used previously in other contexts and we adapted them for the project's purposes. Some were new and a few were created specifically. The tools fall into several different but not discrete groups. A number were associated with the sharing of practice, and triggered dialogue both in preparation and subsequent discussion. For example, for the first whole project gathering, each school group brought an artefact that conveyed something important about their school. This was a way of introducing themselves and a stimulus for dialogue. Deciding what to bring initiated discussion about core values within school groups, and the different artefacts generated interest among project participants. School portraits including a variety of documents and illustrations were a more conventional way of conveying information about each school, again stimulating dialogue and including students in the creation and sharing of these.

Descriptions of national contexts were designed to help us understand practice, and led to conversations about similarities and differences. Vignettes (short descriptive case studies illuminating a practice or issue) were written by an individual or a group, and then used with a variety of structures for debate and discussion. Displays incorporating text, photos, students' work and other images, as well as video recordings, were tools for sharing practice vividly. Displays, a regular feature at all conferences, were a further focus for dialogue captured both verbally and in 'Post-it' notes, adding comment, question and critique to the displays. We also used the more traditional means of presentations and workshops for sharing and discussing practice. The types of tools we recommend rely largely on descriptions of 'what is' and act as a support for discussions about current practice and what might be different in the future.

A second set of tools was much more futures focused than those we have just described. Once people are familiar with practices and contexts, and trusting relationships are formed, they are able to engage in dialogue focused on improving practices in particular situations or bringing different perspectives to bear on the resolution of specific issues and dilemmas. We have used two very tightly structured tools – the 'tuning protocol' and 'critical incident analysis'. They are similar in that one person presents a practice, problem or incident, and the ensuing dialogue follows pre-specified steps or conventions designed to avoid judgement and to assist the presenter in reflecting on the situation from a number of differing perspectives so acting as a prompt to future action.

A third set of tools used structured activities and routines to stimulate, shape and capture the dialogue. 'Table graffiti', where people jot ideas and comments on large sheets of paper, is a way of capturing immediate responses to a statement or question, leading into small group and plenary dialogue. 'Place mats' perform a similar function. A group of five or six (preferably from different country backgrounds) are seated at tables with a large 'tablecloth' divided into 'place-mats'. The process starts with each member of the group writing his or her own personal reflections, followed by a sharing in which key themes are encapsulated in the central space. These are then shared with other groups.

The use of cards with a variety of statements or illustrations is another device to prompt dialogue in different ways. For example, 'the nine card diamond sort' is a well-known prioritising exercise in which groups try to reach consensus on the order of importance of various priorities. Another card exercise is to offer a range of visual images which people select because it says something to them about leadership for learning, and then explain why they chose as they did, that is, the reasons for their choice. Our critical friend to the project, David Perkins, expanded the repertoire, introducing us to 'thinking routines' as developed with his team at Harvard. We used the 'connect, extend, challenge' routine many times in different contexts, asking ourselves 'how does this connect with what we already know and do? How does it extend our thinking and could it extend our practice? And what challenges does it present?'

A fourth group of tools was concerned with recording activities, discussions and ideas which, in turn, promoted subsequent dialogue. Recording activities can be done in a structured way, such as by using the framework of 'conceiving (thinking), believing (acting) and achieving (progressing)' to chronicle developments in a school, and by using a grid with predetermined row and column headings for focusing and recording observations during school visits. Other tools are much more open, such as 'contribution sheets' which can be used at workshops where participants were encouraged to record a comment, question, quotation, image or whatever, as and whenever they feel inclined. These are then added to other contributions projected in a continuously expanding loop, which prompts dialogue among viewers and generates further contributions. Another iterative process in this group of tools is 'the wall' – an actual wall on which people place 'Post-it' notes with ideas, comments, questions and responses.

Some of the most powerful tools for stimulating dialogue are not text based, but rely on images – photographs or drawings. We used photographs taken at different times to remind everyone of our journeys, both literally and conceptually, to recall key contributions and activities, and to make links over time and space. A graphic illustrator, Deirdre Crowley from New Jersey, made a major contribution to the final conference by keeping a rolling record of every presentation and every discussion, a graphic tableau of words and images on scrolls of paper measuring 1.5 metres by 5 metres. This 'complete' record of conference proceedings provided not only a detailed record of what had been said over more than three days but was a vital stimulus to sustaining disciplined dialogue (see Figure 8.1).

A fifth group of tools involved the collection of data through critical friends' and researchers' recorded observations and reflections of lessons, meetings, and documentation of a variety of school activities. They interviewed students, teachers, parents, principals and board members. They shadowed students and school leaders, and collected other data through questionnaires. These are all rich sources of information which can feed into and enrich the quality of the dialogue among school colleagues, critical friends and researchers.

We argue that all of these tools help create disciplined dialogue about leadership for learning. More specifically, they help to make concrete the 'sub-principles', or 'prompts to action' listed below, which reinforce the need for a dialogue about leadership for learning:

- LfL practice should be made explicit, discussable and transferable.
- There should be active collegial inquiry focusing on the link between learning and leadership.
- Coherence will be achieved through the sharing of values, understandings and practices.
- Factors which inhibit and promote learning and leadership should be examined and addressed.

We turn now to address two further matters of overall importance to Principle 3. These concern the purpose and scope of dialogue.

Dialogue purpose and scope

We argue that apart from the fact that disciplined dialogue 'oils' the connection between leadership and learning, it nurtures relationships through which shared values and understandings can be developed. It makes LfL practice explicit and transferable, and helps people seek coherence among leadership activities. One of the main purposes of dialogue is enabling different perspectives to be aired, shared, compared, understood, evaluated and adapted. And for multiple perspectives to be an accepted part of a dialogic process, its scope should not be constrained. Contributions from people at all levels and from all sections of the school, as well as from people outside it, must be valued. We explain more fully what we mean by purpose and scope below, referring to some of our experiences during the Leadership for Learning Project.

Purpose: engaging with multiple perspectives

In Chapter 3 we presented a model of educational learning with four inter-connecting groups and contexts – student learning, teacher learning, school learning and system learning. This extended Knapp *et al.*'s 'wedding cake' model (2003) and suggested that engagement in learning at these four levels promotes collective action within and across groups, aiding the development and use of 'bridging social capital'.

Brad Portin, one of our partners in Seattle, says that 'Professional Learning is informed by the process of an encounter with the *unfamiliar*' (Portin, forth-coming). This is often through the use of data, novel ideas, unfamiliar theories, new stories or new experiences. For us, all groups and contexts can be informed by and are able to learn from the unfamiliar. This approach was acknowledged in the strategies, instruments and tools employed during the project, some of which we have described above. In addition, throughout the project, the unfamiliar was frequently encountered through comparisons and contrasts which both data and experience exposed.

Chapter 4 outlined the application of the LfL Project's comparative methodology across countries and cultures. While this process was essential in an international project, we do not regard it as essential for all schools wanting to move into a leadership for learning framework in the future. What we *do* say is that 'cross boundary' comparison and contrast is essential. This applies as much within schools as it does between them, or between countries for that matter. 'Cross boundary' comparisons are possible between classes and teachers, between departments in large schools, and where there are organised clusters of schools they are possible across schools.

As we have argued above, the development of 'disciplined dialogue' may take time. Where it has not been occurring, where the 'busy-ness' of everyday classroom activity dominates, where the seduction of the mundane flourishes, there is no guarantee that the kind of dialogue needed to bring leadership and learning into focus will be achieved quickly. There must be opportunities for consistent, frequent and adequately resourced 'cross boundary' interchange. This suggests that we do not advocate sporadic forays into concerns for learning or 'here today and gone tomorrow' leadership fads. Our work tells us that there are direct benefits in people wrestling with the perennial questions encountered by schools as they seek to achieve their moral purpose. After all, questions such as: 'What and how should we teach? How do students learn best? How do we know what has been learned?' are enduring. What changes are the students in the school, year by year, the staff and the parents, and, therefore, the interactive dynamic itself. Questions about what and how people learn best are not static; they are in need of constant redefinition in the light of context specific conditions, and changing human agency, so that the school's moral purpose remains in the ascendancy. Comparisons and contrasts among years, class groups, course cohorts, departments, and schools should be used to ensure that habituated or unreasoned practice never takes an unwarranted foothold.

Figure 8.1 A running visual record of conference discussions

Outsiders' perspectives can be used to challenge old habits if they have developed. Much has been written about the power of 'group think' but also about its numbing and debilitating effects on organisations. So, when the potential insularity of in-house conversations is acknowledged, it is but a logical next step to include 'outsiders' in 'disciplined dialogue'. Our experience suggests that university researchers bring views into schools which often create the friction necessary for attention to be given to a particular issue. Critical friends serve a similar purpose. That said, in this day and age, face-to-face dialogue can and should be augmented through 'virtual' means. Asynchronous and real time conversations with various internet tools have been used frequently between countries because of distance but they are just as helpful between schools not very far apart.

During the Leadership for Learning Project, using the means we have referred to above, we scaffolded dialogue around international comparisons and contrasts. We brought university personnel into schools. Data were gathered and reported, and schools engaged with critical friends. This led us to say in support of principle 3, that:

Different perspectives should be explored through networking with researchers and practitioners across national and cultural boundaries.

Different perspectives are indeed important to 'disciplined dialogue' as is the challenge to the familiar that comparisons and contrasts make possible. Schools endeavouring to connect leadership and learning we argue, should make 'boundary crossing' compulsory. It is then that one of the key purposes of dialogue is achieved.

Scope: inclusive of everyone

It remains for us to say something about keeping the link between leadership and learning centre stage. If we have not made the point strongly enough in this chapter, then we reiterate our position here: 'the link between leadership and learning should be a shared concern for everyone'. This is the platform on which principle 3 rests.

We began this chapter with the story of Northside High where it could not be said that concern for leadership for learning was widely shared. Nor was shared leadership. Both are necessary if the explicit values of leadership for learning are to take hold in a school. Too often schools exclude one or other of the groups affected by what they do, not intentionally, but nevertheless effectively. Parents, it has been said, can be hard to enrol in the school's moral purpose because of language difficulties, after hours access problems, disinterest, apathy and a raft of other excuses. Students too can be excluded as too young and inexperienced to know 'what's good for them'. We do not subscribe to either of these views, although we do recognise that inclusive practice is an 'Everest' for many. Modelling practice within the school amongst teachers, school leaders, parents and students will create, in time, the circumstances where the contributions of all parties to focused conversations, indeed to the kind of 'disciplined dialogue' we advocate, will be a constant in every school year. Getting started on an annual journey with new students, teachers and parents using some of the tools we have seen to be effective in scaffolding dialogue about leadership for learning should be of the highest priority. We suggest one of myths perpetuated about teaching, namely, 'If you can't shut 'em up by the end of first term, you're in for a bad year', should be rephrased and trumpeted out loud, 'If you can't open 'em up by the end of the first term, you're definitely in for a bad year'. And we say the "em' applies to everyone.

Conclusion

Gaining a shared and deeply distributed understanding of leadership for learning and its moral purpose cannot be achieved without the power of common language developed through supportive conversations and agreed courses of action. Disciplined dialogue is the key – dialogue that is informed, inclusive and enabling, as the examples we have used in this chapter have shown. We have shown that dialogue must be supported or scaffolded through the use of tools and at least seven general processes:

1 cross boundary comparisons of data and practice;
2 face-to-face inter-school exchanges;
3 virtual inter-school exchanges using internet tools;
4 using the leadership for learning principles as an agenda for dialogue;
5 employing questions derived from the principles as evaluative tools;
6 analysing assumptions against practice; and
7 engaging 'critical friends' and researchers for outside views.

We leave this chapter by offering two further 'tools' which are sets of questions that we hope will further stimulate 'disciplined dialogue'. The first set is about how professionals talk together:

1 Do they listen to each other without interruption?
2 Do they respect each other's viewpoint or do they pontificate, presuming that wisdom comes only with status?
3 Do they accept the discipline of collective problem-solving or prefer to pursue private agendas?
4 Do they stick to the topic in hand or do they digress?
5 Do they feel able to speculate without fear that their contribution will be sidelined as 'theoretical' or 'irrelevant'?
6 In respect of ideas which they have been offered do they ask probing questions, or do they merely hear them and pass them on?
7 In respect of what is novel or unfamiliar, are they prepared willingly to suspend disbelief?

8 Do discussions take thinking forward or do they go round in circles?
9 Do the participants have the skills which all this requires?

(Alexander, 2004: 39)

The second is a set of questions drawn directly from principle 3. The questions for teachers and students act as prompts for both discussion and action; but with inclusivity in mind, either group of questions may be cast in such a way that they can be addressed by parents as well.

Questions for teachers	Questions for students
1 In our school do we talk explicitly about the relationship between learning and leadership?	1 Do our teachers discuss with us how we learn and how we can influence things in the school?
2 Do we share and learn about leadership for learning practices with colleagues from beyond our immediate group?	2 Are we ever involved in discussing learning and leadership with students in other classes or schools?
3 Do we engage in systematic inquiry to improve the links between leadership and learning in our school?	3 Do our teachers investigate problems so that they can improve the way they teach?
4 Do we discuss our values and the extent to which they are reflected in our day-to-day practices?	4 Do we have opportunities to discuss with teachers what is important to us and how this affects our learning?
5 Do we examine factors in school life which either inhibit or promote leadership for learning?	5 Do we have opportunities to discuss with teachers things which help us to learn and things which stop us from learning?
6 In our school, does everyone share a concern with the link between leadership and learning?	6 Do we have opportunities to talk about the way the school is run and how this helps us to learn or not?
7 Do we explore practice through links with researchers?	7 Do we get visitors from universities at our school?
8 Do we network with practitioners in other schools, countries and in other cultural contexts?	8 At our school, do we get visitors from other schools and other countries?

Figure 8.2 Questions for teachers and students

References

Alexander, R. (2004) *Towards Dialogic Teaching: Rethinking Classroom Talk*, Cambridge: Dialogos.

Bottery, M. (2003) 'The management and mismanagement of trust', *Educational Management and Administration*, 31 (3): 245–61.

Czarniawska, B. (1997) *Narrating the Organization: Dramas of Institutional Identity*, Chicago, IL: University of Chicago Press.

Knapp, M.S., Copland, M.A. and Talbert, J.F. (2003) *Leading for Learning: Reflective Tools for School and District Leaders*, Seattle: Centre for the Study of Teaching and Policy, University of Washington.

O'Neill, O. (2002) *A Question of Trust: The BBC Reith Lectures 2002*, Cambridge: Cambridge University Press.

Portin, B. (2004) 'Learning opportunities for school leaders across national boundaries: lessons from an international collaboration of schools', Paper presented at the University Council for Educational Administration annual conference, Kansas City, Missouri, 12–14 November.

Portin, B. (forthcoming) 'Cross national professional learning for school leaders', *International Journal of Leadership in Education*.

Richards, A. (1992) 'Adventure-based experiential learning', in J. Mulligan and C. Griffin (eds) *Empowerment through Experiential Learning*, London: Kogan Page.

Swaffield, S. (2006) 'Scaffolding discourse in multi-national collaborative enquiry: the Carpe Vitam Leadership for Learning project', *Leading and Managing*, 12 (2): 10–18.

Swaffield, S. (2007) 'Light touch critical friendship', *Improving Schools*, 10 (3): 205–19.

Watkins, C. (2005) *Classrooms as Learning Communities: What's In It for Schools?* London: Routledge.

9 Shared leadership (principle 4)

*Joanne Waterhouse and
Jorunn Møller*

Introduction

In Chapter 2, reference was made to the importance of shared leadership. This has been clearly shown to be a significant change in educational leadership literature, putting into deep shadow the primacy of individualistic, iconic or heroic forms of leadership. In Chapter 3, Sue Swaffield argued that leadership for learning is a qualitatively different form of leadership relying on contributions from people across all levels of the school as a tangible expression of the power of 'bridging social capital' in understanding theory and practice. This theme was further elaborated in Chapter 8 where it was shown that 'disciplined dialogue' is best carried across a school when leadership is shared. In the present chapter, we address the concept of shared leadership by discussing the fourth principle developed during the Leadership for Learning Project. As with all five principles, this emerged from our analysis of the data, but was also reflective of the founding values of the project as presented by David Frost in Chapter 5 and reiterated by John MacBeath in the concluding chapter.

Conceptualising leadership

From the outset of the project, learning and leadership were understood as connected.

> We do not assume leadership to be something that resides within the individual at the apex of the organisational pyramid, but as exercised across the community, 'distributive' rather than 'distributed' as delegation, or in the gift of management. We seek out leadership not only in the most likely, but in the most unlikely of places. We expect to find it both in the informal life of the school as well as within its formal structures. It may be assumed as well as delegated, and expressed spontaneously as well as in formalised planning.
>
> (MacBeath *et al.*, 2003: 7)

This perspective on leadership was informed by theories of organisational learning and the significance of social interactions within organisations. It also echoes Gronn's way of conceptualising leadership in which he emphasises the concerted and plural nature of leadership and the importance of influence over conferred authority – 'Managers may be leaders but not necessarily by virtue of being managers, for management denotes an authority, rather than an influence, relationship' (2002a: 428–9).

While the concept of leadership is generally related to a family of terms such as authority, status and power, influence expresses itself in a careful interplay of knowledge and action, and it is conscious of conditions and of change. Foster (1986: 187) has a parallel way of framing the concept when he underlines that 'leadership can spring from anywhere; it derives from the context and ideas of individuals who influence each other. [. . .] Leadership is an act that enables others and allows them, in turn, to become enablers'.

This perspective bears similarities with the way Sergiovanni writes about the phenomenon of leadership 'density' (2001). He argues that high leadership density means that a large number of people are involved in the work of others, are trusted with information, are involved in decision-making, are exposed to new ideas and participate in knowledge creation and transfer. In such a situation, a large number of members of the organisation have a stake in the success of the school. What is interesting for the purposes of shared leadership in organisational contexts is the question of the factors that encourage or inhibit the human capacity to use imagination and to act on it, so creating what is described as a 'learning organisation'.

An organisation could be termed a learning organisation to the extent that it has the capacity to adapt and re-create within itself. Collaboration, teamwork and dialogue are crucial in creating and sustaining such a culture. Leading learning thus needs to be about understanding the issues, fostering the conditions and helping to create the supporting structures – what Senge describes as 'designing the learning processes' (1990: 345). The potent force that shapes behaviour within a learning organisation is the combination of simply expressed expectations of purpose, intent and values, and the freedom for responsible individuals to make sense of these in their own way. 'In this chaotic world we need leaders but we don't need bosses' (Wheatley 1999: 129). This presupposes a quality of leadership which is ecologically aware and 'cognisant of those forces' which impact not only on their own practice, but upon the attitudes and values of the other educators within their organisations, the aspirations and endpoints of their students, and upon those in the wider communities they serve (Bottery, 2004: 25).

The further we mine the organisational literature the more it points us to distributed leadership, a necessary adjunct of complex organisations. However, this is often interpreted as a form of conferred or delegated leadership, perhaps as implied by the term 'distribut*ed*' as against 'distribut*ive*' or dispersed. In a project with three local authorities in England (MacBeath *et al.*, 2002) six forms of distribution were identified from formal delegation by the headteacher at one end to the spontaneous initiative of groups and individuals at the other, assuming leadership in a culture blind to hierarchy and status.

We came to the leadership for learning research in the belief that the most fruitful path to seek an analysis of leadership from a distributed perspective was exploring leadership as an activity 'spread out', in Jim Spillane's terminology. It addresses the relations between structure and human agency in ways that go beyond documenting lists of strategies and skills that leaders use in their work. This perspective on leadership is grounded in activity rather than in position or role, and therefore the unit of analysis is 'concertive actions' (Gronn 2002b: 429) by collaborating pairs or teams, rather than acts by an individual leader.

What follows is a conceptualisation of leadership from a distributed perspective. We then outline the principle for shared leadership that emerged from the project and reflect on how stories from the schools illuminate and inform it.

A distributed perspective on leadership

Distributed leadership has recently received escalating interest within the field of leadership and organisational studies. One reason for this is the growing recognition of the limitations of relying on the single heroic leader. The 'super head' turning schools single handedly is neither realistic nor sustainable. Much of the policy support for distributed leadership has been driven by the recognition that, whether the heroic paradigm for leadership is appropriate or not, it is impossible for enough heroes to exist. Concerns about sustainability of effort, succession planning and recruitment of headteachers have necessitated a shift towards the promotion of leadership skills at other levels in the organisation, with writers asserting that 'sustainable leadership is a distributed necessity and a shared responsibility' (Hargreaves and Fink, 2004: 11). Leadership must be therefore understood as a relational concept, and the practice takes place in the *interactions* of people and their situations. The context determines actions, but at the same time context may be influenced by actions (Gronn, 2003b).

The requirement for teachers to be assessed through a threshold of performance in order to receive incremental additional payments includes attention to leadership opportunities and entitlements for all teachers. Headteachers are expected to recognise, recruit and train for leadership at all levels in the organisation. The standards for headteachers are positioned in a framework that includes leadership of others, such as subject leaders and special needs teachers. It is clear that the standards for each level of leadership are predicated on others in the frame fulfilling their responsibilities.

This 'distributed practice' has been described as 'the exploitation of informal workplace interdependencies in accomplishing tasks' (Gronn, 2003a: 2) and highlights some of the contradictions and confusions at the heart of the policy drive for greater distribution. Accounting for distributive practice and recognising it within the formal structures for responsibility and reward can be inherently problematic. Certainly the stories that emerged from the Leadership for Learning Project reveal cultural restraints and differential developments that place school-wide practice somewhere along a continuum that spans formal individualised structures to more fluid, spontaneous and dispersed forms of leadership.

Some proponents of distributed leadership argue against the separation of the terms 'leadership' and 'management' suggesting that they operate 'in tandem, and are often intertwined' (Spillane *et al.*, 2007: 105). While many practitioners expect their managers to lead and their leaders to manage, we also found instances where this may work against a genuinely distributed perspective, some where inspirational leaders turn out to be very poor managers and some where managers lack the people skills required to encourage followership (MacBeath *et al.*, 2002).

There has been a recent drive in the literature for research into distributed leadership to move beyond description to a normative perspective. A distributed perspective on leadership emphasises practice and process. It is founded on the belief that leadership is open to any member of the organisation and necessitates a focus on the organisation as a whole and leadership activity in particular. Leadership practice is conceptualised as the activity of influence. An activity is both structured and dynamic, it 'has its own internal transitions and trans-formations, its own development' (Gronn, 2000: 87) and has been described as being 'stretched over' the social and situational contexts of the school (Spillane *et al.*, 2001). The unit of analysis can be the enactment of a task or function, it can be the situation and it has been described as behaviour and the dynamic within teams and committees (Gronn, 2003a). It can be 'in-between' the work of two practitioners and can be understood as multiplicative, rather than additional (Spillane *et al.*, 2001).

A study of distributed practice requires an understanding of context and the sense that actors themselves make of the situation. Talking to leaders, observing their work and reflecting with them on the influence and outcomes of their actions can all be significant for the process and enactment of leadership. In this way, 'personal accounts of action often reflect post facto sense-making efforts that refine the complexities of the experience', and the opportunity is created to better 'understand a task as it unfolds from the perspective and through the theories-in-use of the practitioner' (Spillane *et al.*, 2004: 14–15). Increasingly, leadership from a distributed perspective involves a holistic, dynamic concept that is characterised by activity, situation and interaction. The emphasis on process leads to a recognition that 'organisation is as much a structural outcome of action as a vehicle for it' (Gronn, 2000: 30). Most writers remain interested in describing and analysing leadership from this perspective, and resist the call for normative prescription. They want to foster an 'analytic perspective' – to understand how leadership work is spread among leaders, followers and the situation (Firestone and Martinez, 2007).

Other constructs or approaches, such as collaborative, democratic and trans-formational, could all be distributive but are not necessarily. In a distributed perspective, leadership 'is a system of practice made up of a collection of interacting component parts in relationships of interdependence in which the group has distinct properties over and above the individuals who make it up' (Spillane, 2006: 16).

A matter of trust and power

If leadership is viewed through a frame in which relationships are crucial, then the issue of trust is fundamental to the development, nature and sustainability of those relationships. Relational trust has been defined as 'the willingness of individuals to rely upon others and to make oneself vulnerable to others in that reliance' (Mayrowetz *et al.*, 2007: 89). Levels of trust are important to the extent that they enable connections to be made and developed between people whatever their official relationship within more formal, hierarchical settings. In a complex organisation characterised by flexible, dynamic, perhaps pragmatic interactions, it is the degree to which members of that organisation have professional respect for, and relational trust in, each other that enables distributed leadership practice to develop.

Trust in a distributed leadership perspective requires a study of contributory factors. These have been identified to include shared values, complementary temperaments, requisite psychological space and previous experience of collaboration, all factors 'which account for trust in role constellations and couples' (Gronn, 1999: 54).

Trust and power within an organisation are closely interrelated. Trust creates the conditions and mobilises people to action and collaboration. Trust and power both threaten and presuppose each other. Power without trust destroys one's own basis in the long run, and trust without power can hardly survive, because it will always be a potential for 'violence' in a group. In a school, people will have different interests and sometimes there is a need for somebody to stop this kind of 'violence'. Headteachers develop trust through trustworthy uses of power (Møller *et al.*, 2005).

The fourth principle

The principle for shared leadership that emerged from the work of the LfL Project had five discrete elements that were both representative of the data and useful for further and ongoing analysis (Figure 9.1). These elements describe action for the deliberate, conscious sharing of leadership. They encompass

---

Leadership for learning practice involves the sharing of leadership in which:

a) structures support participation in developing the school as a learning community
b) shared leadership is symbolised in the day-to-day flow of activities of the school
c) everyone is encouraged to take the lead as appropriate to task and context
d) the experience and expertise of staff, students and parents are drawn upon as resources
e) collaborative patterns of work and activity across boundaries of subject, role and status are valued and promoted.

Figure 9.1 The fourth principle

behaviours and dispositions and refer to cultural, structural and relational aspects for leadership in a school.

The Leadership for Learning Project provided an opportunity to explore in detail the connection between leadership and learning across different countries and different contexts. Based on our understanding of leadership, we took as our departure point that leadership as an activity is always distributed in an organisation, but in different ways. We wished to explore how it was distributed in the participating schools in order to discuss the notion and the benefits of shared leadership.

Data collection for the project was accounted for in various papers written by the members of the international research team. Stories of practice from the schools in the eight localities illuminated our developing understanding of shared leadership and the development of distributed practice. Inevitably there were accounts that highlighted the different cultural settings, both in terms of individual schools and separate countries. The paradox of the apparent need for control and steerage for effective distribution and increased sharing was endorsed by a number of accounts, particularly in the Northern European countries. Sharing leadership is understood as a journey, an incremental, deliberate shifting of perspectives through the experience of innovation and initiatives. Restructuring was a significant strategy for change and acknowledged as a useful endeavour for learning to share vision for leadership and leadership practice. Central to the journey was the importance of raising the issues, increasing awareness and participating in a research project that demanded attention to the challenges of sharing leadership.

Learning from stories of practice: sharing leadership is a journey of change

The schools involved in the project reported the sharing of leadership variously as an ideal, a challenge and an opportunity. Participating in the project shone a light on the issue and raised awareness. Infusing the fourth principle is a view of leadership as activity rather than role or status. For many participating schools, particularly those with long established hierarchies of responsibility, this proved to be a challenging proposition, particularly in contexts where there were formally designated structures of responsibility, differential rewards and accountability pressures. The evidence is clear that 'heroic' or hierarchical leadership is a view so deeply and systemically entrenched that it can take a long time to shift.

A paradox

There is sometimes a sense that leadership from a distributed perspective may be a result of the exigencies of failed leadership. Perhaps leadership is shared because the principal cannot do the job and the vacuum is being filled by others. It may be that leadership is being shared because the hero is unavailable. More often, it is a development resulting from policy, practice and a vision for sharing leadership that has been inspired by the principal. The creation of roles, focused resources, incentives and recognition can all be critical, leading one group of researchers to conclude 'Effective forms of distributed leadership may well depend on effective forms of focused leadership – leading the leaders' (Leithwood *et al.*, 2007: 55).

During the project we learned how the manifestation or the interpretation of shared leadership practice is quite diverse when we compare different schools. For instance, the Norwegian schools all valued shared leadership, but the manifestation of this value was quite distinct. One of the schools had a strong and charismatic headteacher. She had a clear vision for the school's development, and was constantly working for building consensus among the staff about long-term as well as short-term goals. At another school the headteacher first and foremost, listened to and tried to follow up initiatives coming from the teachers, linking up with a strategy which had been part of the established culture for years. The characteristics of school culture at the first school were described as innovative, risky, and collective. The formal leadership was strong, but at the same time distributed leadership was an organisational quality of the school. At the other school, formal leadership was characterised by a focus on peda-gogical content knowledge, incremental development, and support of teachers. As such, the leadership practice was distributed, but the coordination of actions seemed to be less resilient when compared with the first school.

The paradox is that the more distributed the practice, often the more directed the formal leadership from the top has been or continues to be. In the schools involved in the Leadership for Learning Project, this paradox was articulated in terms of initiatives for sharing leadership and the deliberate re-structuring for opportunities to share.

Structures which support shared leadership

During our collaboration with the schools, we learned that it requires the creation of specific structures to support the idea of shared leadership. At the same time, it should not be underestimated that transforming organisational and cultural structures requires a great deal of time and effort over the long term. In a London school a funding source was used to create opportunities for leadership and learning for leadership. The headteacher describes the impetus:

> Suddenly [the money] comes and I was absolutely clear that even in a deficit budget situation, if we were going to move the school forward I was not going to pay off the deficit. What I was going to do is pay quality time for people to deliver, be accountable to deliver and to share with each other. Teachers need quality time. How do you create that time? If you give them the time there's more than half a chance that they will produce something that is closer to what they would wish to produce in an ideal world.
>
> (Headteacher interview)

Teachers were encouraged to 'bid' for the money to release them so that groups could collaborate on initiatives to improve learning for the pupils. These teams each decided on an inquiry-based project of particular interest to them and planned how they would work together. A teacher talks animatedly about her leadership experience:

> My job as director of learning is actually focused around language development this year. So I've worked on two 'inset' [inservice] days. In particular we're looking at developing writing skills across the curriculum. We've identified that as one of our three focal areas in terms of our development plan. And just getting people feeling quite confident about dealing with writing across a range of subjects. And beginning to invent some of that work. All the teams as well have a writing focus. An extended writing project if you like. So the language work is coming out in different ways. And we've done some 'inset' and that's been my main responsibility as director of learning.
>
> (Teacher interview)

In these ways, principals have led the initiative for sharing leadership. Other examples are more than serendipitous or a stand-alone initiative. They involve re-structuring and long-term changes.

Evidence for this comes from an Australian principal who, recognising the important role of informal leaders, set in place structures which allowed incipient leadership activities to have fuller expression:

> I wanted to put in place some structures that ensured that the people who had been doing a lot of the informal leadership in the school had an opportunity to have that acknowledged so we had some leadership density.
>
> (Principal interview, May 2003)

Restructuring was achieved by breaking the school into four sub-schools, each with a focus on leadership for curriculum and learning:

> [we] have a philosophy that everyone in our school is a leader on our teaching staff whether they're a classroom teacher or someone in admin, right through to the principal. But staff involved in our learning teams have been leaders in the fact that they've selected curriculum and formed . . . what the grade 8 students are going to be doing and then through to grade 9 and . . . we have learning team leaders as well that play specific roles and call meetings and follow protocols that learning teams should be doing.
>
> (Principal interview 2005)

The principal describes the move to this position as a journey involving 'a significant change in their mindset about being in the school and what's important'. She explained that 'focussing on curriculum and pedagogy . . . as our interest, and supporting that through our new leadership structures has been the main priority of . . . staff.' (Principal interview, 2005).

There is a parallel in the London school noted above, where the headteacher set up a system whereby teams of teachers were able to bid for money which would be used to create time for teachers to work collaboratively on initiatives designed to improve pupil learning. The appointment of learning co-ordinators created leadership opportunities to take forward the school's learning agenda. In another Australian school 'transdisciplinary learning teams' were established to lead to curriculum review with a central focus on student learning. This was facilitated by reduction of class sizes in which there would be enhanced opportunities for students to become leaders of their own, and others' learning.

This promotion of collaborative patterns of work typically ran across boundaries of subject, role and status but these patterns were most difficult to accommodate in schools where policy and curriculum pressures, together with tight departmental demarcations between subjects inhibited collaborative leadership.

Raising the issues

How the principle of shared leadership plays out in different cultural contexts has been a source for discussion across country groups. While flatter structures, as in Norway and Denmark, may encourage more freedom and broader participation in activity, in comparison with more hierarchical structures in Austria, Greece, the USA and England, there is greater scope for staff to be left wondering where the boundaries lie and the need therefore to exercise professional judgement and decision-making.

In Denmark principals spoke of struggling with the tension between traditional flat 'democratic' structures and the demands of New Public Management (as described briefly in Chapter 2), seen as foreign to the Danish culture. A Danish principal expressed some of the tensions of a new political climate in which hierarchical decision-making sat uneasily:

> I must provoke, be direct in order to build an appropriate working environment. Leadership should be visible. People must be clear that we have a leader, a vision, and that things are not always straightforward and easy . . . As a principal, I have to be a leader of the department leaders, and not just a member of the 'leadership team'. Some have been unhappy with my role as a 'head leader', thinking instead that I should be an ordinary member of this group. In some ways I've become very alone, working in isolation. In theory we have no hierarchy, but in practice we still have. Of course I have to make some final decisions.
>
> (Principal, Denmark)

In the Danish country report it was said that:

> The conceptions of leadership have been broadened and differentiated for all the stakeholders that we have talked to. Whereas the concept was at first

a 'steering' manager concept that nobody liked, it is now shared and described as an integrated aspect of relations in small groups (of students, of students and teachers, of teachers and of the Senior Management Team) and in the greater community of the whole school. In particular it seems that teachers' conception of themselves as leaders of groups of students has changed significantly: leadership is now seen as an integral part of teaching and of building and maintaining communities.

(Danish report, 2005)

For many schools, particularly in Nordic cultures, shared leadership appears to equate with working together, teamwork, or collaboration. Again it is the mixture of strong leadership from the top and leadership as distributed that emerges as a recurring paradox in Danish and Norwegian data.

Leadership is about overview, identification, empathy, the competence to lay down educational tracks, educational direction and to be visible . . . I like a leader who is committed to both structure and plans and most certainly to education and who has her ears to the ground.

(Danish report, 2005)

This reference to the 'big leader' who lays down the tracks is inherent in the following perspective from another Danish teacher who, while describing leadership as distributed, also refers to another, higher, form of leadership which supports and challenges:

Leadership is a group of people in a school with very clear educational goals, very clear educational visions and who are not afraid of saying so. At the same time this group of people is good at gaining an insight into what is actually going on in school . . . Leadership should be supportive, stretch out a safety net under us and at the same time criticise us sometimes in order to get us up and going: Are some teachers sidetracking or is there a conflict that needs my help?

(Danish report, 2005)

A similar confluence of top-down and distributed leadership is found in Norway where a principal said 'The formal leadership is strong, but at the same time distributed leadership is an organisational quality of the school, the school culture.' This is combined with a description of the school culture as 'innovative, risky, and collective'. To venture into new and untried territory, however, is premised on having the time for proactive leadership which, it was said, was difficult to liberate within the constraints of the school day. The solution, therefore, was to extend teachers' hours to create time for shared leadership activity, a move that appears to have been accepted by staff whose positive responses were reflected in the final questionnaire of the LfL Project.

Risk taking also arises as a theme in a Seattle school where the principal spoke of creating opportunities for teachers to try things out and evaluate things for themselves:

> Teachers feel free and comfortable taking leadership roles. I'm a person who is easy to talk to and to try out ideas on. I give the staff the opportunity to try things out, and then they can determine whether something works or not, or how well it works. They come back to me and we spend time talking about it.
>
> (Principal, US West)

This principal has confidence that her staff will initiate and evaluate activities because of a level of trust among them. So there is room to take risks and make mistakes, recognising and accepting that not all things will prove to be equally effective.

In another Seattle school, the principal acknowledged that shared leadership was a considerable challenge to the status quo and saw any movement in that direction as a slow and pragmatic process, feeling out the strengths and weaknesses of staff:

> As a leader, you must be flexible and fluid . . . and [able to] go with the flow. Every day is different. It's important to involve everyone in leadership . . . to know the staff, recognise their strengths, build on their strengths, move them in a direction you want them to go or they want to go, in moving forward teaching and learning. We're on the right road . . . but still need more shared leadership. In some ways, I feel like we're just beginning.
>
> (Principal, US West)

In this school, teaching staff agreed with the principal's perception with regard to shared leadership. They believed that, although the school had further to go, it was moving in a positive direction. The extent to which shared leadership included young people was a major theme particularly in the Danish, Austrian and Australian contexts. In Denmark it was said:

> One feature of the project work is to find good balances between curriculum demands and student participation. Teachers are now more conscious of where they give students room for decisions and where they make the decisions and they have become better at making that explicit to students.
>
> (Danish report, 2005)

Giving pupils a voice

Sharing leadership involves encouraging everyone to take the lead as appropriate to task and context, including the pupils. There are several examples from the

Leadership for Learning Project schools which demonstrate this part of the principle in action.

In a Greek setting, the opportunity was taken to initiate students into taking the role of teacher and leading the class. This arose from a peer observation activity encouraged by the principal and was considered a radical move for the practitioners involved. During the periods that the pupils were teaching, the teachers strictly confined themselves to the role of the pupil and at the end of the lesson recorded their observations. The pupils – those who became 'teachers' as well as the rest of the class – were also asked to comment on the experience and write their impressions.

> The teachers agreed that the practice had positive results mainly for the pupils who assumed the preparation and teaching of the unit. They benefited both on a cognitive level – they deeply comprehended the units they taught – as well as on issues of personal development. They had taken responsibility and had developed their creativity, and confidence in assuming the role of the teacher. As far as the teachers are concerned, they felt that they had learned from their pupils, as they recognised in the pupils' mistakes their own weaknesses and reconsidered some of their requirements and attitudes towards the pupils. All three of them intend to include the practice in their methodology because the assumption of leadership roles by the pupils not only motivates the students to learn but also expands their own viewpoint.
>
> (Researcher, local report 2004)

In one London school, the example is cited of students being given leadership opportunities at school receptions. These roles are closely circumscribed and latitude for initiative appears to be tightly bounded. This taste of responsibility, however limited, may effect a rise in self-esteem and generate a greater sense of self-efficacy, expanding the boundaries of the student role from passive class-room recipient to a sense of agency. One student confirms that 'it helps us to be more responsible and it gives the teachers a chance to trust students and actually see how responsible some students are'. Another insists that 'When you feel you have got more responsibility you want to act like it more, so that sort of makes you work harder in your lessons. Because you want to live up to the role'. Yet another was clear that there was for him a link between experiencing oppor-tunities to lead and more effective learning. 'When the teacher trusts you, what you're doing and other things around you. That will help you to learn and do more stuff. I concentrate more.'

Student leadership in Denmark was also echoed in comments by students interviewed. Talking about the project one student said:

> It gives you good training in a working pattern that is commonly used in the Gymnasium [High School]. We have great freedom and take respon-sibility for our own learning ... The independent responsibility for

learning makes me inclined to learn more . . . We choose what we want to work with on our own, but the teachers keep tabs on you if you start reducing the demands you make on yourself.

(Student, Denmark)

Within the student group, it was said, members helped to uphold a kind of self-discipline, putting pressure on lazy members, while within the group leadership was characterised as 'spontaneous' and 'shared'.

If somebody gets a good idea in relation to the task or has some kind of insight beforehand, it seems natural that he or she takes on the leadership for a period.

(Student, Denmark)

In both Brisbane and Seattle student leadership was also a theme, as an Australian teacher reports:

There are a lot of students in this school and a lot of students in a leadership role which is very impressive and they take it on quite well too . . . it's not just at the top, it's spread throughout and there are various leaders at various levels.

(Teacher, Australia)

In another Australian school student leadership opportunities arose from a cultural shift towards a systematic focus on learning, setting up a virtuous circle of increased pupil attendance, greater student engagement, and more opportunities for authentic learning.

Examples of shared leadership, where students play a significant role, should not, however, lead to romanticised and sweeping statements about pupils' self-regulating learning in schools. We should not forget that teaching, which involves pupils' participation in planning, evaluation and decision-making, and which open up communications to many more voices, greatly complicates instruction. Pupils' opportunities to learn grow, but so do teachers' intellectual and managerial responsibilities as well (cf. Cohen and Barnes, 1993). Classrooms are places for ongoing social interactions and negotiations, and there is a range of dilemmas implicit in a given method (Berlak and Berlak, 1981). When teachers invite pupils to try out ideas about how to frame problems and to discuss alternative ways to solve them; when they try to cultivate rich thoughts by devising appropriate activities and coaching rather than telling the pupils what to do, they are also left a lot more vulnerable. Qualities like pupils' respect for one another's ideas and their capacities for disciplined argument, and for thoughtful listening, can be encouraged, but not easily. Teachers will have to cope with much greater uncertainty when pupils present ideas that are difficult to understand, and when they get into complicated disagreements. In addition, teachers increase their dependence on pupils. If the pupils do not do the serious work, the teachers will have failed in public.

Summing up

The data emerging from the various project sites suggested that 'shared leadership' is something that principals, teachers and students increasingly aspire to but that it is understood quite differently in different settings. In some instances it was understood in the sense of delegation, while in others it is seen in more bottom-up terms, as initiative spontaneously exercised and as teamwork.

We were made conscious again not only of ways in which language can obscure while apparently uniting, but also how deeply embedded these conceptions are within certain cultures and the time it takes for new forms of shared leadership to emerge and become embedded in thinking and practice.

Two key aspects of the methodology for the LfL Project were (i) a form of portraiture; and (ii) critical friendship (see Chapter 5). Schools were encouraged to portray themselves for illumination and celebration. Critical friends engaged in conversations and reflections with school colleagues to develop the portraits and gain a shared understanding of practice. One of the principles to emerge from the work – principle 3 – is centred on the importance of dialogue. In these ways, the significance of discourse for sharing understanding and making new meaning is emphasised. Similarly, the importance of talking about leadership

Questions for staff	Questions for students
Does everyone have the opportunity to play a part in developing the school as a learning community?	Do we have opportunities to help shape the way our school works? Do we have opportunities to carry out research in order to help improve teaching and learning in our school?
Do the kinds of meetings we have in our school enable a wide range of people to participate in development activity?	In our school do we get the feeling that it is OK to express your opinion and take responsibility?
Is the sharing of leadership evident in the everyday life of the school?	Are we are encouraged to take the lead on certain things?
Is everyone – adults and students – encouraged to take the lead in school appropriate to task and context?	Do our teachers recognise that we have experience of life and abilities that are sometimes useful in learning?
Are there are opportunities for people to work together regardless of subject specialism, status or position in the school?	Do we learn by working with people in different groupings or teams, e.g. a school play or collapsed timetable days?

Figure 9.2 Questions for staff and students

practice cannot be understated in the progress towards a more shared perspective for leadership. Raising the issues, having the conversations and legitimising the discourse all make for greater opportunities for shifting the business of leadership from heroes to mortals. The Leadership for Learning Project offered a critical framework for sharing leadership as a discursive practice. Moreover, our understanding of shared leadership also entails acknowledging that schools are sites of cultural and political struggles, and it is important to support interactions and negotiations that are characterised and distinguished by mutual trust and respect. We conclude this chapter by putting forward a series of questions for staff and students relevant to principle 4 (Figure 9.2). We hope they will stimulate dialogue about sharing leadership which is so critical in actualising its connection with learning.

References

Berlak, A. and Berlak, H. (1981) *Dilemmas of Schooling: Teaching and Social Change*, New York: Methuen & Co.

Bottery, M. (2004) *The Challenges of Educational Leadership: Values in a Globalized Age*, London: Paul Chapman.

Cohen, D.K. and Barnes, C.A. (1993) 'Conclusion: a new pedagogy for policy?' in D.K. Cohen, M.W McLaughlin and J.E. Talbert (eds) *Teaching for Understanding. Challenges for Policy and Practice*, San Francisco, CA: Jossey-Bass Publishers, pp. 240–77.

Firestone, W.A. and Martinez, M.C. (2007) 'Districts, teacher leaders, and distributed leadership: changing instructional practice', *Leadership and Policy in Schools*, 6 (1): 3–36.

Foster, W. (1986) *Paradigms and Promises: New Approaches to Educational Administration*, Buffalo, NY: Prometheus Books.

Fullan, M. (2001) *Leading in a Culture of Change*, San Francisco, CA: Jossey-Bass.

Gronn, P. (1999) *The Making of Educational Leaders*, London: Cassell.

Gronn, P. (2000) 'Distributed properties: a new architecture for leadership', *Educational Management and Administration*, 28 (3): 321–38.

Gronn, P. (2002a) 'Distributed leadership', in K. Leithwood and P. Hallinger (eds) *Second International Handbook of Educational Leadership and Administration*, Dordrecht: Kluwer Academic Publishers.

Gronn, P. (2002b) 'Distributed leadership as a unit of analysis', *The Leadership Quarterly*, 13: 423–51.

Gronn, P. (2003a) *The New Work of Educational Leaders: Changing Leadership Practice in an Era of School Reform*, London: Sage.

Gronn, P. (2003b) 'Leadership: who needs it?', *School Leadership and Management*, 23 (3): 267–90.

Hargreaves, A. and Fink, D. (2004) 'The seven principles of sustainable leadership', *Educational Leadership*, 61 (7): 8–13.

Leithwood, K. (2007) 'Introduction to special issue', *Leadership and Policy in Schools*, 6 (1): 1–2.

Leithwood, K., Mascall, B., Strauss, T., Sacks, R., Memon, N., and Yashkina, A. (2007) 'Distributing leadership to make schools smarter: taking the ego out of the system', *Leadership and Policy in Schools*, 6 (1): 4–36.

MacBeath, J., Oduro, G. and Waterhouse, J. (2002) *Distributed Leadership: A Developmental Process*, Nottingham: Research Report National College for School Leadership.

MacBeath, J., Frost, D., Moos, L., Green, D. and Portin, B. (2003) 'Leadership for learning (the Carpe Vitam project)', Conference paper presented at the American Educational Research Association Conference, Chicago, USA.

Mayrowetz, D., Murphy, J., Seashore-Louis, K. and Smylie, M.A. (2007) 'Distributed leadership as work redesign: retrofitting the job characteristics model', *Leadership and Policy in Schools*, 6 (1): 69–102.

Møller, J., Eggen, A., Fuglestad, O.L., Langfeldt, G., Presthus, A.M., Skrøvset, S., Stjernstrøm, E. and Vedøy, G. (2005) 'Successful school leadership – the Norwegian case', *Journal of Educational Administration*, 43 (6): 584–94.

Senge, P. (1990) *The Fifth Discipline: The Art and Practices of the Learning Organisation*, New York: Doubleday.

Sergiovanni, T.J. (2001) *Leadership: What's in it for Schools?* London: RoutledgeFalmer.

Spillane, J.P. (2006) *Distributed Leadership*, San Francisco, CA: Jossey-Bass.

Spillane, J.P., Halverson, R. and Diamond, J.B. (2001) 'Investigating school leadership practice: a distributed perspective', *Educational Researcher*, 30 (3): 23–8.

Spillane, J.P., Halverson, R. and Diamond, J.B. (2004) 'Towards a theory of leadership practice: a distributed perspective', *Journal of Curriculum Studies*, 36 (1): 3–34.

Spillane, J.P., Camburn, E.M. and Stitziel, A. (2007) 'Taking a distributed perspective to the school principal's workday', *Leadership and Policy in Schools*, 6 (1): 103–25.

Wheatley, M.J. (1999) *Leadership and the New Science*, San Francisco, CA: Berret-Koehler.

10 Shared accountability (principle 5)

John MacBeath

Introduction

Leadership for learning rests on a shared sense of accountability. This is the thrust of the fifth principle connecting leadership and learning. It is a bold statement in a policy climate where accountability is unequivocally seen in the singular, with the 'buck' clearly resting on the headteacher's desk. However, accountability has come to be understood within a policy context and with political overtones that carry very different meetings for those on whom accountability impacts more or less closely. The concept is further confounded by the way in which it translates, or fails to translate, into other languages and other cultural settings. This chapter attempts to shed some light on the confusions which surround the topic and concludes with some suggestions for a positive way forward.

The accountability 'burden'

Bearing the individual burden of responsibility for all that happens within a school is one of the explicit reasons for headteachers and principals retiring early and explains why there is such reluctance among teachers to assume the mantle of headship (OECD, 2001; James and Whiting, 2003; Gronn, 2007). Nor is it simply that senior leaders carry responsibility for the internal workings of the school but they are also held to account for factors that lie well beyond their control. For heads of schools in challenging circumstances (the current euphemism for inter-generational poverty) the notion of shared accountability may seem like a cruel joke. Theirs is the failure when standards do not rise year on year despite competition with schools in more privileged communities and often in the face of insurmountable odds.

The powerful impact of life in turbulent communities is recounted in our three-year study of schools in exceptionally challenging circumstances. The book which emanated from that project (MacBeath *et al.*, 2007) charted the improvement trajectories of eight schools, all with headteachers regarded by Ofsted (the Office of Standards in Education) and the DfES (the Department for Education and Skills) as excellent leaders, all supported by costly intervention strategies running into millions of pounds. The story is a bleak account of unrelenting pressure causing heads to resign, schools being put back into special measures and, in the case of one of the eight schools, finally being closed down. Among the nine lessons for policy with which the final chapter concludes is the following:

> Few schools are adept at introducing and managing innovations success-fully, a capacity massively under-developed in schools on the edge. Demanding that these same schools simultaneously respond to the short-term pressures imposed by performance tables and Ofsted monitoring can produce the institutional equivalent of schizophrenia.
>
> If this view is accepted, prescribing the 'what and how' of school improve-ment in widely differing institutions and social contexts can be counter-productive. Change takes root when staff collectively begin to get hold of a 'powerful idea'. Policy-makers need to become more adept at drawing up menus of the most promising ideas which schools may approach as 'à la carte', while ordering 'off-menu' should be also appraised on its merits.
>
> (MacBeath *et al.*, 2007: 142)

In other words, heads and teachers seeking new ways of improving the learning circumstances for their students may need to divert their energies from the test preparation on which present accountability rests. Simply getting children to attend, to feel secure in their school surroundings, and prepared to engage with what classroom learning has to offer is a necessary precursor to raising and sustaining achievement. Being held accountable against fixed requirements where this occurs is likely to stifle creative improvement action.

The accountability imperative

Accountability by schools to their political masters is not simply an English phenomenon. It is global in character, impacting with varying degrees of intensity on school leadership and on classroom practice. A notion borrowed from the corporate world, it has grown in prominence in education over the last two decades. Accountability rests on two key mutually reinforcing ideas – answerability for actions taken (or not taken) and enforceability, that is, attendant sanctions for failure to comply or deliver. Implicitly this is about the exercise of power. As Day and Klein (1987) observe, constructing accountability requires a definition of relationships between actors, delineating respective positions of power. However, it also implies agency on the part of those being held to account, since they themselves are in positions of power over the lives or welfare of others. So, in the educational field, accountability became increasingly attractive to governments from the mid- to late 1970s onwards as it offered leverage on schools seen to be underperforming and on teachers accused of jeopardising their pupils' futures. This might, in one sense, be regarded as shared accountability but only in a hierarchically devolved context and strictly in the form of upward and individual answerability to a higher authority and not in the collegial sense that 'sharing' might genuinely imply.

It was not coincidental that political interest in accountability grew in proportion to research on school effectiveness, as it was beginning to show that schools could make a difference in spite of children's socio-economic background. This provided policy makers not only with a rationale but with data gathering and analytic tools for comparing schools, devising benchmarks and setting targets. With each passing year the tools and mechanisms of accountability have become more complex, more demanding and more international in scope so that OECD comparative data, for example, have stirred policy makers into even more concerted action and intensified pressure on schools. In the American context Peter Sacks writes:

> Never before had American government been so critical of public schools, and never had so many false claims been made about education in the name of 'evidence' . . . Indeed the 'group-think' quality to the reform crusade has been made possible by widespread trust in several highly questionable beliefs sustained by the powerful coupling of business and political interests.
>
> (Sacks, 1999: 5)

Without any well-grounded evidence, governments in a number of countries have put their faith in a target-driven culture with pervasive influence in health, social welfare, and policing as well as in education. In the UK, complaints from the police service have brought to prominence the diversion of their priorities, making trivial arrests in order to meet government targets.[1] In her Reith Lecture in 2004 Baroness O' Neill spoke of the fraud perpetuated in a range of public services by 'perverse indicators' which in turn were producing perverse practices across a range of public agencies. Nicholls and Berliner (2007) draw similar conclusions and offer parallel examples in the US context in which they cite Campbell's Law, which posits that the greater the social consequences associated with a quantitative indicator (such as test scores), the more likely it is that the indicator itself will become corrupted – and the more likely it is that the use of the indicator will corrupt the social processes it was intended to monitor.

Earl and Fullan, commenting in a Canadian context, but with appeal to wider international relevance, describe school leaders as 'caught in the nexus of accountability and improvement, trying to make sense of the role that data can and should play in school leadership' (2003: 383). The impact of this nexus on the quality and priorities of leadership they link to a reluctance in risk taking and a focus on learning:

> we have found school leaders to be more concerned with accounting than with learning, with control than with teaching, with compliance than with risk-taking, and with public relations than with student experiences.
>
> (Sackney and Mitchell, in press)

This view is echoed by an English headteacher:

> I have three pistols to my head: one is the need to prepare the school for another visit from the inspectors because we are in Special Measures, another is the need to present a case to the local authority which is threatening to close the school and another is the need to improve the attainment figures so we can be lifted out of the status of being 'a school in challenging circumstances'. And then there is the small matter of trying to lead and manage the school on a day-to-day basis and meet the needs of our students and the community.
>
> (quoted in Frost, 2005: 76)

The increased emphasis on standardised testing in England has been widely seen as one of the causal factors of the recruitment and retention crisis (MacBeath, 2006) and a growing disenchantment among English teachers, primarily with what is seen as a vocation now robbed of initiative, spontaneity and ownership (Ball, 2001; Fielding, 2001; Galton and MacBeath, 2002; MacBeath and Galton, 2004) leading to what Brown and Lauder (1991) have termed 'trained incapacity'.

It is remarkable to find close parallels with this in Denmark, a country with a long-standing democratic tradition and commitment to grass roots initiative, but over the last few years neo-conservative forces have been stressing the need for central, state control over content matters and for quality assurance, with schools made financially autonomous and accountable. Schools' test results have been on the Ministry's web site since 2003 accompanied by national testing, binding 'goals' for each stage of schooling. Reiterating the complaint of the English headteacher mentioned above, Moos *et al.* (2001) describe Danish school leaders as left in a 'cross fire' between several competing interests:

> First, there are national objectives for schools that – beyond the demand for basic skills – focus on liberal education, or the development of *Bildung/Dannelse*, meaning the effort to assist and facilitate children to become citizens in a democratic society. Second, there are local authorities' demands for financial accountability, and, thirdly, there is a school culture where teachers are used to being very autonomous and not eager to be managed or led by 'new, strong, visible' school leaders described by the Government and the National Association of Local Authorities.

The greater the pressure from externally driven accountability requirements and the higher the stakes, the more likely it is that schools and teachers will adopt tactical measures to meet targets and/or avoid sanctions. In the United States the famous 'Texas miracle' under the governorship of George W. Bush was shown to be a deception of a high order. An analysis by Boston College's Walt Haney (2000) concluded that the dramatic rise in pass rates for high school students on the Texas Assessment of Academic Skills and decrease in dropout rate was illusory, in part due to a doubling of the numbers 'in special education' (therefore excluded from Grade 10 tests), and a significant rise in grade retention (students held back for another year), including as many as 30 per cent of black and Hispanic students. In fact, rather than the reported 20 per cent increase, Haney's analysis showed a sharp decrease despite heavy coaching for the test. In Chicago, as Leavitt and Dubner (2005) have shown, teachers' cheating on tests has been widespread, not because teachers were intrinsically untrustworthy but because a high stakes environment destroys trust and collegiality.

It is paradoxical that while the nature and impact of learning is now recognised as lying outside schools (Lo, 1999; MacBeath *et al.*, 2007) teachers are increasingly being held more accountable for the performance of those they attempt to teach. As we discussed in relation to our first principle, we know more than ever about the powerful formative influence of the early years, about the effects of deprivation and, most disturbingly, in recent times, about the shaping of children's intelligence, personality and behaviour in those critical inter-uterine years and in early childhood. Yet growing alongside this body of knowledge is the political imperative to make schools more transparent, more effective and more accountable. And the burden falls squarely on teachers to demonstrate that it is good teaching, not environment, not family, not socio-economic factors, not culture, not history, that makes the difference.

Leading for learning

In a market driven system with local management of schools, teachers are held to account through senior leaders, on whom the burden of accountability falls. In almost every country where external accountability has gone hand in hand with devolved management there is a local version of Elmore's 'American' myth:

> Accountability systems, and American views of leadership, tend to treat school leaders or principals as the primary agents of accountability in schools. The mythology of American education is heavily tilted in the direction of 'strong leaders make good schools.
>
> (Elmore, 2005: 11)

It falls to strong leaders therefore to embrace 'instructional leadership', exercised through systems of observation, monitoring, appraisal, benchmarking and targets, a form of internal accountability and self-inspection. While the DfES in England has advocated 'intelligent accountability', school leaders remain to be convinced that policy makers really do understand the nature and complexity of what that means and how it translates into the inner life of schools. In an Australian study, Dempster and Berry (2003) reported that 'over three-fifths (72 per cent) of respondents agreed that the values they considered most important are being overwhelmed by economic rationalism'. Economic rationalism in education they defined as creating an environment where standards are set, where competition is seen as a key performance motivator, and where being held to account against the standards are central to sound schooling. These three policy drivers, teachers feel, are overtaking values such as applauding effort, acknowledging difference, encouraging imagination and stirring creativity. Why a government's almost exclusive emphasis on standards, competition and accountability is so strident, remains at odds for many teachers with their daily experience of children's needs, interests and abilities. As Cuban put it:

> To reformers, teachers are both the problem and solution. Precisely because of this paradox, reformers in every generation have dreamed of teacher-proof curriculum, texts, and other materials to promote designs that leapfrog the teacher and get students to learn. No classroom reform I have ever studied from reading through to using computers or participated in over the last half-century has ever been fully implemented without teachers understanding the change, receiving help in putting it into practice, and adapting it to fit the particular classroom.
>
> (Cuban, 2001: 7)

There is a widespread scepticism as to whether uniform policies can genuinely connect with the environments of twenty-first century schools and whether external accountability measures can ever be fine-tuned and sensitive enough to take account of the inner life of the school. Over a century ago Arnold Tomkins, a New York administrator, wrote:

> The organisation of the school must be kept mobile to its inner life. To one who is accustomed to wind up the machine and trust it to run for fixed periods, this constantly shifting shape of things will seem unsafe and troublesome. And troublesome it is, for no fixed plan can be followed; no two schools are alike; and the same school is shifting, requiring constant attention and nimble judgement on the part of the school leader.
>
> (Tomkins, 1895: 4)

School leaders have always had to be 'nimble of judgement'. What has changed, however, is the scale and scope of the areas in which those judgements now have to be exercised. The tension for leadership is to manage the fit between the external policy world and the internal world of the school, between leadership for learning as seen by government and leadership for learning as seen by schools themselves. The attempt to remain distinctive, reflecting the goals and aspirations of those who constitute the school community, is inevitably in tension with the countervailing forces of public accountability to mandated performance standards. In a faith school context, Gerald Grace has commented on the juggling required in managing successful performance set against the mission of a school rooted in spiritual and human values. The danger is that as schools adapt to each latest fad they lose sight of their own central goals and their own capacity for resistance and self-assertion. As Earl and Fullan (2003) comment:

> Schools that are able to take charge of change, rather than being controlled by it are more effective and improve more rapidly than ones that are not (Rosenholtz, 1989; Stoll and Fink, 1996; Gray *et al.*, 1999). There is not enough time for adaptation by trial and error or for experimentation with fads that inevitably lose their appeal.

Professional accountability

In England, the General Teaching Council (GTCE) has argued for schools to be given more responsibility, a greater role in steering, in shaping their own improvement and with an emphasis on professional accountability to replace the culture of compliance to external mandate. Professional accountability recognises the commitment that teachers bring first and foremost to their pupils, underpinned by a strongly held value position. Its essential tenets as described by Eraut are:

- a moral commitment to serve the interests of clients;
- a professional obligation to self-monitor and to periodically to review the effectiveness of one's practice;
- a professional obligation to extend one's repertoire, to reflect on one's experience and to develop one's expertise;
- an obligation that is professional as well as contractual to contribute to the quality of one's organisation;
- an obligation to reflect on and contribute to discussion on the changing role of one's profession in a wider society.

(Eraut, 1996)

It rests on 'the connective tissue' of trust, a fragile commodity, hard to construct and easy to destroy writes Elmore (1992: 20). Trust, he argues, is a compound of *respect*, listening to and valuing the views of others; *personal regard*, intimate and sustained personal relationships that are the very stuff of professional relationships; *competence*, the capacity to produce desired results in relationships with others; and *personal integrity*, truthfulness and honesty in human concourse.

To sum up, trust lies at the heart of professional accountability. This is a value that does not figure at all in the kind of economic rationalism described earlier. There, it seems to be assumed by policy makers that teachers are not to be 'trusted'. They are assumed not to know what are appropriate standards for learners and they are assumed to be in need of constant ranking through comparative measures with other schools. And above all it is assumed they need surveillance to ensure that they stay on task. Without the trust of governments, their employers and the wider community, there can be no professional accountability. When trust exists, school leaders and teachers are likely to feel the kinds of obligations, outlined by Eraut, as keenly as any other professional group.

Accountability through self-evaluation

The movement from central and local forms of governance to school self-government has been embraced by countries around the world for a mix of motives but with the common assumption that as power is pushed down so accountability is pushed up. Thus inspection, audit, quality assurance and other measures of external accountability have given way to school self-evaluation, often tending to be seen as a form of self-inspection carried out by senior managers who conduct a form of internal accounting but with a weather eye on their external political paymasters.

Common to the varying forms it takes in different countries, self-evaluation is driven by three motives, almost impossible to disentangle – the improvement motive, the economic motive and the accountability motive. From an improvement point of view it is taken as read that well-embedded self-evaluation drives improvement and that improvement is indeed a misnomer if teachers and school leaders are unaware of where they are, where they're going and how they will know when they've arrived. With a compelling improvement motive and strong self-confident evaluation, accountability both internally and externally would seem to follow logically. With schools responsible for their own quality assurance this is good news for government paymasters because the costly burden of external quality assurance and accountability measures are significantly reduced. In England the move to shorter, sharper inspections owed its main driving logic to the Gershon Report (2004) which recommended a saving of over 4 million pounds by, among other cost saving devices, making schools responsible for their own self-evaluation. The presentation of the new relationship with schools was couched in terms of intelligent accountability and learning-centred self-evaluation. The trinity of principles was spelt out by the DfES as:

1　Intelligent accountability should be founded on the school's own views of how well it is serving its pupils and its priorities for improvement.
2　Strong self-evaluation should be embedded in the school's day-to-day practice.
3　Effective self-evaluation should ask the most important questions about pupils' learning, achievements and development.

The three principles were amplified in the 2004 DfES document *Towards Intelligent Accountability for Schools* to include 36 recommendations as to changes in the relationship between accountability and self-evaluation. The vision of the future, therefore, was one in which schools would grasp the logic of their accountability through the kind of strong internal professional accountability argued for by Elmore and others (2005). The Standing International Conference of Central and General Inspectorates in Europe (SICI) argued for a model of improvement and accountability in which external inspection would focus on the following question:

> How effective is the school in achieving continuous improvement through evaluating the quality of its own provision and taking action to build on its own strengths and address its weaknesses?

This rationale for strong self-evaluation accompanied by lighter touch external verification resonates with policy shifts in many other countries of the world. In Hong Kong, for example, the Education and Manpower Bureau radically reformulated its quality assurance policy to one in which self-evaluation would be the bedrock of accountability. The policy initiated in 2002, entitled School Development and Accountability (SDA), embraced intelligent accountability though self-evaluation frameworks, and performance indicators, professional development for principals, the tools of self-evaluation and evaluation both summative and formative. As the Impact Study over three years showed, change followed Rogers' classic innovation curve (Figure 10.1).

The slow nature of change may be explained by the time it takes to find a reconciliation among the three driving motives of improvement, accountability and economy. What the Impact Study in Hong Kong was able to demonstrate, as in England and elsewhere, was that these implicit tensions can only be reconciled when schools grasp the opportunity to tell their own story according

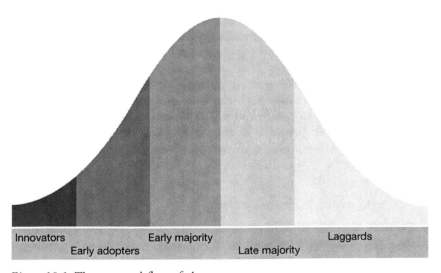

Figure 10.1 The pace and flow of change

to their own values, priorities and criteria. Out of strong self-knowledge and evidence of improvement, accountability can flow as a natural consequence. There is an abundance of examples internationally which attest to how the accountability agenda can be met through bottom-up self-evaluation initiatives. A common characteristic of these is captured by the leadership for learning principles but most saliently in the third principle, that of dialogue. It is through the shared dialogue among all stakeholders that quality and effectiveness are both problematised and realised. It is this form of storytelling that illuminates quality and drives improvement. Without self-evaluation for improvement, however, accountability comes to be seen as imposed and a burdensome extra. When driven by purely economic motives self-evaluation becomes ritualised and resented.

Ben Jaafar (2006) participated in two pan-Canadian studies investigating the constructions and effects of educational accountability policies, from which she and her colleagues 'concluded that Canadian educational accountability is best described as a hybrid model of results-oriented EBA [economic-bureaucratic accountability] and process-oriented EPA [ethical-professional accountability]' (Ben Jaafar, 2006: 64). Her subsequent analyses position the Canadian perspective as 'inquiry-based accountability' (Ben Jaafar, 2006: 69), in which all measures, including large-scale and classroom-based assessments, are seen as entry points into professional discussions about learning experiences, opportunities, outcomes, and desires, which can be used to inform and direct attention and action so as to achieve the greatest learning benefits for all students. This approach to accountability is consistent with the goals of learning-centred leadership, but it is not an approach that is commonly acknowledged or valued in the accountability literature. We therefore see a need to reconstruct the discourse to raise the profile and the status of inquiry-based accountability.

In Canada at McGill University, Bill Smith's programme of school self-assessment activities was set in a top-down accountability context but was able to show that schools thrive as learning communities 'through approaches which connect leadership to learning'. The project, *Schools Speaking to Stakeholders*, developed frameworks for internal accountability which gave teachers the confidence and equipped them with the tools to account to external quality assurance agencies. *Schools Speaking to Stakeholders* was a close and coincidental cousin of the National Union of Teachers' (NUT) project, *Schools Speak for Themselves*, in which indicators were developed from the ground up by pupils, teachers and parents.

The leadership for learning story

The Trenton example of self-evaluation is one of lateral and professional accountability, reflecting a quite different form from that familiar to schools in London, Athens, Brisbane or Oslo for example, yet a shared commitment to self-evaluation was one of the main driving forces for these eight disparate teams of researchers to come together in the first place. All brought to the project a belief in the power of schools to speak for themselves through the acoustic of students, teachers and parents. In New Jersey the model described was built from more than a decade of self-evaluation and appreciative inquiry in different parts of the United States. At the other end of the country Brad Portin in Seattle had been engaged in the KEYS school self-evaluation project whose rationale he describes in these terms:

> The initiative's theory-of-action holds that school improvement can be set in motion through a reflective tool (such as the KEYS instrument) acting as a mirror, stimulating action, providing a source of important issues to attend to, and offering an organising rubric for a variety of activities that schools might pursue. The KEYS strategy, thus, places its bets on the power of the process, one that encourages schools to begin down a path of clearer understanding of strengths and weaknesses towards a vision of what they might do to improve their service to students.

The assumption of the KEYS project was that the improvement and accountability processes had to be built school-by-school, with, and by, the unique configuration of people who comprised the school community. The elements of the KEYS approach provide immediate parallels with belief systems in all of the other participating countries and in many senses describe the intentions of the LfL Project itself, encouraging schools to adopt a deliberative process to bring to light connections between leadership and learning that might otherwise have remained hidden.

The process, which we have described as holding up a *mirror* to the school, surfaces that which is not seen in everyday action, which might otherwise remain hidden without a deliberative process to bring it to light. The result is a portrait (however incomplete and perception-bound) that encourages school personnel to look more closely at their action, programmes, culture, and capacities and how those elements influence their efforts to improve education.

In Innsbruck Michael Schratz had published widely on self-evaluation and engaged in pioneering work with schools on self-evaluation through photo inquiry, the LfL Project offering the opportunity to test this process in the challenging climate of US East middle schools and high schools. Michael Schratz had also played a leading role in the 18-country European Project (MacBeath *et al.*, 2000) which was able to demonstrate that in cultures as far removed as Iceland and Greece, schools could develop a sense of their own professional accountability regardless of the prevailing political climate.

Within that project, Greece had become a committed player despite some initial scepticism. This provided the impetus for our Greek partners to become involved in the LfL Project through George Bagakis, a tireless advocate of self-evaluation in his country, and with a commitment to use that experience in researching leadership for learning. As in Greece, *Schools Must Speak for Themselves* had been translated into Danish and Lejf Moos had also been a long-standing advocate of self-evaluation. Together with Jorunn Møller in Norway, he led the vanguard of resistance to the imposition of borrowed and transplanted models of self-evaluation, arguing for the need to grow them from their own cultural roots.

From Queensland, the Australian team brought to the project lengthy experience in school renewal in the Catholic school sector and extensive involvement in school development in government sector schools. Both sets of experiences relied heavily on school-led evaluations conducted collaboratively by school staff and both produced plans for improvement in existing practices or different approaches to persistent problems.

While the Leadership for Learning Project was not essentially about school self-evaluation, the eight research teams shared a common commitment to the underpinning values of school-led inquiry and to exploring ways in which, through being attuned to the voices of teachers, students and parents, we can better comprehend learning, leadership and their interrelationship. In this sense the seeds of the five LfL principles were already sown.

Despite these seminal values being held in common and an understanding of accountability as an integral aspect of school self-evaluation, there was difficulty in arriving at a common understanding of how to deal with account-ability to external authorities. Finding common ground with regard to the very different kinds of national tensions between school autonomy and government mandate was also not easy. This fifth 'accountability' principle was in fact a late entry to our suite. That it was suggested by the US (New Jersey) team was of itself significant as the *No Child Left Behind* policy was bearing down hard on American schools, a force which leadership could not ignore and which impinged in a daily way on classroom learning and the work of teachers. While in Athens, accountability appeared to be of least concern to teachers, the reconciliation of learning and performativity agendas were, in practice, equally problematic.

The implicit nature of accountability in some places and its highly explicit nature in others set in train a dialogue which served to tease out the essential common elements. It aroused vigorous debate when the fifth principle was introduced at the final (2006) Athens conference. It was a late addition to the set of four but one that had a compelling rationale given the policy framework within which all 22 LfL schools were working, external accountability exert-ing an explicit policy pressure to a greater or lesser degree. It arose from what was perceived as a need for 'intelligent accountability', that is, not a slavish compliance with external indicators and inspection criteria but a self-knowledge and self-confidence to recognise, in Fullan's terminology, what is worth fighting for. Nonetheless, the concept, or perhaps simply the terminology, aroused heated debate, met with terms such as 'delicate', 'challenging', 'complex' and 'worrying'. Despite attempts at definitions and clarification, pleas were made repeatedly for 'greater clarity' and a shared understanding that could be accepted across countries and cultures. The fifth principle attempted to provide that clarity.

The fifth principle

Leadership for learning rests on a shared sense of accountability by:

- taking account of political realities and exercising informed choice as to how the school tells its own story;
- developing a shared approach to internal accountability as a precondition of accountability to external agencies;
- maintaining a focus on evidence and its congruence with the core values of the school;
- reframing policy and practice when they conflict with core values;
- embedding a systematic approach to self-evaluation at classroom, school and community levels;
- maintaining a continuing focus on sustainability, succession and leaving a legacy.

The first of the these six aspects of the principle re-asserts the importance of schools speaking for themselves but with a strong political sense of where the challenges lie and, as the further elaboration of the principle asserts, can only be accomplished with the self-confidence that evidences informed choice. Choice in the way of telling one's own story rests, however, not only on empirical evidence but also on core values, and the sustainability of these is the legacy that leadership leaves to the next generation of teachers and students. We might have assumed that realising these principles might be easier in some of our participant countries than others but while the pressure of league tables, targets, high stakes testing, and external accountability were less acute in Greece and Austria, and only beginning to be felt in Norway and Denmark, all school staff were experiencing an inexorable tide of change and the 'loose-tight paradox' (Day, 2000) of local decision-making responsibilities alongside increased public scrutiny and external accountability. All were experiencing in differing ways the tension between political pressures on attainment and their own commitment to a broader set of educational goals for their students. All participating countries were touched by PISA comparisons, and the need to compete in a global educational economy. As Jorunn Møller (2002: 13) has argued in a Norwegian context:

> Improving the ranking becomes an aim in itself, not the efforts to understand and discuss how schooling could be improved, and what goals are most important to achieve . . . The problem is that the information gained from these studies is often too technically flawed to serve as an accurate measure of national effectiveness.

In all of the seven countries of the LfL Project, PISA was a silent and insidious presence.

Nowhere among the eight sites of the project was accountability made more explicit as a public, professional and personal responsibility than in New Jersey.

The most pointed description of the tensions between improvement and accountability comes from a District Superintendent in a US East city. Torch Lytle, who was a keen supporter of the Leadership for Learning Project and a highly progressive system leader, said the following:

> One of the biggest challenges in NCLB [No Child Left Behind] is trying to improve learning in the schools. I worry that principals, not necessarily teachers, get preoccupied with AYP [Average yearly Progress] . . . and I've seen my role as protecting the district from NCLB and Average Yearly Progress.

As District Superintendent with a keen interest in promoting leadership for learning, Lytle has tried to support senior managers in dealing with the dilemmas they faced in having to demonstrate a continuous rise in students' test scores or be subject to the sanctions imposed by NCLB and AYP or alternatively focus on deep authentic learning. For Lytle, the priority is to help staff sustain the moral purpose of education, through engaging students in meaningful activities and critical conversations. His firm belief is that in a climate where learning is led and leading is learned, test scores will look after themselves. In the year 2005/6 Lytle made the difficult decision to remove several long-term principals from schools in which there was no evidence of a focus on learning and no sense of accountability to that moral purpose. This was an unprecedented step in a context where once someone had become a principal, he/she could remain in the position until they decided to retire.

As to the impact on the schools themselves, the New Jersey team reported that a focus on learning as a fundamental aspect of accountability had led to significant change. Involvement in the project had, it was claimed, clarified the importance of a focus on learning and the conditions for learning as a counterbalance to a focus on statutory standard assessments alone. This had given the impetus to developing a shared approach to internal accountability as a precondition of accountability to external agencies. An expression of increased self-confidence in tuning it to the core values of the school was made evident in the ongoing engagement of principals and teachers, not only in internal dialogue but also in communication with parents centred on students' learning. In one school the example is given that 'when decisions about learning issues are taken, the principal phones all parents who express concerns in order to inform them and discuss with them relevant issues'.

While the US East school district was, as a community, facing federal policy imperatives, schools were, it was said, given a new-found sense of their own efficacy by 'focussing on deepening learning through engaging students in meaningful activities and exciting conversations'. Two of the staff in two of the schools gave a particularly high agreement rating to the following questionnaire item:

> In this school we stand by our values and principles in meeting external pressure.

At the end of the Leadership for Learning Project each country's research team was asked to submit a report structured around the five LfL principles. Some of those reports, such as the one from New Jersey quoted above, reveal accountability as an explicit policy pressure, while in other countries it has to be teased out from cultural modus operandi. In these contexts, accountability did not figure explicitly in the discursive repertoire but was embedded in the way in which teachers experienced their responsibility and to whom they viewed themselves as answerable.

Being held to account for student performance was a dilemma for leadership in those places where the stakes were judged to be highest. But although, in Austria, for example, accountability demands assumed a lower profile than in the US or UK, there was, nonetheless, pressure exerted by external authorities rather than by the schools themselves, attributed to the changing political landscape. Senior leaders used this as a lever to persuade teachers of the need for change, to provide a more explicit rationale for their pupils' learning and share more openly with their colleagues. As the Austrian project report described it, the critical friend also played a crucial role in helping staff understand the changing political context in which they were now working and the need to sharpen the focus on shared approaches to learning-centred practice. The establishment of the Leadership Academy in Innsbruck, led by Michael Schratz, was a system-wide initiative to embed a learning-centred conception of leadership in the inner life of schools.

A sense of disquiet about accountability was reported by the Greek research team. Accountability simply did not figure in the professional discourse and teachers struggled to find an appropriate Greek translation for a concept seen by them as deeply puzzling. However, Greek teachers had a strong sense of duty to their students and to their principals, combined with an absence of professional learning conversations and a profound reluctance to assume responsibility outside their own classroom. For two of three Greek principals this was such a significant cultural barrier to change that, it was felt, it would take a generation to shift the professional mind set. Yet, this has to be set alongside a hunger among Greek teachers to learn more about their craft. At the numerous conferences organised by George Bagakis and his team it was a constant source of surprise to researchers from other countries that more than a hundred teachers would attend an all-day conference on a Saturday running on into the early hours of the evening. Staff from English schools re-visiting the same Athens school two years on could hardly believe the change in attitudes and practice that had taken place within that short time.

While accountability was not a theme explicitly addressed in these Greek conferences the focus on learning and the knowledge creation which flowed from it led to a sharper awareness of what teachers owed to their colleagues as well as to their students. The statement in the fourth principle 'developing coherence among leadership activities and demonstrating how they impact on learning' contains within it an expression of rich internal accountability in which teachers' dialogue and peer observations acquire a more critical edge.

One of the activities which featured in the LfL conferences for the 22 partici-pating schools was for teachers and senior leaders to prepare vignettes, short stories of practice which were then shared with colleagues from other schools, other countries. This process, a form of accountability in itself, helped signifi-cantly to make the connections between learning and leadership and what it means to open up practice to the scrutiny of others.

Ann Lieberman's experience with American teachers provides confirming evidence of the link between a learning conversation and a leadership impulse. She also found that teachers with no official status beyond that of classroom teacher were impelled into leadership activity by virtue of the new way in which they were framing their individual and shared learning. These teachers with whom she worked returned to their school after summer workshops experienc-ing a strong sense of accountability to their colleagues who had not had the same enriching professional development opportunity which they themselves had enjoyed. The parallels with the LfL Project are striking. There was a significant strand of evidence within the schools that the building of confidence and mutual self-assurance was leading both to a more distributed form of leadership and within that to a more developed sense of professional accountability (Lieberman and Friedrich, 2008).

In London, leadership teams in the three schools joined forces to plan a conference, bringing together the entire teaching staff from these three schools to focus on learning and leadership and to embed a stronger sense of internal accountability within a high pressure/high stakes political context. The government's Leadership Incentive Grant (LIG) was used creatively to give time and space for teachers off-timetable to support their colleagues in greater risk taking in pedagogy and sharing of leadership.

In the report from the Seattle team, it was through a 'continuity of partici-pation' in the project that staff involved were able to build and to sustain, over time, a sense of self-efficacy which they described as 'a cornerstone of account-ability both within the school and in relation to external stakeholders'. The school within a school which grew out of involvement in the project was the initiative of one classroom teacher who enlisted the support of her colleagues in a shared enterprise with an explicit underpinning of professional accountability.

In Norway, responsibility is identified as a key feature of the development of leadership teams and shared leadership practice, in common with Denmark where responsibility is implicit in the way teams are organised:

> In the self-governing teams there is no formal leader. Instead, they make use of everybody's resources by talking about teaching, students and learning.
>
> (Denmark report)

As in other aspects of the principles there is evidence of a slow movement to some common ground but from very different starting points. What is held in common is that, however accountability is understood, it has to confront top-down mandates that disempower rather than empower teachers. When there is strong internal support and conviction, as many of these LfL schools report, there is resilience and vitality to tell the school's story in their own register and in terms of their own core values.

Conclusion

Our work in the Leadership for Learning Project has reinforced our view that if leadership and learning are to be connected consciously, then shared accountability must be developed amongst school staff. Doing so requires a commitment to understanding the inner workings of the school and the significance of school-led evaluation. Without this commitment, accountability remains as an external demand requiring coercive extrinsic motivation, dampening the excitement and intrinsic motivation of planning and action for innovation and improvement. With this in mind, we leave the chapter by putting forward a series of questions (Table 10.1) derived from principle 5 which we believe

Table 10.1 Questions for staff and school leaders

Principle No 5. Leadership for learning practice involves a shared sense of accountability in which:	*Questions for staff and school leaders*
5 (a). a systematic approach to self-evaluation is embedded at classroom, school and community levels	Is a systematic approach to self-evaluation embedded at classroom and school levels? Is self-evaluation extended to the parents and community?
5 (b). there is a focus on evidence and its congruence with the core values of the school	Is our self-evaluation based on evidence? Does our self-evaluation reflect our shared core values?
5 (c). a shared approach to internal accountability is a precondition of accountability to external agencies	In our school are we firstly accountable to each other?
5 (d). national policies are recast in accordance with the school's core values	In our school do we stand by our values and principles in meeting external pressures?
5 (e). the school chooses how to tell its own story taking into account political realities	Do we decide how best to portray our school to external stakeholders and authorities taking into account political realities?
5 (f). there is a continuing focus on sustainability, succession and leaving a legacy	Do we make systematic efforts to ensure that the school has the capacity to improve and be successful in the future.

schools committed to learning should ask themselves. Most of the questions are for members of staff and school leaders but two are important to ask students because their views are critical to how seriously the school takes its interest in shared accountability.

Questions for students

• Are we asked our views on how well the school works?
• Are my parents asked for their views on how well the school is run?

The questions for staff members and school leaders are linked to principle 1 and each of its six elaborations. Again, answers to these questions can become prompts to action in connecting leadership and learning.

Note

1 Newspaper reports 17 May 2007.

References

Ball, S.J. (2001) 'Labour, learning and the economy', in M. Fielding (ed.) *Taking Education Really Seriously: Four Years Hard Labour*, London: RoutledgeFalmer.

Ben Jaafar, S. (2006) 'From performance-based to inquiry-based accountability', *Brock Education*, 16 (2): 62–77.

Brown, P. and Lauder, H. (1991) 'Education, economy and social change', *International Studies in Sociology of Education*, 1 (1&2): 3–23.

Cuban, L. (2001) 'Improving urban schools in the 21st century: do's and don'ts or advice to true believers and skeptics of whole school reform', OERI Summer Institute, CSR Grantees Conference, July.

Day, C. (2000) 'Teachers in the twenty-first century: time to renew the vision', *Teachers and Teaching: Theory and Practice*, 6 (1): 101–15.

Day, P. and Klein, R. (1987) *Accountabilities: Five Public Services*, London: Tavistock.

Dempster, N. and Berry, V. (2003) 'Blindfolded in a minefield: dilemmas in ethical decision making', *Cambridge Journal of Education*, 33 (3): 457–77.

Department for Education and Skills (2007) *Towards Intelligent Accountability for Schools*, London: DFES.

Earl, L. and Fullan, M. (2003) 'Using data in leadership for learning', *Cambridge Journal of Education*, 33 (3): 383–94.

Elmore, R.F. (1992) 'Why restructuring alone won't improve teaching', *Educational Leadership*, 49 (7): 20–8.

Elmore, R. (2005) *Agency, Reciprocity, and Accountability in Democratic Education*, Boston, MA: Consortium for Policy Research in Education.

Eraut, M. (1996) 'Developing the professions: training, quality and accountability', in P. Gordon (ed.) *The Study of Education: Inaugal Lectures: End of an Era? Vol. 4*, London: Woburn Press, pp. 168–89.

Fielding, M. (ed.) (2001) *Taking Education Really Seriously: Four Years' Hard Labour*, London: RoutledgeFalmer.

Frost, D. (2005) 'Resisting the juggernaut: building capacity through teacher leadership in spite of it all', *Leading and Managing*, 10 (2): 83.

Galton, M. and MacBeath, J. (2002) *A Life in Teaching?* London: National Union of Teachers.

Gershon, P. (2004) *Releasing Resources to the Front Line*, London: HM Treasury.

Gray, J., Hopkins, D., Reynolds, D., Wilcox, B., Farrell, S. and Jesson, D. (1999) *Improving Schools: Performance and Potential*, Buckingham: Open University Press.

Gronn, P. (2007) 'Grooming next generation school leaders', in N. Dempster (ed.) *The Treasure Within: School Leadership and Succession Planning*, Canberra: The Australian College of Educators.

Haney, W. (2000) 'The myth of the Texas miracle in Education', *Education Policy Analysis Archives*, 8 (41) http://epaa.asu.edu/epaa/v8n41/.

James, C. and Whiting, D. (1998) 'The career perspectives of deputy headteachers', *Educational Management and Administration*, 26 (4): 26–34.

Johnson, S.M. (2004) *Finders and Keepers*, New York: Jossey-Bass.

Lashway, L. (2003) 'Finding leaders for hard-to-staff schools', *ERIC Digest*, 173, December.

Leavitt, S.D. and Dubner, S.J. (2005) *Freakonomics*, London: Allen Lane.

Lieberman, A. and Friedrich, L. (2008) 'Changing teachers from within: teachers as leaders', in J. MacBeath and Y.C. Cheng (eds) *Leadership for Learning: International Perspectives*, Amsterdam: Sense Publishers.

Lo, L.N.K. (1999) 'Knowledge, education and development in Hong Kong and Shanghai', *Education Journal*, 27 (1): 55–91.

MacBeath, J. (2006) 'The talent enigma', *International Journal of Leadership in Education*, 9 (3): 183–204.

MacBeath, J. and Galton, M. (2004) *A Life in Secondary Teaching?* London: National Union of Teachers.

MacBeath, J., Jakobsen, L., Meuret, D. and Schratz, M. (2000) *Self-Evaluation in European Schools: A Story of Change*, London: Routledge.

MacBeath, J, Gray, J., Cullen, J., Frost D., Steward, S. and Swaffield, S. (2007) *Schools on the Edge: Responding to Challenging Circumstances*, London: Paul Chapman Publishing.

Moos, L. (2002) 'Cultural isomorphs in theories and practice of school leadership', in K. Leithwood and P. Hallinger (eds) *Second International Handbook of Educational Leadership and Administration*, Dordrecht: Kluwer, pp. 359–94.

Moos, L., Moller, J. and Joahnnsen, O. (2001) 'School leaders' working conditions: a cross case analysis of school leaders' opinions in Denmark', Norway and Sweden', UMEA Conference, September.

Møller, J. (2002) 'Democratic leadership in an age of managerial accountability', *Improving Schools*, 5 (2): 11–20.

Nicholls, S.L and Berliner, D.C. (2007) *Collateral Damages: How High Stakes Testing Corrupts American Schools*, Boston, MA: Harvard Education Press.

OECD (2001) *Teacher Exodus – The Meltdown Scenario*, Paris: Education Policy Analysis.

O'Neill, N. (2004) *A Question of Trust*, Cambridge: Cambridge University Press.

Portin, B., Beck, L., Knapp, M. and Murphy, J. (2003) *Self Reflective Renewal: Local Lessons for a National Initiative*, New York: Praeger.

Rogers, E.M. (1995) *Diffusion of Innovations*, New York: The Free Press.

Rosenholtz, S.J. (1989) *Teachers Workplace: The Social Organization of Schools*, New York: Teachers College Press.

Sackney, L. and Mitchell, C. (in press) 'Leadership for learning: a Canadian perspective', in J. MacBeath and Y.C. Cheng (eds) *Leadership for Learning: International Perspectives*, Rotterdam: Sense Publishers.

Sacks, P.J. (2001) *Standardized Minds: The High Price of America's Testing Culture*, New York: Da Capo Press.

Stoll, L. and Fink, D. (1996) *Changing Our Schools*, Buckingham: Open University Press.

Tomkins, A. (1895) *School Administrator*, New York, quoted in K. Riley (1998) *School Leadership and School Culture*, Washington, DC: World Bank.

11 Leaving a legacy

Helping schools to collaborate in a climate of competition

David Frost, John MacBeath and Jorunn Møller

In the many conference presentations of the Leadership for Learning Project we were challenged, particularly from American and British audiences and others steeped in the school effectiveness tradition, as to the outcomes of the project. Our response was always to question the equating of 'outcomes' with measures of student attainment which we regard as weak proxies for the real work of schools. As mentioned in Chapter 5, to try and measure or compare student attainment over a three-year period in eight country sites would have been a distraction and have produced, at best, highly ambiguous data. We saw the potential to affect policy and practice and to build capacity for leading learning at school and inter-school level as outcomes worth pursuing.

Educational research has been criticised for being piecemeal rather than cumulative, for failing to engage with stakeholders and users in order to ensure take up or impact with 'findings', published in the hope that policy makers or practitioners will take notice and make changes (Hargreaves, 1998). There are important questions for any research project about the project's legacy. This chapter illustrates ways in which the LfL Project sought to address this concern by promulgating a continuing live discourse.

Practical and intellectual tools

The legacy of the project was not just a set of insights and recommendations, rather it can be characterised as a set of intellectual and practical tools to help people fashion their own discourse. The use of the word 'tools' here draws on activity theory (Engeström, 1999a), a way of explaining the socio-cultural world in which we pursue our aspirations through the use of 'mediating artifacts'. Artifacts of various kinds help us, for example, to clarify our vision of possible futures, create strategic pathways and diagnose and explain our practices (Engeström, 1999b).

In the LfL Project the tools we were seeking to leave behind a set of principles for practice, a conceptual framework, developmental strategies and practical tools to support professional and organisational learning. The key principles for practice were offered as a framework for a wide range of discursive activities such as reviewing practice, consulting colleagues, students and other stakeholders or identifying priorities for development. Another key resource was the conceptual framework offered as a way of understanding the interrelationship of learning and leadership, both conceptualised as agential activities. In addition, a range of techniques and instruments were offered for use in situations such as professional development workshops and self-evaluation activities.

This is illustrated by two examples. The first is a collaboration between a school in Nessoden, Norway (Bakkelokka) and a school in Yorkshire, England (Whitby) in which they came together to share ideas and embed the five LfL principles in their future planning and ongoing practice. The second is where a cluster of six secondary schools and two special schools in an English municipality used the tools and processes of the Carpe Vitam Project to assist them in developing a more collaborative approach to the development of practice.

Example 1: learning across national boundaries

It is within an international context that day-to-day practice opens to question 'the way we do things round here' and the application of common principles receives its sternest test. It requires a standing back from the familiarity of the everyday, what Czarniawska (1997) has termed 'outsidedness', a form of knowing by difference rather than by similarity:

> It aims at understanding not by identification ('they are like us') but by the recognition of differences – 'we are different from them and they are different from us; by exploring these differences we will understand our-selves better.'

> (Czarniawska, 1997: 62)

This proposition was rigorously tested over two professional development days in which staff of the two schools met in Norway and explored the five LfL principles. Starting with a Monday morning session, staff in groups 'talked out' the principles, making sense of them for themselves before dividing into pairs to consider further applications to their own schools and classrooms. This led to presentations to colleagues on the Tuesday afternoon, with each presentation framed by the question – What does this mean for us next year? The results were gathered in the form of tables written on flip charts. Each table indicated the meaning that participants took from the 'sub principle' or 'prompt to action' as we have called them elsewhere in this volume. The next column in the table specified how the 'prompt to action' translated into practice in the Norwegian and the English schools respectively. The tables show how these conversations sparked ideas and led to a resolve to reframe practice to bring it closer to the 'prompt to action' in question. Many things proved to be similar based on shared values, but some things were distinctive to the respective cultures. The use of time, the size of school, requirements to report measures of attainment and the deployment of staff (such as teaching assistants) for example, were important differences.

A focus on learning as an activity

This principle reflects a particular way of defining learning but also highlights the importance of strategies to keep the focus on learning rather than allowing energy and attention to be diverted to other dimensions of schooling.

Leadership for learning practice involves maintaining a focus on learning as an activity in which:

a everyone is a learner;
b learning relies on the effective interplay of social, emotional and cognitive processes;
c the efficacy of learning is highly sensitive to context and to the differing ways in which people learn;
d the capacity for leadership arises out of powerful learning experiences
e opportunities to exercise leadership enhance learning.

At the reporting back stage colleagues from the two schools were able to talk about what the principle meant to them, how practice differed between the two schools and what needed to be done. Notes of the discussion were presented in tabular form, for example:

Prompt to action	*What it means*	*What we do in our schools*
Everyone is a learner.	That we share the same language. That we feel we are learning for life; that everyone gets something out of it.	Similar: we have dialogue and think it's important to talk and *do* what we talk about. Different: Bakkelokka pupils have time set aside to review their learning.

Prompt to action	*What it means*	*What we do in our schools*
The efficacy of learning is highly sensitive to context and to the differing ways in which people learn.	An awareness of this enables us to adapt to our learners.	We have both done work on analysing learning styles. But pupil learning reviews are built in at Bakkelokka. Whitby could take this on board. Talking to pupils informs teachers so much and helps students understand differences.

Conditions for learning

This principle highlights the complexity of strategic action to create the optimum learning environment.

Leadership for learning practice involves creating conditions favourable to learning as an activity in which:

a cultures nurture the learning of everyone;
b everyone has opportunities to reflect on the nature, skills and processes of learning;
c physical and social spaces stimulate and celebrate learning;
d safe and secure environments enable everyone to take risks, cope with failure and respond positively to challenges;
e tools and strategies are used to enhance thinking about learning and the practice of teaching.

In the discussion of this principle the cultural and structural differences are again evident as the English school is a specialist school with different forms of funding, incentives and rewards, accountability and it is subject to greater performativity pressures than its Norwegian counterpart. The open plan design and collegial nature of the Norwegian school provides a more relaxed atmosphere for reflection and casual conversation. Nonetheless, the deeper lying values appear to be shared, both schools affirming the importance of self-expression, opportunity for students to fail with support, ownership of learning, emphasis on social skills, peer-led and team-led dialogue. The principle that learning is for everyone is a shared aspiration that the cultures in their respective schools model, nurturing the desire and ability to learn and go on learning. Below is an example of how the teachers reported back on their discussions.

Prompt to action	*What it means*	*What we do in our schools*
Safe and secure environments enable everyone to take risks, cope with failure and respond positively to challenges.	Safe to succeed or fail in the learning process at times.	Students are secure when more than one person helps with their subject learning. Open structures remove the fear of failure.

Creating an LfL dialogue

This principle might be recognised by some as 'pedagogic dialogue' but, in the Carpe Vitam Project, the way the link between leadership and learning has been characterised means that the leadership part of the equation is also pursued in a conscious and deliberate way.

Leadership for learning practice involves creating a dialogue about LfL in which:

a   LfL practice is made explicit, discussable and transferable;
b   there is active collegial inquiry focusing on the link between learning and leadership;
c   coherence is achieved through the sharing of values, understandings and practices;
d   factors which inhibit and promote learning and leadership are examined and addressed;
e   the link between leadership and learning is a shared concern for everyone.

In this particular workshop, this principle was set aside for later discussion.

Shared leadership

This principle reflects the value of the centrality of leadership to any successful learning community.

Leadership for learning practice involves the sharing of leadership in which:

a   structures support participation in developing the school as a learning community;
b   shared leadership is symbolised in the day-to-day flow of activities of the school;
c   everyone is encouraged to take the lead as appropriate to task and context;
d   the experience and expertise of staff, students and parents are drawn upon as resources;
e   collaborative patterns of work and activity across boundaries of subject, role and status are valued and promoted.

How leadership is shared generated a lively discussion as it is in this respect that cultural differences come most conspicuously to the fore. While aspirations for sharing of leadership are similar in the two countries, who the leaders 'are' and their role and status in the school is a function of a long tradition, not only of schooling but of cultural history. In Hofstede's (1991) categorisation of national cultures, comparison between Norway and the UK reveals a significant gap on four of the five dimensions – femininity as against masculinity, the collective as against individuality, long-termism as against short-termism and 'power distance' (a measure of degrees of separation between those with most power and those with the least power). These dimensions refer both to the culture generally but also to how these are reflected in organisations such as schools. It was clear from the reporting back from the group discussions that it is not only that there are different structures, organisation of subjects and the nature of meetings but also that these reflect the differing attitudes and expectations people bring with them in trying to identify and establish common ground.

Prompt to action	What it means	What we do in our schools
Shared leadership is symbolised in the day-to-day flow of activities of the school.	Participants in pupils' learning include teacher, classroom assistants, parents, pupils, etc. Everyone can learn from each other. Shared culture for learning.	The use of a Learning Platform involving pupils, staff, and parents – huge potential here. Whitby – monitoring days. Whitby and Bakkelokka – parents' meetings – but not enough time to discuss issues and involve parents.

The extract from the reporting-back posters included above illustrates how the power of international comparison was evident in the group discussion. Participants were clearly able to find common ground and identify foci for development.

Accountability

The fifth principle was perhaps the most contentious in this cross-country conversation. The concept of accountability threw cultural differences into even sharper relief.

Leadership for learning practice involves a shared sense of accountability in which:

a a systematic approach to self-evaluation is embedded at classroom, school and community levels;

b there is a focus on evidence and its congruence with the core values of the school;

c a shared approach to internal accountability is a precondition of accountability to external agencies;

d national policies are recast in accordance with the school's core values;

e the school chooses how to tell its own story taking account of political realities;

f there is a continuing focus on sustainability, succession and leaving a legacy.

In England accountability has become closely associated with inspection, performance management, 'league' tables and other government measures designed to raise standards, make schools more transparent and encourage parental choice. Norway has, until recently, been largely free of state intervention but is slowly, and with some reluctance, accommodating to a more top-down style of government. However, as the reporting back on the group discussion indicated, teachers in both countries' schools see their primary locus of accountability as internal and mutual, exemplified in words such as 'loyalty', 'sharing', 'empowerment' and the 'collective'.

Prompt to action	*What it means*	*What we do in our schools*
A shared approach to internal accountability is a precondition of accountability to external agencies.	To progress together. Identify the direction we want to go in. Link between internal and external evaluation and identify ways forward.	Bakkelokka – need to formalise and evaluate the important and possible. Whitby – accountable to many masters. Strong focus on self-evaluation. Bakkelokka – selective in choice of what is to be evaluated.

Prompt to action	What it means	What we do in our schools
There is a continuing focus on sustainability, succession and leaving a legacy.	Loyalty to ideas and sharing empowered colleagues. It is 'in the life-blood'. Collective thinking Sharing and spreading of ideas – a template for the future.	In Bakkelokka – focus on the vision. Empowering people through teams and opportunities to work together. Widening our horizons. Collective responsibility – in action, thought and deed. Whitby – is checked by governors, critical friends, LAs, Ofsted, *et al.* Bakkelokka – research and feedback in collaboration with Oslo University.

Schools in both countries reaffirmed a strong commitment to self-evaluation and found that the LfL principles helped to frame, and focus on, the important as against the expedient.

This exercise shared between the staff of two schools may be seen as a journey between theory and practice, testing the theory against what is feasible within political and cultural constraints, and testing the practice against values held to be self-evident. Following the initial analytical task described above, the teachers engaged in discussion activities to identify 'good ideas', 'wishes for the future' and 'lines of inquiry'.

The good ideas were displayed as illustrated below.

Good ideas for Bakkeloka	Good ideas for Whitby
Toolbox of learning strategies A space/area for pupils with special needs Systematic and formal self-evaluation with clear priorities Design and use of portfolios	Pupil learning reflection, dialogue, diaries A teaching team for Year 7 Design and use of portfolios Pupils as leaders

These 'good ideas' generated a number of challenges for professional development and cultural change. It was decided that these could be met by identifying practical lines of inquiry that would enable teachers to pursue the good ideas back in their own schools. These 'lines of inquiry' included questions such as:

- How do we/can we get the best from our staff?
- How do we/can we involve students in their own learning and in the running of the school?

- How do we/could we shape the curriculum and the way we organise learning?
- How do/could our schools lead change?

The final stage of this cross-country seminar focused on the future and in clarifying hopes and aspirations. For the staff at Bakkelokka, a key theme was concerned with being able to stretch the more able pupils to achieve their full potential whereas the teachers from Whitby expressed a desire to be able to teach children instead of subjects. Both schools were concerned to be able to adapt and modify the curriculum to meet the needs of all pupils. More specifically the flip chart listed the following aspirations:

1 To develop at Bakkelokka a better system which offers pupils with special needs fail-safe support to progress and thrive within their year group.
2 To plan at Whitby a radical new approach to teaching and engaging Year 7 pupils which will involve them in their learning and its process.
3 To make practical provision for an enduring conversation between our two schools, to involve staff and pupils, to ensure continued challenge and inspiration.

The challenge of leading change

Both schools could agree on one key issue – that in both contexts there was a need for change, not simply a question of tinkering at the edges but a more fundamental rethinking of prior assumptions and embedded routines. Reshaping the school curriculum and devising imaginative ways of re-organising learning would, like any change, be uncomfortable and would meet some resistance. Recognising and building on what the respective schools were already doing well was, therefore, an essential starting point. Both schools were already providing support and challenge for students but were aware that they could still do this better. Both schools were providing opportunities for independent learning, and reflection on learning but were aware that they would benefit from enhanced time and space to explore issues further. Teamwork and opportunities to work flexibly within and across teams were embryonic but with existing strengths and commitment to build on. Clarity of aims and how to achieve them were common priorities but could clearly be made more explicit and systematic. In summary, change would be accommodated through:

- mutual reflection, support and critique in which differences are seen as strengths and sustainability is vouchsafed through continuity;
- encouraging confidence to try out new things, not being afraid of failure;
- thinking, reflecting and *acting* collectively so that new practice can spread throughout the organisation and stay there, creating more quality time for this to happen;
- 'seeing' that change has an impact on practice, so that we can see for ourselves that it 'survives' and can account for it.

Wish lists and promissory notes generated in the enthusiasm of workshops and the heady atmosphere of 'away' days, either physically or as a temporary escape from daily routine, may quickly dissipate back in the 'real world'. Commitment to a continuing learning exchange, specific targets and mutual accountability between the two schools was designed to ensure that the momentum continued. This, it was agreed, would include exchange of staff and students, not simply as cultural tourists but in both cases with a specific focus which each school could learn from. Systems would be established to promote communication on a regular basis, building a framework to talk together, with protocols and portfolios for sharing practice. The two schools would continue to share and adapt what they were particularly good at and run joint projects, starting with a joint technology project.

A calendar and timeline were agreed for the following year with implementation from September 2007 to December through the creation of a learning platform, website and web forums, the design of electronic portfolios followed by a Spring to Summer plan to extend and widen the scope of activities.

Example 2: a cross-town collaboration to meet a socio-economic challenge

A second example of the legacy is the Carpe Vitam LfL Stevenage Extension Project which involved six out of the seven secondary schools and two of the special schools in the town. The project helped in the development of collaborative relationships among these eight schools.

The town of Stevenage in Hertfordshire exemplifies many of the issues confronting schools trying to cope with an unfair share of the nation's challenging children in a competitive market driven system. After 30 years of educational reform there are still large numbers of children in the UK not able to access the cultural goods that the state school system has the potential to deliver. The 1960s policy of trying to create common, or 'comprehensive' schools as they were known, failed to solve the problem, as did attempts in the 1970s to establish a common core curriculum. The bringing in of a compulsory National Curriculum at the end of the 1980s was intended to guarantee every child's entitlement to a good education but for reasons too complex to examine here, a wide variation in educational outcomes has persisted. An examination of the indicators of academic performance over some years suggests that almost all of the schools in the town faced a common problem. The most commonly used indicator of educational outcomes in the UK over the last 15 years is the percentage of pupils achieving a grade between A* and C in the GCSE examination they sit at the age of 15 or 16 years. In 1995 two out of the eight secondary schools in Stevenage scored in the low 20s, two more scored in the low 30s and two more in the low 40s.

Only one of the Stevenage schools scored above the national average and that school was the only one with a religious affiliation, the means to operate a degree

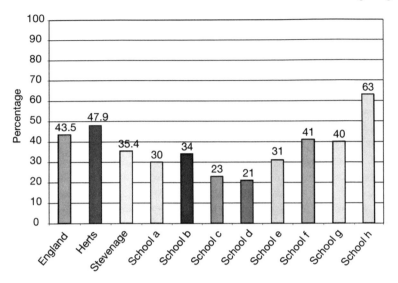

Figure 11.1 Percentage of GCSE grades A*–C in 1995

of selection. Four years later, in 1999 the situation had improved to some extent. Two schools scored in the high 20s, three schools scored in the 30s and one school scored in the 60s only five percentage points behind the school with the religious affiliation.

While this evidence of progress is to be celebrated, nevertheless these figures are consistently below both the national average and the average scores for the

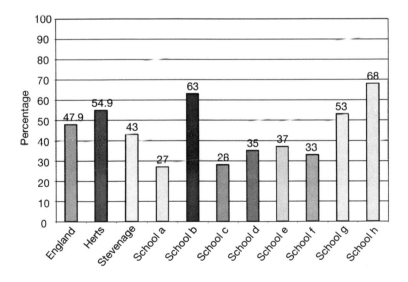

Figure 11.2 Percentage of GCSE grades A*–C in 1999

county of Hertfordshire in which Stevenage is located. It is perhaps unsurprising that the socio-economic indicators reflect a similar pattern. Public records show that housing in Stevenage is predominantly 'aimed at blue collar families', that 'residents are less well qualified' than the majority of people in Hertfordshire. There are 'worrying health characteristics', 'teenage conception is double the Hertfordshire average' and 'there are pockets of serious deprivation in the town' (Stevenage Borough Council, 2006).

This challenging socio-economic environment combines with the effects of a policy climate that encourages competition between schools to make improvement trajectories fragile. In 2002, one of the schools, Barnwell, came under a lot pressure from school inspectors because their levels of measured attainment had fallen to just 20 per cent from a high of 33 per cent in 1997. A more detailed account of the school's struggle to improve can be found elsewhere (Frost, 2005), but it is interesting to note that the school was able to reverse this trend within three years. Meanwhile, one of the other schools within walking distance of Barnwell, Collenswood School, was not able to do this. In 1997 their results were very similar to Barnwell's but from 2001 to 2005 their results steadily declined. The inspectors were not able to find evidence of the capacity for improvement and so the local authority decided to close the school. Some of the staff were interviewed for teaching posts at Barnwell School which was expanding to take in the children from the condemned school.

The kind of competition described above is problematic in all sorts if ways. First, it exerts pressure on schools which can lead to short term tactical measures to try to improve the results. This was recently admitted by an arm of government in the UK when the head of the QCA, Ken Boston, said the following:

> In many schools too much teaching time is taken up with practice tests and preparing for the key stage tests in English, mathematics and science – at the expense of actual teaching in these core subjects and other areas.
>
> (*Guardian*, 11 August 2007)

Just one week after Ken Boston's remarks, the front page of the *Observer* carried a piece in which the deputy head of the London Institute for Education, Dylan Wiliam, called for reform of the examination system because of the tendency to drill for tests that are too fact based and do not encourage critical thinking (*Observer*, 19 August 2007). The constant threat of censure and even closure hanging over the schools in towns such as Stevenage makes it difficult to enable teachers to focus on the development of long-term capacity and sustainable learning for all students. Collaboration seemed to offer the best way forward so when the 'Stevenage 14–19 Partnership' was established under the Strategic Area Review and the headteachers seized the opportunity. Such partnerships were established in order to broaden the range of specialist courses that could be offered within the town (Secretary of State for Education and Skills, 2005), but in the Stevenage case the headteachers took the radical decision to appoint one of themselves as a full-time coordinator.

The impetus to collaborate

A website declares that the Stevenage 14–19 Partnership:

> . . . brings together the town's six 11–19 community schools – Barclay, Barnwell, Heathcote, Marriotts, Nobel, Thomas Alleyne – North Hertfordshire College, Lonsdale and the Valley special schools and the Stevenage Education Support Centre. All these centres are working together and with our partners to transform the educational culture in the town and, through collaboration at 14+, to broaden and enhance opportunities and learning pathways for all young people.
>
> (Stevenage 14–19 Partnership website)

The statement on the Stevenage website 'transforming 'the educational culture in the town' and enhancing 'opportunities . . . for all young people' suggests much more than collaboration for the purposes of increasing vocational curricula or raising test scores. The headteachers in Stevenage had higher aspirations.

An opportunity arose for the Cambridge LfL team to support this work and add further impetus to the move towards collaboration. One of the schools, Barnwell, had been involved in the LfL Project as an 'associate school' and members of staff had participated in the international conferences. The senior leadership team at Barnwell had embraced leadership for learning principles and invited the Cambridge team to put a proposal to a meeting of the headteachers at one of their regular 14–19 Partnership meetings. It was a modest proposal: to use one of the main data gathering instruments, the questionnaire, in all of the schools in the partnership as a stimulus to building a discussion about leadership for learning across the town. It was agreed that the project would proceed from the beginning of the 2006 academic year, each school having identified a project coordinator and having been provided with a critical friend to help interpret the survey data and support subsequent planning. A small group of senior staff had met with members of the LfL Project team to look carefully at the survey instrument. The decision was taken to revise the instrument in the light of what we had learnt during the three year life of the project and to build it round the five principles. This collaborative ethos was carried forward to the first project team meeting where the discussion moved from an interest in collecting comparative data towards taking collective responsibility for educational outcomes in the town as a whole.

At the first team meeting concern was expressed about 'innovation overload' and the fatigue experienced by teachers arising from the relentless pressure of external inspection and local authority target setting. The school coordinators knew their schools and wanted to avoid the layering on of what would be seen to be 'yet another project'. It was suggested that instead of presenting the project to school staff as a major new initiative, the Carpe Vitam LfL approach could build on innovative projects already underway in Stevenage schools. It rapidly became clear that the Stevenage schools already had intellectual capital in abundance.

> Intellectual capital is one of the invisible assets of an organisation and complements its financial capital and physical assets. Schools are evidently rich in the intellectual capital of the teachers and staff, but also of the students, their families and communities.
>
> (Hargreaves, 2003: 4)

How could this knowledge and intellectual capital be made liquid? One of the strategies employed in the original LfL Project was portraiture.

> . . . 'portraiture,' the term I use for a method of inquiry and documentation in the social sciences. With it, I seek to combine systematic, empirical description with aesthetic expression, blending art and science, humanistic sensibilities and scientific rigor.
>
> (Lawrence-Lightfoot and Hoffmann Davis, 1997: 3)

Portraiture as used in the original project was adapted and focused on innovative practices that corresponded with the LfL principles. It was agreed that the project's critical friend would visit each of the schools and produce a visitor's portrait drawing on her conversations with project coordinators, framed by the five LfL principles. This led to the publication across Stevenage of a collection of brief but vivid portrayals of practices that reflected leadership for learning aspirations. Each of the key principles was illustrated and exemplified by several vignettes; for example, the shared leadership principle was reflected in the following:

> One aim of the redesigning of the meeting structure at the Barclay School was to allow staff at all levels of the school to take the lead in developing and monitoring their own work. Regular Cluster Meetings are a good example of this policy in action. Made up of 10 Form Tutors and two attached Learning Mentors, Cluster Groups set their own agendas and chair their own meetings.

Such vignettes were assembled in a visually appealing way with text boxes, graphics and the schools' logos. The textual content of the booklet was sent to each school coordinator to check for integrity and the resulting booklet, 'Exploring LfL Activity', containing more than 40 vignettes, was made available to all staff in the eight schools.

Redesigning the questionnaire

In the initial discussion with colleagues from Barnwell School it had become clear that the survey instrument would be more useful if it were to be redesigned to reflect the five principles that had emerged through the LfL Project. Together with the conceptual framework, the principles provided the underpinning structure of the questionnaire, with two sets of questions for each of the five key principles: one for staff and one for students. School coordinators were asked to identify additional questions that would reveal the extent to which collaborative practice across Stevenage were both valued and evident in practice.

A significant issue in the design of the survey instrument was the language used. In the original project we had wrestled with the challenge of translation into different cultures and languages, but in this case the focus was more centrally on intelligibility in a very local sense, relying on school coordinators to vet the questions in the light of how students and staff might interpret them. In order for there to be a close correspondence between the questions for staff and for students and the LfL principles, the team devised a table making it possible to read across from a principle to staff questions to student questions. Such a procedure, as we found in the larger international study, is not simply a technical exercise but creates a dialogue around the principles and enhances shared understanding.

As in the original project, the questionnaire was administered to all Year 8 students in six schools. There is always a danger with surveys of this kind that, if there is a significant time lag between the administration of the questionnaire and the availability of the results, the fast moving pace of events in the school may well render the survey redundant. The research team therefore moved quickly to carry out the analysis. At the next meeting of the school coordinators they presented a booklet containing a variety of tables and graphs, including:

- chart showing, item by item, teachers' view of the extent of practice compared to its value;
- chart showing, item by item, students' view of the extent of practice compared to its value;
- list of the five most and least evident practices (teachers' view);
- list of the five most and least evident practices (students' view);
- chart showing, item by item, teachers' view of the importance of practices compared to its prevalence in practice;
- chart showing, item by item, students' view of the importance of practices compared to its prevalence in practice;
- list of the five most and least important practices (teachers' view);
- list of the five most and least important practices (students' view);
- chart comparing staff and student's views about the extent of collaboration between Stevenage schools;
- chart comparing staff and students' views about the importance of collaboration between Stevenage schools.

The project's critical friend explained each output in the booklet and facilitated a discussion about the different ways in which the data could be used. What emerged from this discussion was the identification of further outputs that the coordinators' believed would be useful. In particular the idea of a summary sheet for staff in each school and a differently worded one for students was requested. The outputs listed above were of interest to the coordinators and to their colleagues on senior leadership teams but, even to those accustomed to looking at data outputs, they are quite challenging and require time to study them properly. The critical friend visited schools to support the discussion with senior leaders about the implications of the data, but the audience for these outputs remained restricted. In contrast, the simple sheets exemplified in Figure 11.3 were more immediately accessible and could be used in a wide variety of team meetings and staff development contexts. They constituted an effective tool for stimulating and nourishing a wider discourse about leadership for learning.

Making innovative practice visible

The survey was seen to be of considerable value, but the booklet containing the initial portraits led the coordinators team back to the question of how innovative practices could be made visible; not so these practices could be simply mimicked but because educational ideas travel well when represented in tangible activities and materials. It was considered important to nurture a dialogue about leadership for learning amongst staff, students and others within Stevenage as a whole and so it was necessary to make visible those practices that corresponded with the LfL principles and to represent them in such a way that people would be able to talk about them and subsequently adapt them for use in their own contexts. The aim went deeper than that though. It is not simply a matter of transfer of practices, strategies and techniques; it is also about the pedagogical ideas that are embedded within them. The 'Exploring Leadership for Learning' booklet had provided more than 40 brief vignettes, mere glimpses of the innovative practices already in use, but they were scant and superficial. What was needed were richer accounts of those practices, 'fatter' vignettes, more detailed and nuanced, which could be created by eliciting accounts from key individuals or groups involved in, or touched by, the practices concerned. Members of the research team were subsequently invited to visit three of the schools to trial this strategy.

The cases the research team agreed to examine in the first instance were: the 'Partners in Learning' Project at Nobel School, the development of 'vertical tutoring' at Barclay School and an innovation in assessment for learning techniques at Barnwell School, referred to as 'response to learning'. Each study began with as simple series of questions:

- How did this practice originate? What problem was it intended to respond to?
- What is the scope of the activity – who is involved, when, where?
- How does it work? Who does what? What does it look like?
- In what ways does it correspond with the LfL principles?

What did you tell us?

The Carpe Vitam LfL project: The Stevenage expansion

Six schools in Stevenage are working together to learn more about the type of leadership which supports good learning in your school.

We wanted to start by discovering more about what you think about learning and your school. You helped us to do this by completing a questionnaire in the Autumn Term.

In the questionnaire you were asked to tell us about what was really important to you compared to what you thought was happening.

For example, you might think that it is really important to have occasions when staff can learn from one another across faculties but in reality, this hardly ever happens.

You told us these things were really important to you:

- Providing students with feedback that helps them to improve their work
- Making systematic efforts to ensure that the school has the capacity to improve and be successful in the future
- Encouraging everyone in our school to be a learner
- Having a culture which nurtures the learning of everyone
- Setting learning tasks that provide students with the right level of challenge

You told us these things were not very important to you:

- Talking explicitly about the relationship between learning and leadership
- Everyone in the school sharing a concern with the link between leadership and learning
- Extending self-evaluation to include the parents and community
- Exploring practice through links with researchers
- Networking with practitioners in other countries and other cultural contexts

Update for staff

You told us these things happen a lot in your school:

- Systematic efforts to ensure that the school has the capacity to improve and be successful in the future
- Encouraging everyone in the school to be a learner
- Members of the senior leadership team see themselves as learners
- Building a culture which nurtures the learning of everyone
- Collaborating with other schools in order to secure the best possible education for all youngsters in Stevenage

You told us these things don't happen very much:

- Setting learning tasks that provide students with the right level of challenge
- Creating physical and social spaces that stimulate and celebrate learning
- Networking with practitioners in other countries and in other cultural contexts
- Drawing upon the experience and expertise of staff, students and parents as resources for learning
- Everyone in the school sharing a concern with the link between leadership and learning
- Extending self-evaluation to include the parents and community

What is interesting about this?

What do you think should happen now?

The project schools

Blahdiblah School

Blahdibli School

Blahdiblon School

Blahdiblue School

Blahdibly School

Blahdibling School

Figure 11.3 Data output sheet for staff

- What conditions make this practice possible or what conditions enhance it?
- How effectively does it work and what needs to be done to make it work better?

From these questions were developed interview and observation schedules to be used by the researcher who would visit each school to try to capture a rich portrayal of the practice concerned – a 'thick description' in the ethnographic tradition. It is interesting to note in passing that the researcher in this case, Ozgur Bolat, was a research student from Turkey; this brought a fresh perspective to these practices in English schools. In each case the research team produced a report for the schools concerned. These were between 2,500 and 4,000 words long with headings such as:

- aim of the innovation;
- how it works;
- benefits for teachers;
- benefits for students;
- benefits for the whole school;
- developing the project;
- challenges and issues.

The research team showed draft reports to the school coordinators and asked them how they might be used. These documents were seen to be very helpful to the teachers who were directly involved – serving as evaluative feedback – but, in order to nurture the LfL dialogue across the schools, it was important to have something that could easily be accessed by very busy teachers, leading to summaries, sufficiently brief to be able to fit on one side of A4 paper (see example in Figure 11.4).

These summaries were to be distributed throughout the project schools so that any teacher who recognised the potential of the practice described in outline there could ask for a copy of the full report and make contact with the staff directly involved in the particular practice.

From data to discourse

After six months of the project's existence not only was there a rich body of quantitative and qualitative data, but an intense dialogue within the project team that included a coordinator from each school. The challenge was to draw teachers into a Stevenage-wide discourse and beyond that, students, parents and other community stakeholders. While a conference was proposed, it was dismissed as too costly and likely to be seen as an unwanted intrusion. Instead it was suggested that teachers should be invited to engage in inter-school visits, the value of which had been amply demonstrated in the original LfL Project. The approach adopted had the following key characteristics, designed to avoid any association with inspection:

The Carpe Vitam Leadership for Learning Project: Stevenage Extension
Portraying innovative practice in Stevenage Schools
The Case of 'Partners in Learning' at Nobel

What is it?
Students observe lessons and give teachers feedback.

Why?
To support teacher self-evaluation by providing relevant feedback and foster student voice.

How it works

Selection of participants
- Announcement in assemblies, invitation to participate
- 25-30 students selected
- Both experienced and newly-qualified teachers

Training
- Building social bonds in relaxed surroundings (hotel) with casual clothes
- Team building games and activities
- Students and staff discuss worries/concerns
- Practice observation using videos
- Code of conduct discussed
- Training in giving constructive feedback

Observation
- Teacher and the student observer negotiate lessons to be observed
- Students often observe same teacher in different lessons
- Negotiated focus
- Some use pre-designed observation sheet
- Frequency of observations not fixed – 6–9 lessons a term

Feedback
- Immediately after the lesson or during a break time or lunch time
- Meetings last between 20 and 30 minutes
- Feedback directly to teacher, verbally and in confidence, sometimes written feedback
- Sometimes teachers give feedback on the students' feedback

How does it help?
- Self-awareness of and reflection on classroom practice
- Awareness of students' learning needs
- More relevant feedback
- Student voice
- Student exercising leadership and taking responsibility for their learning
- Students understanding of teaching and learning process
- Confidence building, improved behaviour, trust building

What are the issues?
- Providing feedback to students about their feedback
- Time for feedback sessions
- Students missing classes
- Staff meetings to maximise teacher learning
- Widening participation

Find out more
Contact Barry Burningham at Nobel School
BarryBurningham@nobel.herts.sch.uk

Figure 11.4 Case study summary sheet

- a focus on particular innovative practices;
- collaboration rather than individualistic;
- illumination rather than judgemental;
- use of LfL principles as a lens through which to observe practices;
- raising questions and identifies issues.

While those individuals participating in the visits would come away with an enhanced understanding of the nature of the innovative practices they had seen, in order to spread knowledge more widely, each visit would result in materials that could be practical use in supporting ongoing collaboration. Each visiting team was, therefore, provided with guidelines to structure their inquiries and the resulting report.

Developing leadership capacity across the town is an ambitious goal. It is difficult to predict the direction in which a project such as this may unfold because the strategy is quite properly an emergent one. The headteachers have oversight and their appointed school coordinators play their part in the direction and planning of the project. The recently announced proposals for the re-organisation of secondary schooling in Stevenage will take advantage of the Building Schools for the Future programme and will inevitably impinge on the way the legacy of LfL continues to be used.

Outcomes and capacity building

What were the outcomes of the Leadership for Learning Project? Statistical evidence of raised student attainment in the short term or a sea change in the culture and capacity of schools to grow deep and sustainable learning? Impatient governments may prefer the former but if two years after the official end of the project, schools in England, Norway and elsewhere are continuing to make the connections, then hopefully policy makers may look again at the language of outcomes and the assumptions that lie behind it.

While there is no single or immutable legacy from the LfL Project, what it can offer is a set of discursive tools which may be taken up in many different ways. The two examples presented here demonstrate that such tools can be adopted and adapted to enable schools in a variety of contexts and cultures to examine and develop their own practice.

References

Bell, D. (2005) *The Annual Report of Her Majesty's Chief Inspector of Schools 2004/05*, Press conference opening remarks: 19 October 2005. Ofsted. Online. Available HTTP: http://www.ofsted.gov.uk (accessed 31 August 2007).

Czarniawska, B. (1997) *Narrating the Organization: Dramas of Institutional Identity*, Chicago, IL: University of Chicago Press.

Engeström, Y. (1999a) 'Activity theory and individual and social transformation', in Y. Engeström, R. Mietten and R.L. Punamäki (eds) *Perspectives on Activity Theory*, Cambridge: Cambridge University Press.

Engeström, Y. (1999b) 'Innovative learning in work teams: analyzing cycles of knowledge creation in practice', in Y. Engeström, R. Mietten and R.-L. Punamäki (eds) *Perspectives on Activity Theory*, Cambridge: Cambridge University Press.

Frost, D. (2005) 'Resisting the juggernaut: building capacity through teacher leadership in spite of it all', *Leading and Managing*, 10 (2): 70–87.

The Guardian (2007) 'Drilling pupils for exams wastes time, says watchdog', by James Meikle, 11 August.

Hargreaves, D.H. (1998) 'A new partnership of stakeholders', in J. Rudduck and D. McIntyre (eds) *Challenges for Educational Research*, London: Paul Chapman Publishing.

Hargreaves, D.H. (2003) 'From improvement to transformation', Keynote lecture International Congress for School Effectiveness and Improvement, Sydney, Australia, 5 January 2003.

Hofstede G. (1991) *Cultures and Organisations: Software of the Mind*, London: McGraw Hill.

Lawrence-Lightfoot, S. and Hoffman Davis, J. (1997) *The Art and Science of Portraiture*, San Francisco, CA: Jossey-Bass.

The Observer (2007) 'Scrap these "19th-century" GCSEs says expert', by Anushka Asthana, Education Correspondent, 19 August.

Perkins, D.N. (2003) 'Making thinking visible', New Horizons for Learning. Online. Available HTTP: http://www.newhorizons.org/strategies/thinking/perkins.htm (accessed 13 November 2007).

Department for Education and Skills (2005) '14–19 Education and Skills', White Paper presented to Parliament, Nottingham: DfES.

Stevenage Borough Council (2006) 'East of England plan – examinations in public', Appendix B: Issues facing Stevenage in 2006, Stevenage Borough Council, 5374.

12 Leadership for learning
Towards a practical theory

Neil Dempster and
John MacBeath

Most voyages of exploration have destinations in mind and when reached, the voyage is at an end. In the leadership for learning journey, our destination is clear: understanding learning, leadership and the links between the two. We embarked on our travels through the Carpe Vitam Project but we are still on the 'longue durée' towards understanding. We feel that we have passed and charted a number of important headlands and points along the way and that we are now better equipped to continue the expedition. What are those important headlands and points? To step back from the seafaring metaphor, we ask in this final chapter: 'What have we learned about leadership for learning that makes it qualitatively different from other conceptions of leadership?' We also ask what implications our understanding carries for policy makers, for practitioners, for school self-evaluation and improvement.

There are at least seven defining features of leadership for learning which we are prepared to summarise at this stage. They build on preceding chapters and with particular reference to Chapter 3 in which the connecting links between leading and learning are explored. We restate these defining features here as foci for wider discussion and critique as well as stimuli for the quality of professional dialogue that enhances individual and shared understanding.

Defining features of leadership for learning

Leadership and learning are conceptualised as activities both of which inform each other. No one can be immunised against leadership and no one can be quarantined from involvement in learning. Indeed in quite material ways when one is learning, as a bare minimum, the self is leading; when one is learning with others, leadership often moves fluidly from group to individual as does what is learned. The defining feature about a leadership for learning framework is that individuals and collectives are able to be self-consciously reflective about: (i) what and how they are learning; (ii) how they are led; (iii) by whom and why; and (iv) what they are learning about leadership and their own learning as a result.

A second defining feature best describes leadership for learning as the antithesis of hierarchical leadership, by foregrounding the vital part that leaders, students, teachers and parents play in fostering learning and sharing leadership. This implies that leadership should be taken as a right and responsibility for all, never being seen as a bonus from an organisational icon or a gift from a benevolent dictator. Putting it another way, we see leadership primarily as activity while recognising that position carries a weight of expectation and a particular form of responsibility and accountability.

A third defining feature is the moral commitment on which both learning and leadership rest and which unites them in a single purpose. We have argued that both learning and leadership are distinctive forms of activity, but in a school context they are moral activities because they are always tested against the 'good'. Do those activities ultimately serve the purpose of the good life, the good society, the common good? Do they equip learners and leaders to make the wisest choices not only for themselves but for those they work with and those they serve? As we have seen from the accounts of school principals, the higher the command the greater the dilemmas in doing the right thing, but as Bennis and Nanus (1985) famously wrote, it is doing the right thing as opposed to doing things right that dignifies leadership and distinguishes it from management.

A fourth defining feature is the importance of human agency in taking hold of the levers of change. While 'rudder' and 'compass' are essential in ensuring that a vessel moves freely through the water, both rely on human agency to read and interpret the flow of information, with the end in mind. We have described this as 'disciplined agency', connecting activity, context and moral purpose. Human agency is not haphazard. It is intentional, engaging disciplined people in disciplined thought, and disciplined action. Our use of the term 'disciplined' is not to be confused with deference or conformity or with student behaviour in schools as it sometimes is. We apply the term to the unerring attention given by people to act together to improve the leadership and learning circumstances in which they find themselves. In this sense, they are disciplined by their conjoint moral endeavour.

A fifth defining feature rests on the knowledge that strength, resilience and creativity lie in a school's distributed intelligence. It is worth repeating the old adage that *no one person holds all of the wisdom*. The shared wisdom of the group is much more powerful in releasing ideas than the wisdom of the one can ever be. When leadership and learning are treated as quite separate concepts, it hampers the ability of shared wisdom to deal with the challenges which a school faces. In such circumstances teachers, students and parents tend to defer to those in positions of authority, looking to them for resolution. As shared wisdom is gathered in a school, however, we are able to see quite tangibly, the intertwining of leadership and learning. When people come together to express their ideas and multiple perspectives are brought to bear on salient issues, we are reminded again that we learn as much from our differences as from our commonly held precepts. It is this kind of action that keeps alive the 'bridging social capital' to which we referred in Chapter 3, that is, the conscious linkage of people with organisational power and authority and those without it – a question of tuning to the right 'bandwidth' so as to hear the weakest as well as the strongest voices.

A sixth defining feature is the nature and quality of the dialogue in which people engage in Leadership for Learning schools. We have called this 'disciplined dialogue' because all of the conversations of importance are directed towards understanding the school's moral and strategic purpose and how people can be brought together to help in achieving its desired ends. The dialogue is disciplined because it is not based on hearsay, folklore, personal anecdote, rumour or playground myth. Disciplined dialogue is based on information of substance about the school, quantitative and qualitative data about matters critical to understanding learners' needs, achievements, dispositions, preferences and aspirations. The same applies to parents, teachers and positional leaders. Without disciplined dialogue professional conversations are often undirected, piecemeal and based on stereotypic information and generalisation drawn from personal experience – the sample of one.

The seventh and final defining feature of leadership for learning is the repertoire of strategies and tools which a school can draw on to mine its hidden capital, to tune in to the acoustic of the school, to facilitate disciplined dialogue, to encourage distributed intelligence, to ensure, as the Chinese dictum has it, 'All of us is better than one of us'. With a 'spread out' sense of agency, tools and strategies are the enabling devices which connect leadership and learning. They feed people's capacities for analysis, interpretation, creativity and innovation and they do so on the basis of the evidence that is brought forward for discussion. These are hallmarks of the learning school, the intelligent school and the school committed to authentic in-depth self-evaluation.

To sum up, we argue that when these features are implemented in schools there is a very practical theory at work. Leadership for learning is not a 'theory' so tightly empirically based that it may be replicated in different settings with the same variables for predictable results. Theories of this kind in the social sciences are 'as scarce as hens' teeth'. What we have is a combination of concepts which, when coupled with human agency of the kind we have described, lift leadership and learning to a prominence in schools where surprising things are possible.

Principles and questions for the self-evaluating school

In relation to each of the five principles and their accompanying prompts to action we have raised questions for teachers, students and senior leaders. These may be seen providing both a framework and a number of critical questions for the self-evaluating school. There will be obvious overlaps with inspection protocols such as Ofsted, Estyn or for HMI in Scotland and Northern Ireland and similar protocols elsewhere in the world, but we hope that these serve a broader purpose. Inquiry, undertaken voluntarily, collectively and not simply for the purpose of an impending inspection, may offer a more penetrating view of a learning school and the impact of leadership on its inner life.

In a context where governments are increasingly dictating the parameters of audit, performance management and quality assurance it was the desire for a more reflective authentic self-evaluation process that provided the incentive for some of the countries to sign up to the Project. Although we came to it late in the life of Carpe Vitam, the fifth principle of shared accountability gave us a further critical dimension to self-evaluation because it focused attention on how schools tell their story, to whom and with what authority and moral conviction.

Together, the five principles which we elaborated in Chapters 6 to 10 grew out of the collective experience of participating teachers, principals and school board members and were shaped through the conversations that took place in and between conferences and workshops. The fact that strands of these conversations continue beyond the life of the project tells us something significant about the vitality of a form of inquiry whose destination is never finally attained. Each question generates a further question, leading people deeper and deeper into further knowledge and understanding.

At the end of our story, the benefits of the Carpe Vitam Project might be judged in terms of the individual teachers who took part, and whose testimony runs through many of the chapters. More broadly, benefits or 'outcomes' may be judged by the impact on policy and practice in individual schools, 22 out of the 24 which started remaining at the end. In some cases, as we have seen in previous chapters, the impact was profound and lasting. We might evaluate the project's benefits in respect of the impetus it gave to other associated schools, such as those described in Chapters 11 and 12, who used the tools and approaches and continue to do so. We might also ask to what extent it has informed and challenged policies of national and local government. In respect of this last criterion we might point to a number of local authorities and school districts which have used both principles and tools to inform practice. However, we cannot claim, at least as yet, to have influenced national policies, but we do believe there are important messages for policy makers in all the countries from which the Carpe Vitam schools were drawn.

Issues for policy

Each of the five principles has implications for the development of government policies, not simply in the UK but in all seven countries of our study and beyond.

Our first principle, a focus on learning, implies a shift in the balance of policy towards a stronger emphasis on learning as life wide and lifelong, developing criteria and indicators which give greater weight to achievements other than exam performance. If imaginative pedagogy is to be encouraged and teaching to the test discouraged it means releasing the pressures on teachers and engaging professionals in finding new and creative ways to assess the quality of learning. Policy needs to build from the ground up as well as the top down, attuned more sensitively to professional experience.

In England the government is committed to addressing conditions for learning through Building School for the Future programme. There is, however a danger of physical architecture taking precedence over pedagogical architecture. School design needs to reflect the flow of learning across subjects and avoid replicating the physical separation of subject departments clustered in their own domains, symbolically sealed from one another. Providing opportunities for teachers and students to visit radical school redesign in other countries can stretch the imagination and stimulate a vision of what a school for the twenty-first century could be and feed into planning of new schools.

Yet we are reminded of the famous quote at the beginning of the 1963 Newsom report 'It could be all glass and marble, sir, but it's still a bloody school'. Conditions for learning are greater than the sum of the physical parts. They are the social, emotional and psychological conditions which provide the breathing space, the reflection time and above all the trust that distinguishes the intelligent school from the 'bloody' school.

Our third principle asserts the importance of dialogue, the lifeblood of professional learning. The quality of dialogue is enhanced when teachers have opportunities to research their practice, to travel both physically and virtually beyond their own schools. Policy makers might consider the cost benefits and professional enhancement of a minimum funded entitlement annually for personal professional development with a promise of study leave after a given length of service. This might be for one school term, say once every five years. While this clearly represents a significant cost to the government it has to be weighed against attrition, burnout and long term sick leave. It may ultimately prove more cost effective.

Shared leadership is the fourth principle. The current 'crisis' in recruitment and retention of school leaders will not be addressed, but rather exacerbated, by increasing targets, heightening the rhetoric and raising the stakes for individual heads. What is happening at the leadership level cannot be fully grasped without having some understanding of what is going on at the teacher level. Individuals will become, and remain, headteachers if the position represents the most attractive activity to pursue among all activities available to them. It must be desirable in terms of ease of entry and overall compensation, which includes salary and benefits but also the kinds of rewards derived from headship, including working conditions and personal satisfaction.

Parents and pupils, along with teaching and support staff need to feel that they have a vital leading and learning role to play within the school community as well as beyond its immediate physical boundaries. Parents need to have access to the kind of information which steers the away from simplistic judgements about quality and encourages them to engage in dialogue with teachers and with children about the purposes of education in a changing world. None of this can be achieved by dictat but by providing a framework which provides school staff with professional breathing space and helps parents to form judgements based on deep and lasting measures of quality.

Our fifth principle addresses the accountability issue. It posits a recasting of responsibility and accountability, promoting an internal accountability which rests on mutual trust and a strong sense of collegiality. External accountability is acceptable and motivating when it moves beyond duty or compliance to external demands and builds on schools' own intrinsic commitment to essential educational values.

The autonomous school in competition for clientele is no longer an option for the twenty-first century. If schools are to collaborate, sharing expertise, offering mutual support, exchanging staff they need to be enabled to do so within a framework which explicitly encourages and rewards collaboration. If schools are to exploit opportunities to learn from others, there need to be mechanisms for schools to build capacity together.

OECD studies conclude that securing diversity of provision within schools rather than between schools is most likely to be the best route for any government to take if it wishes to enable all young people to reach high standards of achievement and for teachers to be in a position to promote it. Policy needs, therefore, to direct its attention to the communities which schools serve rather than focusing simply on schools themselves.

Conclusion

Finally, we have argued throughout this book that leadership for learning is qualitatively different from other kinds of leadership. We acknowledge that implementing such an inclusive 'five point' leadership framework is not necessarily easy. Making theory practical probably never has been. This is because it is hard to create a school culture where disciplined dialogue and shared leadership are the principal means of developing deep understanding of learning, of fostering a stimulating learning environment and accepting professional and public accountability for the outcomes students are achieving. Each one of these five contributing concepts has an extensive literature, but consistent with the old axiom – the sum is greater than the parts – we leave this work encouraged by what we have learned about the distinctive form of leadership that schools now need. We also go forward with the knowledge that a practical theory provides the means for new learning in new contexts with new people always with a view to the moral purpose of education – enhancing the lives of learners.

References

Bennis, W. and Nanus, B. (1985) *Leaders: The Strategies for Taking Charge*, New York: Harper and Row.

Central Advisory Council for Education (1963) *Half Our Future (The Newsom Report)*, London: HMSO.

Index

Note: page numbers in *italics* denote figures or tables